Recipes From

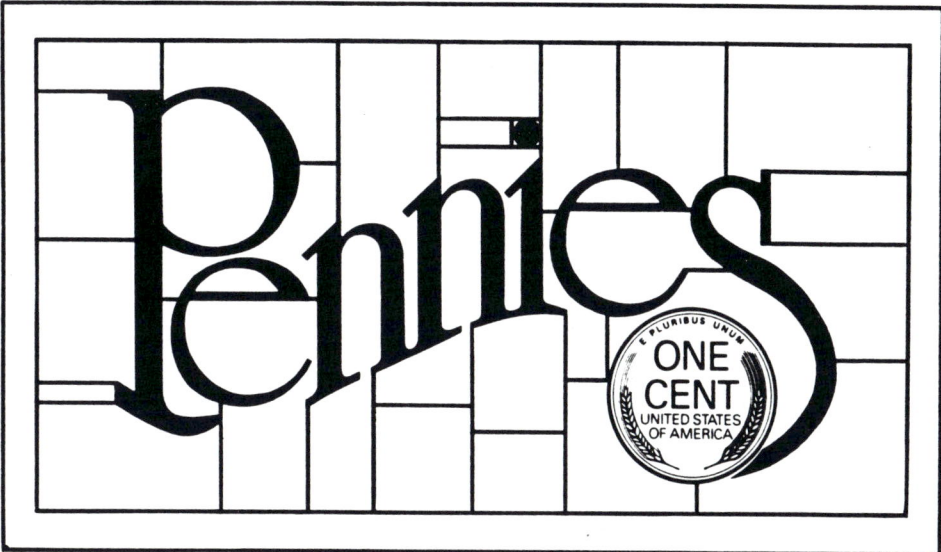

Penny Greenwood selected the recipes and assisted in rewriting and editing them. **Cheryl Massengill, Jean McCoy,** and **Norma Stuart** tested the recipes. **Cheryl Massengill, Joy Schwentker,** and **Peggy Parker** provided data entry. **Lisa Linn** edited and rewrote the recipes. **Mike Pezzoni** provided art work and layout. **Harriet Janes** provided technical assistance.

Recipes from Pennies

Contents

Salads

HALF MOON BAY ARTICHOKE SALAD

Dressing
3/4 cup oil
1/4 cup white wine vinegar
1 teaspoon sugar
1/2 teaspoon salt
1/2 teaspoon paprika
Dash pepper

Salad
1 (9-ounce) package frozen artichoke hearts, cooked and drained
1 (8-ounce) package frozen green beans, cooked and drained
6 cups assorted salad greens, torn into bite-sized pieces
1/4 cup thinly sliced onion
8 to 10 cherry tomatoes, halved
2 ounces (1/2 cup) crumbled blue cheese

1. In medium bowl, combine all dressing ingredients.
2. Add cooked artichoke hearts and beans; toss lightly.
3. Refrigerate until chilled - about 3 hours.
4. In large bowl, toss dressing mixture with salad greens, onion, tomatoes, and cheese.
5. Serve immediately.

Yield: 8 to 9 servings

TABOOLEY

1 cup medium-fine bulgur (cracked wheat), cooked
1/2 cup olive oil
Juice of 4 lemons (about 3/4 cup)
1 bunch scallions, finely chopped, including green part
2 large bunches parsley, chopped
4 large tomatoes, very finely chopped
1 small bunch celery, very finely chopped
2 small cucumbers, very finely chopped
Vegetable salt to taste
Romaine lettuce leaves

1. In a large ceramic or glass crock, make a layer of the bulgur.
2. Add the olive oil and lemon juice.
3. Layer the vegetables in the order listed, scallions first and cucumbers last.
4. Sprinkle vegetable salt over the top.
5. Cover the crock loosely; store in the refrigerator until ready to serve - at least 24 hours, and up to two weeks.
6. To serve, toss the salad so that all ingredients are well mixed.
7. Check seasonings.
8. Salad may be served on a bed of lettuce, or Lebanese style: wrapped by the fingers in single leaves of lettuce and eaten out-of-hand.

Yield: 6 to 8 servings

BULGUR SALAD WITH BROCCOLI, RADISHES, AND CELERY

1-1/2 cups broccoli florets, cut into small pieces
1/2 cup plus 2 tablespoons chicken stock, preferably homemade
3 tablespoons plus 1/2 teaspoon red wine vinegar
1-1/2 teaspoons Dijon mustard
3/4 teaspoon coarse salt
1 medium garlic clove, minced
1/4 teaspoon freshly ground pepper
1 cup medium bulgur

1/3 cup diced red radishes
1/3 cup diced celery
1/4 cup sliced green onion
1-1/2 tablespoons olive oil

1. Steam broccoli florets until crisp-tender; pat dry. Set aside.
2. Bring stock, 3 tablespoons vinegar, mustard, salt, garlic, and pepper to boil in medium saucepan.
3. Stir in bulgur.
4. Cover; set aside until stock is absorbed - about 15 minutes.
5. Turn bulgur into bowl; fluff with fork.
6. Stir in broccoli, radishes, celery, onion, oil, and remaining vinegar, if desired.
7. Serve at room temperature.

Yield: 6 servings

BEAN SALAD

1 medium onion, chopped
1 small jar of pimientos
1 can French green beans, drained
1 can Shoe Peg corn, drained
1 can baby lima beans, drained
1 can small green peas, drained

Marinade
1 cup sugar
1 cup vinegar
1/3 cup oil

1. Combine vegetables in a large bowl.
2. Mix together marinade ingredients.
3. Pour marinade over vegetables and mix.
4. Refrigerate for several hours before serving.

Yield: 6 servings

STUFFED AVOCADO SALAD

3 ripe avocados
1 cup finely chopped, fresh pineapple
2 oranges, peeled and separated into sections
12 acerolas* or maraschino cherries
1/2 cup olive oil
1/4 cup vinegar
1/4 teaspoon fresh lime juice
1/2 teaspoon salt
1/8 teaspoon ground pepper
1 tablespoon sugar (optional)
Lettuce leaves, washed and drained

1. Cut avocados into halves, lengthwise.
2. Remove seeds and scoop out pulp, being careful not to break shells.
3. Cut avocado meat into 1/2-inch cubes and combine with pineapple.
4. Mix thoroughly with dressing made by mixing together the olive oil, vinegar, lime juice, salt, pepper, and sugar.
5. Fill shells with the mixture; serve on lettuce leaves on individual plates with orange sections around.
6. Garnish with acerolas or maraschino cherries and serve cold.

*An acerola is a West Indian cherry.

Yield: 6 servings

HOT CHICKEN (OR TURKEY) SALAD

2 cups chopped chicken or turkey
4 hard cooked eggs
2 cups diced celery
1/2 cup chopped, toasted almonds
1/2 teaspoon salt
2 tablespoons grated onions
2 tablespoons lemon juice
1 cup mayonnaise
1 cup crushed potato chips
1/2 cup grated cheddar cheese

1. Combine meat, eggs, celery, almonds, salt, onions, and lemon juice.
2. Mix well and fold in mayonnaise.
3. Pour into a greased casserole.
4. Top with potato chips and cheese.
5. Bake at 450F for 12 minutes, or until cheese melts.

Yield: 4 servings

GAZPACHO SALAD WITH CHEESY GUACAMOLE DRESSING

Note: To prepare dressing in food processor or blender, cut avocado in large pieces and process until smooth. Add remaining ingredients; process just until blended.

2 envelopes unflavored gelatin
1/2 cup cold water
1/4 teaspoon salt
2 cups tomato juice
3 tablespoons lemon juice
Dash of hot pepper sauce
1 cup (1 medium) chopped cucumber
1 cup (1 medium) chopped tomato
1/2 cup chopped green pepper
1/4 cup thinly sliced green onions

Dressing
1 cup (1 medium) mashed, peeled avocado
1 to 2 teaspoons thinly sliced green onions
1/4 teaspoon salt
2 tablespoons lemon juice
1 (3-ounce) package cream cheese, softened

1. In medium saucepan, soften gelatin in cold water; stir over low heat until dissolved. Remove from heat.
2. Add salt, tomato juice, lemon juice, and hot pepper sauce; blend well.
3. Chill until slightly thickened but not set - about 45 minutes.
4. Stir in cucumber, tomato, green pepper, and onions.
5. Pour into 5-cup mold or individual molds.
6. Refrigerate until firm.
7. Meanwhile, in small bowl, combine all dressing ingredients; mix well.
8. Cover; refrigerate to blend flavors at least 30 minutes or until served.
9. To serve, unmold gelatin onto lettuce-lined plate and spoon on dressing.

Yield: 8 servings and 1 cup dressing

HOT ORIENTAL CHICKEN SALAD

Note: Crisp chow mein noodles may be used for garnish; or for a heartier entree, serve over chow mein noodles.

2-1/2 quarts (3 pounds) cooked chicken, diced
3 cups (1 pound) celery, chopped
1-1/2 cups (8-9 ounces) water chestnuts, sliced
2/3 cup prepared French dressing
5 cups (1-1/4 pounds) cheddar cheese, very sharp, shredded
5 cups (2 pounds) seedless green grapes
5 cups (2-1/2 pounds) dairy sour cream
1/4 cup flour
1 tablespoon prepared yellow mustard
1 teaspoon salt
1/4 teaspoon white pepper, ground
1 cup (3 ounces) almonds, sliced

1. Mix together chicken, celery, water chestnuts, and French dressing.
2. Stir in cheese; add grapes; mix gently.
3. Cover with plastic wrap; let marinate for about 1 hour; or chill until time for final preparation.
4. Combine sour cream with flour, mustard, salt, and pepper; mix well.
5. Sift sour cream mixture into chicken mixture.
6. Divide salad mixture into two 9x13-inch casseroles.
7. Sprinkle about 1/2 cup or 1-1/2 ounces almonds over top of each pan.
8. Bake at 325F until bubbly - about 25 to 35 minutes.

Yield: 35 servings

EXOTIC LUNCHEON SALAD WITH CHICKEN

2-1/2 to 3 pounds cooked chicken, cut into chunks
1 (8-ounce) can water chestnuts, sliced
1 pound seedless grapes
2 cups celery, chopped
2-3 cups slivered almonds, toasted (save 1/2 cup for garnish)
2-3 cups mayonnaise
1 tablespoon curry powder
1 tablespoon soy sauce
2 tablespoons lemon juice
Lettuce, Boston or Bibb
1 (20-ounce) can pineapple chunks

1. Combine first five ingredients.
2. Combine mayonnaise, curry powder, soy sauce, and lemon juice; toss with chicken; chill several hours.
3. Spoon into a bed of lettuce or individual plates.
4. Sprinkle with pineapple and rest of almonds.

Yield: 6 to 8 servings

MEXICAN CHEF'S SALAD

Note: We like to substitute taco meat for the shrimp. Spoon in the beans, then the taco meat and continue according to the directions, skipping the shrimp.

4 cups lettuce, shredded
1 cup Ortega diced green chilies
1/2 cup green onions, sliced
1/4 cup oil
2 tablespoons red wine vinegar
2 flour tortillas, fried crisp in shape of bowl*
1 cup refried beans, heated
10 large shrimp, cooked
1 large avocado, pitted, peeled, sliced lengthwise
2 tomatoes, cut in thin wedges
1 whole jalapeno
1/2 cup longhorn cheese, shredded
2 tablespoons Romano cheese, grated

1. Toss together lettuce, chiles, green onions, oil, and vinegar.
2. Spoon 1/2 cup refried beans into each tortilla bowl.
3. Add 2 cups lettuce mixture, mounding it like a volcano.
4. Around lettuce, alternate shrimp, avocado slices, and tomato wedges. Save 1 shrimp.
5. Add 1 jalapeno.
6. Sprinkle with longhorn and Romano cheeses.
7. Top with 1 shrimp.

*When frying, place small bowl or other weight in center of tortilla.

Yield: 4 servings

SALAD BREAD 'N BOWL

Dough (bread bowl)
1 package Pillsbury Hot Roll Mix
1/2 teaspoon dill weed
3/4 cup hot tap water (115-125F)
1 egg
Coarse ground salt

Filling (shrimp salad)
3 cups cooked medium shrimp, cut into pieces*
2 cups cooked rice
3/4 cup chopped celery
1 carrot, shredded
3/4 cup mayonnaise or salad dressing
1 tablespoon lemon juice
1 (10-ounce) package frozen peas or cut asparagus, cooked and drained
Leaf lettuce

For Dough
1. Generously grease outside of six 10-ounce custard cups.
2. Invert and place on cookie sheet.
3. In large bowl, combine yeast from foil packet with flour mixture and dill weed.
4. Stir in hot tap water and egg; mix until dough forms a ball.
5. Cover; let rise on wire rack over bowl or pan to which boiling water has been added, until light and doubled in size - 30 to 45 minutes.
6. On well-floured surface, knead dough until no longer sticky - 1 to 2 minutes.
7. Roll 1/4 dough into 8-inch round; cut into six 2-1/2-inch dough rounds.
8. Place on top of each inverted custard cup.
9. Divide remaining dough into 6 equal parts.
10. Roll each to 30-inch rope.
11. Coil around cup, starting at edge of dough rounds and coiling down sides of cup.
12. Pinch seams of rope together; seal rope to dough rounds by pinching seams.
13. Brush gently with milk; sprinkle lightly with coarse salt.
14. Cover; let rise in warm place until almost doubled - about 20 minutes.
15. Heat oven to 375F.
16. Bake 20 to 25 minutes or until light golden brown.
17. Remove from cup immediately; cool on wire rack.

For Filling
1. In large bowl, combine all filling ingredients except lettuce; mix well.
2. Refrigerate until serving time.
3. Line bread bowls with lettuce; spoon chilled salad into bowls.
4. Serve immediately.

*One and one-half pounds of medium-sized raw shrimp, cleaned, equal 3 cups cooked shrimp.

Yield: 6 servings

SEAFOOD SALAD

1 head cauliflower
1/2 pound (approximately) Alaskan king crabmeat
20 large cooked shrimp, peeled, sliced 3/8-inch thick
1/2 cup chopped onion
1 tablespoon minced parsley
1 tablespoon chopped, fresh dill weed
1/4-1/2 cup dairy sour cream

Sauce
1 egg yolk, boiled and grated
1 egg
1/2 teaspoon salt
2 teaspoons Dijon mustard
3 drops Tabasco sauce
2 teaspoons wine vinegar
1 cup vegetable oil

1. Shred cauliflower very finely and combine with crabmeat and shrimp; add onion, parsley, dill, and sour cream. Mix well.
2. To make sauce, place egg yolk, egg, salt, mustard, Tabasco, and wine vinegar in blender and turn on lowest speed for 2 seconds.
3. Begin pouring oil very slowly into blender while turning speed once again on lowest; increase flow until all oil is used and sauce is thick.
4. Blend sauce into the seafood salad; mix well.
5. Garnish salad with fresh parsley, lemon twists, and cauliflorets, or whole cooked shrimp.

Yield: 6 servings

STRAWBERRY SALAD

Note: This is my favorite congealed salad. Whenever I see it at a pot-luck supper I always get it.

6 ounces strawberry Jell-O
2 cups boiling water
20 ounces frozen strawberries
1 (13-1/2-ounce) can crushed pineapple
2 large bananas, diced
2 tablespoons lemon juice
1 cup dairy sour cream
1 teaspoon sugar
1/4 teaspoon ground ginger
Dash of salt

1. Dissolve Jell-O in boiling water. Add strawberries, bananas, and lemon juice.
2. Pour half of Jell-O in mold; chill until set.
3. Combine sour cream, sugar, ginger, and salt. Spread over set Jell-O.
4. Pour remaining Jell-O over dressing.
5. Chill until set.

Yield: 6 servings

ROAST BEEF IN VINAIGRETTE

Note: The marinated version is called Salade de Boeuf.

1-1/2 cup cooked roast beef, cold, cut in thin slices or julienne strips
1 medium onion, finely chopped
2 handfuls fresh parsley (no stems), finely chopped
1 large hard-cooked egg, chopped
1/2 stalk celery, chopped (optional)
1-2 cloves garlic, chopped
6 tablespoons tarragon vinegar
3/4 cup olive oil
5 leaves butter lettuce, chopped

1. Blend all sauce ingredients and serve either as a sauce over the roast beef, or marinate the beef in the sauce overnight.
2. Add the chopped lettuce at serving time.

Yield: 4 servings

PASTA SALAD

Note: My former catering partner and good friend came up with this wonderful recipe. The first time I had it was at a tailgating party; its been a favorite ever since. It's the only pasta salad my backyard neighbor can get her husband to eat!

If you cannot find rotelli in your grocery store, another short noodle may be substituted, but it won't look as good!

This recipe must be made ahead.

1 pound rotelli (spiral shaped noodles)
1 package Italian dressing made up with olive oil and wine vinegar
1/2 cup Parmesan cheese
4 ounces salami, diced
1 package frozen green peas, thawed
1 Bermuda onion, diced
1/4 cup pitted black olives, cut in half
1/4 cup green olives, cut in half

1. Cook rotelli until al dente (not quite totally soft all the way through the noodle but still palatable).
2. Prepare the package of dressing, substituting the olive oil and wine vinegar for the salad oil and cider vinegar. Marinate the pasta in the dressing.
3. Add the Parmesan, salami, green peas, onion, and both kinds of olives. Allow flavors to blend for at least 3 hours, but overnight would be better.

Yield: 10 servings

LEMON TAHINI DRESSING

1/4 cup tahini
1/4 cup tamari
1/2 cup oil
1/3 cup lemon juice
1/4 cup onion, minced
2 tablespoons green pepper, minced
1 small stalk celery, minced
2 teaspoons white pepper
About 1/4 cup water

1. Blend the onion, green pepper, celery, tamari, and tahini.
2. Add the lemon juice and pepper; blend on high speed.
3. Add the oil, and, with the blender running, enough water to reach desired consistency.

Yield: 2 cups

DIJON SALAD

Note: This recipe must be made several days ahead.

1 pound lean pork, cooked and thinly sliced
2 tablespoons olive oil
1/4 cup wine vinegar
2 green onions, minced
2-3 large potatoes, cooked and diced
1/4 cup wine vinegar
4 tablespoons olive oil
1/4 cup red onion, chopped
1 teaspoon Dijon-style mustard
Salt
Freshly ground pepper
1 head romaine lettuce
2 roasted green or red peppers, cut julienne
2 green onions, thinly sliced
2 tablespoons capers

1. Combine pork, oil, vinegar, and green onions; cover; refrigerate 1 to 2 days.
2. Combine potatoes, vinegar, oil, red onion, mustard, salt, and pepper; toss.
3. Cover; refrigerate overnight.
4. Arrange lettuce leaves on large platter.
5. Add peppers to pork mixture; toss.
6. Arrange potato salad over lettuce in a ring; sprinkle with onions.
7. Mound pork in center; top with capers.

Yield: 4 to 6 servings

CELERY SEED DRESSING

1/2 cup sugar
1 teaspoon dry mustard
1 teaspoon salt
1 to 2 teaspoons celery seed
3 tablespoons onion, grated
1 cup salad oil
1/3 cup vinegar
Few sprigs of lemon thyme

1. Combine sugar, mustard, salt, and celery seed.
2. Add onion.
3. Beating constantly, gradually add salad oil and vinegar.
4. Garnish salad with lemon thyme.

Yield: 1-1/2 cups

Soups

SOPA DE MAIZ (MEXICAN CORN SOUP)

Note: This meal-in-one soup is terrific with fresh or frozen corn. We used canned corn.

Soup
3-1/2 cups fresh corn kernels (8-12 ears)
1 cup chicken stock
1/4 cup butter
2 cups milk
1 garlic clove, minced
1 teaspoon oregano
Salt and freshly ground pepper
1-2 tablespoons canned chilies, rinsed and diced
1 whole cooked chicken breast, boned and diced
1 cup diced tomatoes
1 cup cubed Monterey Jack, Muenster, or Fontina cheese
2 tablespoons minced parsley

Tortilla Squares
Oil for deep frying
6-8 corn tortillas

For Soup
1. Combine corn and chicken stock in blender or food processor and puree.
2. In 3-quart saucepan, combine butter and corn mixture; simmer slowly 5 minutes, stirring to keep corn from sticking to bottom of pan.
3. Add milk, garlic, oregano, salt, and pepper; bring to a boil.
4. Reduce heat; add chilies; simmer 5 minutes.
5. May be frozen or stored in refrigerator at this point.
6. To serve, reheat soup slowly.
7. Divide chicken and tomatoes among 6 bowls.
8. Remove soup from heat; add cheese; stir until melted.
9. Ladle into bowls; sprinkle with parsley and tortilla squares.

For Tortilla Squares
1. Preheat oil to 375F in electric skillet, deep fryer, or large pan.
2. Stack tortillas on cutting board and slice into 1/2-inch squares.
3. Drop a handful at a time into oil and stir with wooden spoon until crisp and golden - about 3 minutes.
4. Drain on paper towels.
5. Store up to 6 weeks in a covered container in a dry place. Good with soups and salads.

Yield: 6 servings

SPINACH SOUP

2 (10-ounce) packages frozen leaf spinach, thawed, or 2 pounds fresh
   spinach
4 tablespoons butter
2 cups homemade meat broth or 1 cup canned chicken broth mixed with
   1 cup water
2 cups milk
1/4 teaspoon nutmeg
5 tablespoons freshly grated Parmesan cheese
Salt, if necessary

1. Cook, squeeze dry, and chop the spinach.
2. Saute the spinach in the butter for 2-3 minutes over medium heat.
3. Add the broth, milk, and nutmeg.
4. Bring to a simmer, stirring often.
5. Add the Parmesan cheese and cook for 1 more minute, stirring two or
three times.
6. Salt to taste.
7. Serve immediately.

Yield: 5 to 6 servings

CORN CHOWDER I

4 ounces salt pork, diced (about 1/2 cup)
1 medium onion, thinly-sliced (about 1/2 cup)
4 cups corn - 2 cups pureed, 2 cups whole kernels (from about 6 ears)
2 medium potatoes, cut into 1/2-inch dices (about 1-1/4 cups)
4 cups chicken broth
2 cups light cream
Salt and freshly ground pepper
Pinch cayenne pepper (optional)
1 tablespoon chopped parsley

1. In a large pot, render salt pork of fat - about 5 to 10 minutes,
until pork is crisp.
2. Remove pork pieces with a slotted spoon and reserve for garnish.
3. Saute onions in pork fat until tender - about 3 minutes.
4. Add corn kernels, both whole and pureed.
5. Stir in potatoes and chicken broth.
6. Bring to a boil; reduce heat; simmer for 10 minutes, or until
potatoes are tender.
7. Add cream; season to taste with salt, pepper, and optional cayenne;
stir in parsley.
8. Serve immediately, garnished with salt pork.

Yield: 9 cups

CORN CHOWDER II

Note: Dairy sour cream may be substituted for part of the milk.
Good reheated.

3 slices bacon
1 medium onion, chopped
1 cup sliced raw potato
1-1/2 to 2 cups fresh, frozen, or canned corn
3 cups boiling water
Salt and pepper
1 tablespoon sugar
2 cups milk, or 1 cup milk and 1 cup cream
2 egg yolks, beaten
2 tablespoons butter
1/4 to 1/2 cup chopped parsley

1. Fry bacon until crisp.
2. Reserve 1 tablespoon bacon drippings.
3. Remove bacon and crumble.
4. Saute onion and potato in reserved drippings until onion is golden.
5. Add bacon and blend.
6. Stir in corn; add boiling water, salt, pepper, and sugar.
7. Cook until vegetables are tender.
8. Gently blend in milk or cream.
9. Stir 1/2 cup hot soup into egg yolks; blend into soup.
10. Add butter and parsley.

Yield: 6 servings

CREAMY ONION SOUP

1-1/2 cups butter (3 sticks)
4 cups white onions, sliced
1-3/4 cups flour
12 cups beef stock
1/2 teaspoon cayenne pepper
1-1/2 tablespoons salt
1 egg yolk
2 tablespoons cream
Toasted bread rounds
1 cup grated Parmesan cheese

1. Melt butter in a 6-quart soup kettle.
2. Add onions; reduce heat to very low; cook until onions are translucent. (Be careful not to brown onions in the first stage of cooking.)
3. Add flour; cook 5-10 minutes more, stirring occasionally.
4. Blend in beef stock very slowly.
5. Add salt and cayenne; bring to a boil.
6. Reduce heat; simmer about 15 minutes.
7. Remove kettle from heat.
8. Beat together egg yolk and cream; add a little of the soup; mix
quickly; add to the soup kettle.
9. Serve in soup cups; top with toasted rounds of bread sprinkled
with grated Parmesan cheese.
10. Brown quickly under broiler and serve immediately.

Yield: 10-12 servings

CREAMY TOMATO SOUP

2 tablespoons olive oil
2 tablespoons butter
1 medium onion, chopped
2 medium carrots, chopped
1 celery rib, chopped
1 tablespoon minced garlic
2/3 cup long-grain brown rice
1 (35-ounce) can Italian plum tomatoes, with their liquid
3/4 teaspoon dried dill weed
3/4 teaspoon basil
2 teaspoons salt
1/4 teaspoon pepper
1-1/2 cups milk
1/2 cup heavy cream

1. In a large saucepan or stockpot, heat the olive oil and butter until the butter is melted.
2. Add the onion; saute over moderate heat until softened and translucent - about 3 minutes.
3. Add the carrots, celery, and garlic; saute for 5 minutes.
4. Add the brown rice; saute for 1 minute longer.
5. Add the tomatoes, mashing them with the back of a spoon to break them up.
6. Add the dill, basil, salt, pepper, and 6 cups of water.
7. Bring to boil; reduce heat; simmer, uncovered, for about 45 minutes, stirring occasionally, until the rice is tender.
8. Puree half of the soup in a blender or food processor and return it to the remaining soup in the pot.
9. Stir in the milk and cream; season with salt and pepper to taste.
10. Heat gently just until hot.

Yield: 6 to 8 servings

FRESH TOMATO SOUP

2 medium white Bermuda or other sweet onions, slivered (about 1-1/2 cup)
1 inner rib celery with leaves, trimmed, cut into 1/4-inch diagonal
   slices
1 small clove garlic, crushed
8 fresh sage leaves
1 tablespoon olive oil
8 large or 12 small, fresh, ripe tomatoes (about 3-1/2 pounds), peeled
2 cups chicken broth, preferably homemade
1 teaspoon (or to taste) salt
Freshly ground pepper

1. Combine onion, celery, garlic, sage, and oil in a large, heavy
saucepan; saute, stirring, over low heat until vegetables are coated
with oil.
2. Cover saucepan; sweat vegetables, uncovering occasionally to stir,
until very soft - about 25 minutes.
3. Place tomatoes in large, shallow sieve set over bowl; break up
tomatoes with fingers, rinsing off seeds under cold water.
4. Press pulp in sieve to extract as much juice as possible; cut up
tomatoes coarsely, leaving pieces fairly large.
5. Add strained tomato juice and cut-up tomatoes to onion mixture in
saucepan.
6. Add chicken broth; salt and pepper to taste.
7. Heat to boiling; reduce heat to low; simmer, uncovered, 10
minutes.
8. Remove from heat; serve hot or cold.

Yield: 6 to 8 servings

FRESH TOMATO BISQUE

2 pounds ripe tomatoes (about 6 tomatoes)
1 medium onion, sliced thin
1 tablespoon butter
1 bay leaf
1 heaping tablespoon brown sugar
2 whole cloves
1 teaspoon salt
1/2 teaspoon black pepper
2 teaspoons finely chopped, fresh basil
1 pint light cream
1 cup milk
6 large croutons
Butter
2 tablespoons chopped chives

1. Skin and seed the tomatoes. To seed, cut tomato in half and squeeze with your hands. Rinse away remaining seed with cool water.
2. Saute onion in butter; add the tomatoes, chopped.
3. Add bay leaf, sugar, cloves, salt, pepper, and basil.
4. Simmer, stirring occasionally, until tomatoes are thoroughly cooked - about 25 minutes.
5. Remove bay leaf and cloves; transfer mixture to blender to puree (or strain through a coarse sieve).
6. Add cream and milk; heat through.
7. Serve topped with toasted, buttered croutons; sprinkle with chopped chives.

Yield: 6 servings

VEGETABLE SOUP

1 cup dried Cannellini or Great Northern beans, sorted
6 cups water
6 cups beef broth
1 (16-ounce) can whole, peeled tomatoes, undrained
2 medium onions, diced
8 ounces green beans, cut into 2-inch pieces (about 2 cups)
2 medium potatoes, diced
1 small fennel bulb or 2 stalks celery, diced
1 small bunch fresh parsley, tied together
1 large garlic clove, minced
1 cup alphabet pasta
10 ounces escarole, shredded (about 6 cups)
2 small zucchini, diced
1 (10-ounce) package frozen peas
1/4 cup olive oil
Salt and freshly ground pepper

1. Place beans in stockpot; cover with cold water; soak overnight.
2. Drain beans.
3. Cover with 6 cups water, broth, tomatoes (and liquid), onions, green beans, potatoes, fennel, parsley, and garlic.
4. Bring to boil over high heat.
5. Reduce heat to medium-low, cover partially; simmer until beans are tender - about 80 minutes.
6. Add pasta.
7. Cover and cook 5 minutes.
8. Add escarole, zucchini, peas, and oil.
9. Cover and cook until escarole wilts - about 5 minutes.
10. Season with salt and pepper.
11. Discard parsley.
12. Ladle soup into bowls.
13. Garnish with minced parsley.

Yield: 4 quarts

CUCUMBER SOUP

3 medium cucumbers, peeled, diced, and seeds removed
1/2 medium onion, diced
3 tablespoons butter
1/4 teaspoon thyme
1/4 teaspoon dill weed
1 small bay leaf
3 tablespoons butter
3 tablespoons flour
3 cups chicken broth (made with 1-1/2 teaspoons base), warmed
1 cup evaporated milk
Juice of 1/2 lemon
Salt and pepper to taste

1. Melt 3 tablespoons butter; saute cucumber and onion with thyme,
dill weed, and bay leaf until onion becomes transparent.
2. Remove bay leaf and puree the cucumber and onion mixture.
3. Melt 3 tablespoons butter; add flour all at once to make a roux.
4. Slowly add the chicken stock and milk.
5. Add lemon juice and pepper.
6. Cook 20 minutes.
7. Add puree.
8. Chill 2 to 3 hours.
9. Garnish with diced cucumber, lemon slices, mint, or parsley.

Yield: 4 servings

LEMONY BASIL MUSHROOM SOUP

1/4 cup margarine or butter
1-1/4 cups chopped onions
1 pound fresh mushrooms, sliced
3 celery stalks, sliced
2 carrots, sliced
4 garlic cloves, minced
6 cups water
3 (10-3/4-ounce) cans condensed chicken broth
1 (10-3/4-ounce) can condensed cream of chicken soup
1/2 cup chopped fresh basil (1 tablespoon dry basil leaves and one
   10-ounce package frozen chopped spinach, thawed, can be substituted
   for fresh basil)
1 teaspoon fresh ground pepper
1 teaspoon lemon juice
1/2 cup uncooked wild rice
1/4 cup uncooked regular rice
1 lemon, sliced (optional)
Grated Parmesan cheese (optional)

1. Melt margarine in a 6-quart Dutch oven.
2. Saute onions, mushrooms, celery, carrots, and garlic in margarine
for about 5 minutes.
3. Stir in water, chicken broth, chicken soup, basil, pepper, lemon
juice, wild rice, and regular rice.
4. Cover; simmer over low heat until wild rice is tender - about 40
minutes.
5. Serve garnished with lemon slices and Parmesan cheese, if desired.

Yield: 16 one-cup servings

SPINACH SOUP PRINTANIER

2 medium carrots, pared, cut into 1/4-inch dices
3 tablespoons unsalted butter
2 tablespoons all-purpose flour
6 cups chicken stock
1 pound fresh spinach, stemmed, washed
1/2 pound fresh asparagus, trimmed, cut into 1/4-inch dices
1 medium zucchini, trimmed, cut into 1/4-inch dice
1 cup (lightly packed) stemmed watercress
1 cup cream fraiche*
2 teaspoons fresh lemon juice
3/4 teaspoon salt
1/8 teaspoon freshly ground white pepper

1. Blanch carrots in medium saucepan of boiling salted water 3 minutes; drain in colander.
2. Rinse under cold running water to cool; reserve.
3. Melt butter in large, noncorrosive saucepan over medium-low heat.
4. Whisk in flour until smooth; cook 4 minutes, stirring constantly.
5. Whisk in chicken stock in thin stream; cook, whisking, until liquid is simmering and thickened.
6. Stir in spinach, one handful at a time; cook until just tender - about 3 minutes.
7. Puree, in batches, in blender or food processor; return to saucepan.
8. Increase heat to medium.
9. Add asparagus and zucchini to saucepan; simmer until tender - about 4 minutes.
10. Stir in watercress, cream fraiche, lemon juice, salt, pepper, and reserved carrots.
11. Reduce heat to low; cook soup, stirring frequently, until just heated through - about 2 minutes.
12. Serve immediately in warmed soup bowls.

*To make 1 cup cream fraiche, shake 2 tablespoons active-culture buttermilk with 1 cup heavy cream (not ultrapasteurized) in sterilized jar. Let stand, loosely covered, in warm place until thickened - 12 to 14 hours. Stir well. Refrigerate, covered, up to 10 days.

Yield: 8 servings

DILLED POTATO SOUP

Note: This versatile soup is delicious hot or cold. An excellent accompaniment: cream cheese on a bread board with fancy rolls or crackers.

1 cup butter
3 cups yellow onions, finely chopped
6 cups carrots, grated
1 tablespoon dried dill weed
1/2 cup powdered chicken bouillon
2-3 teaspoons salt
6 cups water
6 cups milk
8 cups potato flakes
6 cups whole milk
6 cups whole milk again

1. Melt butter in two-gallon kettle.
2. Saute onions and carrots in butter 10 minutes over medium heat.
3. Stir in dill weed.
4. Combine powdered chicken bouillon, salt, water, and milk in another two-gallon kettle.
5. Heat to boiling.
6. Stir in potato flakes until moistened.
7. Whip by hand until fluffy.
8. Stir carrot mixture and milk into potatoes.
9. Puree entire mixture.
10 Cover and chill.*
11 When ready to serve, stir in additional milk.

*If soup is to be served hot, stir in additional milk at this time.

Yield: 60 4-ounce servings

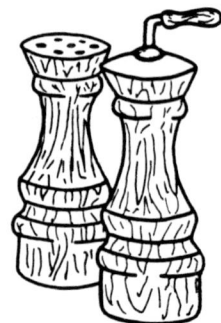

BARLEY MUSHROOM SOUP

Note: Barley absorbs a lot of liquid. If this soup is to be made many hours before serving, it may be necessary to cut back on the amount of barley or increase the water and adjust spices accordingly.

1-1/2 cups onion, chopped
2 cloves garlic, crushed
2 tablespoons oil
2/3 cup barley
2 stalks celery, chopped
4 cups mushrooms, sliced
1 teaspoon dill weed
1/4 teaspoon pepper
6 cups water
6 tablespoons tamari

1. Saute onions and garlic in the oil.
2. When the onions are soft, add half the barley.
3. Saute 3 minutes.
4. Add the celery, mushrooms, dill, and pepper.
5. Saute three to five minutes more; add the water and the other half of the barley.
6. Simmer for 1 hour; add the tamari during the last ten minutes.

Yield: 6 servings

SICILIAN MUSHROOM SOUP

4 cups beef stock
1-1/2 cups hot water
1-1/2 tablespoons olive oil
1-1/2 tablespoons unsalted butter
1 medium onion, finely chopped
1 medium clove garlic, crushed
8 ounces fresh mushrooms, trimmed, wiped clean with a dampened paper
   towel, thinly sliced
1 (16-ounce) can imported Italian plum tomatoes (preferably of the San
   Marzano type), drained, finely chopped, or 1 fresh ripe medium
   tomato, peeled, seeded, finely chopped
Salt
Freshly ground pepper
1 tablespoon finely chopped, fresh parsley
2 eggs
4 to 6 slices (each 1/2-inch thick) French or Italian bread, toasted
3/4 cup freshly grated Parmesan cheese

1. Make beef stock.
2. Heat 4 cups stock in heavy medium saucepan over medium heat to
simmering.
3. Meanwhile, heat oil and butter in noncorrodible, heavy, medium-sized
saucepan over medium-high heat.
4. When foam subsides, add onion and garlic; saute, stirring, until
onion is transparent - about 1 minute.
5. Add fresh mushrooms; saute stirring frequently, until almost all
mushroom liquid has evaporated - about 6 minutes.
6. Add hot water, the tomatoes, hot stock; salt and pepper to
taste; reduce heat to low.
7. Adjusting heat to maintain gentle simmer, cook soup, uncovered,
until flavors are blended - about 20 minutes.
8. Just before serving, stir parsley into soup.
9. Beat eggs with fork in small bowl until light and fluffy.
10. Holding bowl about 15 inches above simmering soup, pour in egg in
thin, steady stream, beating liquid in saucepan constantly with fork;
the egg will spin out into threads.
11. When all the egg has been added, remove soup from heat.
12. To serve, place a piece of bread in each of 4 warmed soup bowls;
ladle hot soup over bread slices, dividing evenly.
13. Serve immediately, accompanied by the grated Parmesan.

Yield: 4 servings

SPINACH VELVET SOUP

Note: Also known as tapioca starch, tapioca flour is used like cornstarch as a thickener and is available in health food stores.

Prepare immediately before serving, or spinach will lose its bright green color.

6 cups chicken stock
12 ounces fresh spinach
2 tablespoons sugar
3 egg whites
1 tablespoon water
1/4 cup tapioca flour
2 tablespoons finely chopped Smithfield ham
2 tablespoons peanut oil
2 teaspoons (or to taste) salt
1 teaspoon Oriental sesame oil

1. Make chicken stock.
2. Remove tough stems from enough spinach leaves to measure 6 cups, packed.
3. Rinse leaves in several changes of cold water until thoroughly free of grit.
4. Fill large heavy saucepan halfway with water; add sugar.
5. Heat over high heat to boiling.
6. Add spinach; stir gently until water returns to boil.
7. Drain immediately; rinse spinach under cold running water until cold; drain again.
8. Squeeze as much liquid as possible from spinach; mince fine with sharp heavy knife. Set aside.
9. Beat egg whites and 1 tablespoon water in small bowl with fork until combined but not foamy; set aside.
10. Stir together tapioca flour and 1/3 cup of the stock in second small bowl until blended and smooth; set aside while you heat remaining 5-2/3 cups stock to boiling in heavy, medium-sized saucepan over high heat.
11. Add 1 tablespoon of the ham; reduce heat to medium.
12. Simmer, uncovered, 5 minutes.
13. Re-stir tapioca mixture to blend; whisking constantly, add to soup in slow, steady stream.
14. Continue to whisk until soup is thickened and clear - about 30 seconds; stir in peanut oil.
15. Increase heat to high; whisk in spinach.
16. Heat soup to boiling, then remove from heat.
17. Hold bowl containing egg white mixture about 6 inches above soup; stirring soup gently, add egg whites in slow, steady stream.
18. Let stand without stirring 30 seconds, then stir to distribute egg white strands.
19. Season with salt; stir in sesame oil.
20. Remove soup to warmed tureen; sprinkle with remaining 1 tablespoon ham.
21. Serve immediately.

Yield: 6 to 8 servings

FRENCH ONION SOUP

Note: Stock may be refrigerated in a covered bowl, but needs boiling up every 2 or 3 days to prevent spoilage; or it may be frozen for several months. If your stock lacks savor, boil it down in a large kettle (after degreasing) to concentrate it.

Beef Stock

2 or more quarts sawed beef bones, including knuckles and some meaty scraps attached; plus veal and poultry bones, raw and/or cooked
2 large carrots, scrubbed and roughly sliced
3 large onions, peeled and roughly chopped
Sufficient cold water to cover all ingredients
1 large leek, washed (optional)
3 celery ribs with leaves, washed
1 tablespoon coarse or kosher salt (or table salt)
1 large herb bouquet tied in washed cheesecloth (8 parsley sprigs, 1 large imported bay leaf, 1 teaspoon dried thyme, 4 whole cloves or allspice berries, 3 large cloves garlic, unpeeled)

Onion Soup

3 tablespoons butter
1 tablespoon olive or cooking oil
6 cups quite thinly sliced yellow onions (about 1-1/2 pounds)
1/2 teaspoon sugar (helps the onions to brown)
1 teaspoon salt
2 tablespoons flour
2 quarts homemade stock, heated
2 cups dry white wine or dry white French vermouth
Salt and pepper as needed

For Beef Stock

1. Spread the bones and meat scraps (except for poultry) and the carrots and onions in a roomy roasting pan; set in the upper middle level of a 450F oven and roast for 40 or more minutes, turning and basting ingredients several times with accumulated fat until nicely browned.
2. Transfer to a large soup kettle, leaving fat in pan.
3. Discard fat and deglaze pan (pour in a cup or so of water and set over heat, scraping coagulated roasting juices into the liquid).
4. Pour into the kettle; add enough cold water to cover ingredients by 2 inches.
5. Bring to a simmer; skim off gray scum that will rise to the surface for several minutes; add rest of ingredients.
6. Cover partially; simmer slowly 4 to 5 hours at least, adding more water if needed to cover ingredients.
7. Strain into a large bowl; chill; peel coagulated fat off surface, and your stock is finished.

Yield: 2 quarts

For Onion Soup

1. Melt butter with the oil in a heavy-bottom, 1-quart pan; stir in the sliced onions.
2. Cover the pan; cook slowly for 15 to 20 minutes (or cook them in a 350F oven), stirring up occasionally, until onions are tender and translucent.
3. Raise heat to moderately high; stir in sugar and salt; cook 20 to 30 minutes more, stirring frequently, until onions have turned a fine, deep caramel brown.
4. Lower heat to moderate; blend in flour; cook, stirring, for 2 to 3 minutes.
5. Remove from heat; blend in 2 ladlefuls hot stock.
6. Stir in the rest, and the wine.
7. Season lightly to taste; bring to a boil; simmer slowly, partially covered, for 30 minutes.
8. Carefully correct seasoning.
9. Serve as is, with a bowl of grated cheese and toasted French bread, or float the French bread sprinkled with grated cheese on top of the soup and place under the broiler until cheese melts and starts to brown.

Yield: 2 quarts

LEEK AND ASPARAGUS BISQUE

1/4 cup (1/2 stick) unsalted butter
1 pound fresh asparagus tips, preferably white (if unavailable, drained
    canned white asparagus tips can be substituted)
5 to 6 medium leeks, white part only, thinly sliced
1 quart rich chicken or veal stock, preferably homemade
1 teaspoon sugar
Salt and freshly ground pepper
2 cups whipping cream

1. Melt butter in large, heavy saucepan over medium-low heat.
2. Add asparagus and leeks; cook until slightly softened, stirring occasionally - about 10 minutes.
3. Add stock; simmer until vegetables are tender - about 15 minutes.
4. Puree mixture in blender or processor.
5. Strain through fine sieve back into saucepan.
6. Stir in sugar.
7. Season with salt and pepper.
8. Simmer over medium heat 15 minutes.
9. Blend in cream; simmer 5 minutes.
10. Ladle soup into bowls and serve.

Yield: 6 to 8 servings

CREAM OF ALMOND AND ZUCCHINI SOUP

4 tablespoons butter
1 medium onion, minced
2 medium zucchini, unpeeled and well scrubbed
2/3 cup slivered almonds, toasted
4 cups chicken broth
3/4 cup heavy cream
1 tablespoon brown sugar (or more, to taste)
1 tablespoon Grand Marnier
1/4 teaspoon cinnamon
1/2 teaspoon nutmeg

1. Melt butter in a large kettle; add minced onion; cook over medium heat until softened.
2. Add zucchini, sliced thin, and 1/3 cup almonds.
3. Cook for an additional 5 minutes, until zucchini just begins to soften.
4. Add chicken broth and simmer for about 30 minutes, or until mixture is reduced by one-third.
5. Add the additional 1/3 almonds and simmer for 10 minutes.
6. Stir in cream, brown sugar, Grand Marnier, cinnamon, and nutmeg to stock; simmer over low heat, while stirring, until soup is thoroughly heated. Do not boil.

Yield: 6 servings

TOMATO CORN POTATO CHOWDER

French's Soup's On French Onion Soup Base, prepared according to package
    directions, to yield 10 cups
10 cups tomato puree
1-1/2 cups milk
1 teaspoon tarragon
1 teaspoon basil
1/4 cup sugar
1-1/4 teaspoons salt
2/3 cup French's Complete Idaho Potato Granules
2-1/2 pounds whole-kernel, canned corn, drained

1. Combine soup base, puree, milk, and seasonings; simmer on medium
heat for 15 minutes.
2. Gradually add potato granules, stirring constantly until blended.
3. Add corn; simmer for 15 minutes.

Yield: 25 1-cup servings

GAZPACHO

1 cup tomato, peeled and finely chopped
1/2 cup green pepper, finely chopped
1/2 cup celery, finely chopped
1/2 cup cucumber, finely chopped
1/4 cup onion, finely chopped
2 teaspoons parsley, snipped
1 teaspoon chives, chopped
1 small clove garlic, minced
2-3 tablespoons wine vinegar
2 tablespoons olive oil
1 teaspoon salt
1/4 teaspoon black pepper, freshly ground
1/2 teaspoon Worcestershire sauce
2 cups V-8 juice
Croutons

1. Combine ingredients in bowl. Puree 1/2 in food processor and
return to bowl.
2. Cover and chill thoroughly - at least 4 hours.
3. Serve in chilled cups.
4. Top with croutons.

Yield: 1 quart

VICHYSSOISE

Note: Vichyssoise is traditionally served very well chilled as a first course. It may also be served hot. If leeks are not available, substitute green onions. For extra seasoning, add a dash or two of nutmeg.

1 pound leeks
1/2 cup chopped onion
1/4 cup butter or margarine
1 pound potatoes (3 medium), pared, cut into 1/2-inch cubes (2 cups)
1/2 teaspoon salt
Dash white pepper
2 (13-3/4-ounce) cans clear chicken broth
2 cups milk
1 cup light cream, chilled
1/2 cup snipped chives
Crushed ice

1. To trim leeks, cut off roots and tips and most of the dark green, leaving some of the light green.
2. Wash leeks thoroughly and drain. (If leeks are very sandy, it may be necessary to remove the outer leaves and wash and drain them again.)
3. Using a sharp knife, slice the leeks crosswise - about 1/4-inch thick. This should yield approximately 2 cups of leek slices.
4. Have chopped onion ready; combine with sliced leeks.
5. Melt butter or margarine in a 5-quart Dutch oven or kettle.
6. Saute leeks and onion over medium heat until they are soft and golden - about 5 minutes.
7. Stir occasionally with a wooden spoon.
8. Be careful that leeks and onion do not brown; if they do, the soup, which should be creamy white, will be discolored.
9. Add potato, salt, pepper, and chicken broth to leek mixture.
10. Bring to boiling; reduce heat and simmer, covered, 45 minutes, or until potato is soft, almost mushy. This is important to ensure that the soup will be smooth.
11. Remove from heat.
12. Put potato-leek mixture into blender container, 2 cups at a time; blend at low speed until mixture is smooth. Puree should measure 5 cups.
13. In a small saucepan, heat milk until bubbles form around edge of pan.
14. Add hot milk to potato/leek mixture; mix well with wire whisk.
15. Refrigerate, covered, 6 hours or overnight.
16. Before serving, gradually add light cream; mix well.
17. Pour into 8 chilled soup cups; top with 1 tablespoon chives; surround with crushed ice.

Yield: 8 servings

SOUPE AU PISTORE

Note: Vegetable/broth mix can be cooked ahead of time, then reheated before serving, adding tomato sauce just before serving.

2 quarts chicken broth (may substitute 7 chicken bouillon cubes with 2 quarts water)
3 medium potatoes, peeled and cut in small cubes
1/2 pound fresh green beans, cut up, or 1 can cut green beans
3 carrots, peeled and sliced
1 medium onion, chopped
1 teaspoon salt
1/4 teaspoon pepper
1/2 pound zucchini or crookneck squash, sliced or 1 package frozen zucchini, sliced
1 (16-ounce) can kidney or navy beans, drained
2 cloves garlic, mashed
1 (6-ounce) can tomato paste
1 teaspoon dried basil
1/2 cup Parmesan cheese, grated
1/2 cup parsley, chopped, or 1/4 cup dried parsley flakes
1/4 cup olive oil

1. Combine chicken broth, potatoes, green beans, carrots, onions, salt, and pepper in a large pot or Dutch oven.
2. Bring to boil; reduce heat; simmer for 10 minutes.
3. Add zucchini and kidney or navy beans.
4. Cook 10 minutes or until tender.
5. Meanwhile, mix garlic, tomato paste, basil, cheese, and parsley.
6. Using wire whip, gradually beat in oil until mix is a thick sauce.
7. Just before serving, stir sauce into hot soup; heat through quickly.

Yield: 8 servings

SESAME-EGGDROP SOUP

1/2 ounce dried black mushrooms (optional)
1-1/2 cups boiling water (if you use mushrooms)
1 tablespoon peanut or soy sauce
3 thin slices fresh ginger root
2 tablespoons Chinese sesame oil
2 tablespoons sesame seeds
1 large carrot, cut into matchsticks
6 minced scallions (separate greens and whites)
Few dashes of salt and pepper
4 tablespoons tamari sauce
4 cups stock or water
3 medium-sized tomatoes, chopped
1 tablespoon wine vinegar
1 cup steamed green peas
2 large eggs, beaten

1. Soak mushrooms in boiling water for 15 to 20 minutes.
2. Strain through cheesecloth; reserve the water to use as part of
the stock.
3. Remove and discard the mushroom stems; slice the caps into strips.
(This addition is optional, because black mushrooms are expensive.
Although they're very delicious, the soup will also be fine without
them.)
4. In a kettle or a large saucepan, quickly saute ginger slices in peanut or soy oil for several minutes.
5. Remove and discard the ginger.
6. Add the sesame oil, sesame seeds, carrots, and scallion whites
(save the greens).
7. Salt the mixture lightly; grind in some fresh black pepper.
8. Saute over medium heat for 5 minutes, stirring frequently.
9. Add the soy or tamari, stock or water, and chopped tomatoes.
10. Cover; let cook over medium heat about 10 minutes more. At
this point, the soup is ready to rest until just before serving time.
11. About 10 minutes before serving time, add the vinegar, peas, and
optional black mushrooms.
12. Heat the soup to a gentle boil.
13. Stir the soup in a circular direction with a long chopstick;
drizzle in the beaten egg in a thin, steady stream.
14. Continue stirring the simmering soup for about 5 more minutes.
15. Serve topped with minced scallion greens.

Yield: 4 servings

ALMOND SOUP

2 tablespoons butter, melted
2 tablespoons instant-dissolving flour
2 tablespoons grated onion
3 cups chicken broth
1-1/2 cups finely ground almonds
1/4 teaspoon basil
1 teaspoon sugar
1/4 teaspoon ground mace
1/4 teaspoon dry mustard
1/4 teaspoon paprika
1 clove garlic, minced
Salt and pepper to taste
1 cup whipping cream
2 tablespoons sweet sherry
Slivered, toasted almonds to garnish

1. Combine butter and flour in a saucepan; blend until smooth. Cook 1 minute.
2. Add onion; cook 2 minutes.
3. Stir in chicken broth; cook, stirring constantly, until thickened.
4. Combine almonds, basil, sugar, mace, mustard, and paprika; stir into soup.
5. Cook 20 minutes over medium-low heat.
6. Add garlic, salt, and pepper.
7. Remove from heat; whisk in cream.
8. Heat slowly; do not bring to a boil.
9. Add sherry just before serving.
10. Garnish with slivered, toasted almonds.

Yield: 6 servings

MONTEREY JACK CHEESE SOUP

2 cups chicken broth
1 cup finely chopped onion
1 cup peeled and diced tomatoes
1 (4-ounce) can chopped green chilies
1 teaspoon garlic, minced
6 tablespoons butter
6 tablespoons all-purpose flour
5 cups hot milk
1/2 teaspoon salt
1/8 teaspoon pepper
3 cups coarsely grated Monterey Jack cheese (3/4 pound)

1.   In a large saucepan, mix chicken broth, onion, tomato, green chilies, and garlic.
2.   Bring to boil over high heat; cover.
3.   Reduce to moderate heat and simmer 10 minutes or until vegetables are tender.
4.   In a medium-sized, heavy saucepan, melt butter over moderate heat.
5.   Remove from heat and stir in flour.
6.   Return to heat and cook 3 minutes, stirring constantly.
7.   Stir in 3-1/2 cups hot milk, 1/2 cup at a time.
8.   Cook about 7 minutes until smooth and thickened.
9.   Remove broth mixture from heat and stir into the milk mixture, 1/4 cup at a time.
10. Return to heat.
11. Add remaining 1-1/2 cups milk, salt, pepper, and cheese, stirring constantly until cheese is melted and soup is well heated.

Yield: 8 servings

CAULIFLOWER CHEESE SOUP

5 heads cauliflower, cut into small florets
4 bottles of beer
16 cups water
4 cups butter, divided
4 cups flour, divided
3-4 dashes cayenne pepper
1/2 teaspoon black pepper
1/2 cup Dijon mustard
12 cups milk
6 to 8 cups sharp cheddar cheese, shredded

1. Cook cauliflower in beer and water until tender.
2. Drain; reserve (separately) stock and cauliflower.
3. Melt 2 cups of the butter; add 2 cups of the flour; cook for 1 minute.
4. Gradually add reserved stock, stirring constantly to make a smooth sauce.
5. Cook until thickened, stirring constantly. Set aside.
6. Melt remaining butter; add remaining flour; cook for 1 minute.
7. Stir in cayenne pepper, black pepper, and Dijon mustard.
8. Gradually add milk, stirring constantly to create a very smooth sauce.
9. Cook until very thick, stirring constantly.
10. Add cheese; stir until cheese is melted. Remove from heat.
11. Gradually add first sauce to cheese sauce.
12. Blend in reserved cauliflower.
13. Heat over low heat just until hot. Do not let it scorch.
14. Adjust seasonings and serve.

Yield: 2 gallons

CREAM OF CHEESE SOUP

Note: WONDERFUL!

1/2 cup minced carrots
3/4 cup minced celery
2 cups chicken broth
2 tablespoons onion
3 tablespoons butter or margarine, melted
1/4 cup plus 1-1/2 teaspoons all-purpose flour
2 cups milk
1/2 pound processed American cheese, cut into 1/2-inch cubes
Freshly chopped parsley (optional)

1. Combine first 3 ingredients in a small saucepan; simmer 10 minutes or until vegetables are tender.
2. Saute onion in butter in a medium saucepan; add flour, stirring well.
3. Cook 1 minute, stirring constantly.
4. Gradually add milk and chicken broth mixture; cook over medium heat, stirring constantly, until thickened and bubbly.
5. Remove from heat; add cheese; stir until cheese melts.
6. Garnish with parsley, if desired.
7. Serve immediately.

Yield: 4 cups

CREAM OF CHICKEN SOUP

Use Cream of Cheese Soup and add pulled chicken from freezer.

CHEESE AND LEEK SOUP

1/4 cup (1/2 stick) butter
1 cup chopped leek, white part only
1 cup chopped onion
3/4 cup chopped celery
3 cups chicken broth
1 (8-ounce) package cream cheese, cubed
1 cup dairy sour cream
Salt and freshly ground white pepper
Whipping cream (optional)
Chopped green onion, chives, or parsley

1. Melt butter in heavy medium saucepan over low heat.
2. Add leek, onion, and celery; cook until soft but not brown, stirring occasionally - about 10 minutes.
3. Add broth; simmer 10 minutes.
4. Puree in batches in blender.
5. Return to saucepan.
6. Mix cream cheese and sour cream in processor until smooth.
7. Add to soup; stir over low heat until heated through; do not boil.
8. Season with salt and pepper.
9. Thin with whipping cream if desired.
10. Ladle into bowls.
11. Garnish each with chopped green onion, chives, or parsley.
12. Serve immediately.
Yield: 8 servings

ZUCCHINI SOUP

1 large onion, chopped
6 small zucchini, cubed
1 teaspoon curry powder
1/2 teaspoon dry mustard
3 cups chicken broth
3 tablespoons uncooked rice (not instant)
Salt and pepper
1-1/2 cups milk
Chives for garnish

1. Combine all ingredients except milk.
2. Cover and simmer for 45 minutes.
3. Cool and puree.
4. Add milk.
5. Reheat to boiling.
6. Garnish with chives.

Yield: 6 servings

CHEESY ANYTIME SOUP

1/4 cup butter or margarine
1/4 cup plus 2 tablespoons all-purpose flour
1 (10-3/4-ounce) can chicken broth, undiluted
2 cups milk
1/4 teaspoon white pepper
2 tablespoons chopped pimientos
1/4 cup plus 2 tablespoons dry white wine
1/2 teaspoon Worcestershire sauce
1/4 teaspoon hot sauce
2 cups (8 ounces) shredded sharp cheddar cheese

1. Melt butter in a heavy saucepan over low heat; add flour, stirring until smooth.
2. Cook 1 minute, stirring constantly.
3. Gradually add the broth and milk; cook over medium heat, stirring constantly, until thickened and bubbly.
4. Stir in pepper.
5. Add next 4 ingredients.
6. Heat to boiling, stirring frequently.
7. Remove from heat; add cheddar cheese; stir until melted.
8. Serve immediately.

Yield: 5 cups

BEER-CHEESE SOUP

1/2 cup shredded carrot
1/4 cup finely chopped onion
1/4 cup butter or margarine
3 tablespoons all-purpose flour
1 teaspoon instant chicken bouillon granules
1/2 teaspoon salt
1/4 teaspoon dry mustard
1/8 teaspoon ground ginger
1/8 teaspoon pepper
3 cups milk
1-1/2 cups shredded cheddar cheese
1/2 cup beer

1. In a medium-sized saucepan, cook shredded carrot and chopped onion in butter or margarine until tender.
2. Stir in flour, instant chicken bouillon granules, salt, dry mustard, ground ginger, and pepper.
3. Stir in milk all at once, mixing till smooth.
4. Cook and stir over medium heat till thickened and bubbly.
5. Cook and stir 1 minute more.
6. Reduce heat; add cheddar cheese and beer; continue cooking and stirring until cheese is melted and soup is heated through.

Yield: 4 servings

BROCCOLI CHEESE SOUP

2 (10-ounce) packages frozen chopped broccoli
3-1/2 cups chicken broth
20-30 fresh mushrooms, sliced
1 cup finely chopped celery
1/2 cup chopped green onion
2 tablespoons finely chopped, fresh parsley
2 tablespoons butter
2 teaspoons garlic powder
1/2 teaspoon cracked pepper
1/2 teaspoon fresh pepper, grated
1-1/2 cups grated mild or medium cheddar cheese
1/2 cup dairy sour cream
1/2 teaspoon Tabasco sauce

1. Cook broccoli according to package directions. Drain.
2. Puree in blender with 1-1/2 cups chicken broth.
3. In a medium-sized saucepan, simmer pureed broccoli with remaining chicken broth over medium heat while preparing the vegetables.
4. In a skillet, saute vegetables in butter until onions are transparent.
5. Season with garlic powder and pepper; add to the broccoli.
6. Cover; cook over low heat for 30 minutes.
7. Stir in grated cheese and sour cream.
8. Season with Tabasco; serve when cheese is melted.

Yield: 6 servings

CHICKEN ALMOND SOUP

1/4 cup (1/2 stick) unsalted butter
1/4 cup all-purpose flour
1 quart whipping cream
3 cups strong chicken broth (preferably homemade)
2 tablespoons (1/4 stick) unsalted butter
3 tablespoons minced celery
2 tablespoons minced onion
1/4 cup toasted almonds, finely chopped (in processor)
1-1/2 cups minced, cooked chicken
1/8 teaspoon freshly ground white pepper
Salt
Sliced, toasted almonds (garnish)

1. Melt 1/4 cup butter in medium-sized saucepan over low heat.
2. Stir in flour.
3. Cook, stirring, 2 minutes; do not brown. Remove from heat.
4. Heat cream and broth in large, heavy saucepan over medium heat.
5. Gradually whisk 2 cups hot cream into flour mixture, then whisk back into remaining cream mixture.
6. Let soup simmer until thickened, stirring frequently.
7. Meanwhile, melt remaining 2 tablespoons butter in small saucepan over medium-low heat.
8. Add celery and onion; cook until soft - about 5 minutes.
9. Add chopped almonds; cook 1 minute.
10. Stir vegetable mixture into soup.
11. Add chicken and seasoning; simmer 5 minutes.
12. Ladle into heated bowls.
13. Garnish each serving with sliced, toasted almonds.

Yield: 2 quarts

CREAM OF CHICKEN SOUP WITH APPLES

3 tablespoons butter
2 cups chopped onion (10 ounces)
1 cup chopped carrot (6 ounces)
1 cup chopped celery (4 ounces)
1 tablespoon butter
3 medium-sized red apples (12 ounces), cored and sliced (4 cups)
4-1/2 tablespoons all-purpose flour
2 tablespoons (1/4 stick) butter
5 cups chicken broth (preferably homemade)
2 tablespoons applejack or Calvados
1/2 teaspoon dried marjoram, crumbled
1/2 teaspoon salt
Freshly ground white pepper
2 cups diced, cooked chicken
1 to 2 teaspoons cider vinegar (optional)

1. Melt 3 tablespoons butter in a large, heavy saucepan over high heat.
2. Add onion; saute 2 minutes.
3. Reduce heat to medium-low; cook, stirring occasionally, until onion is transparent - about 4 minutes.
4. Add carrot, celery, and 1 tablespoon butter.
5. Increase heat to medium-high; saute until vegetables are slightly tender - about 7 minutes.
6. Add apples.
7. Reduce heat to low, add flour and 2 tablespoons butter; stir 2 minutes.
8. Blend in broth, Applejack, marjoram, salt, and pepper.
9. Increase heat to medium; cook until soup thickens.
10. Stir in chicken.
11. Taste and adjust seasoning, adding vinegar if soup is too sweet.
12. Serve hot.

Yield: 4 to 6 servings

CHICKEN RIVVEL CORN SOUP

1 (about 4 pounds) stewing chicken, cut up
3-1/2 quarts boiling water
2 onions, chopped
1 cup chopped celery and leaves
8 ears sweet corn
2 hard-cooked eggs, sliced
Salt and pepper
1 cup flour
1 egg, well beaten
1/4 cup milk

1. Simmer chicken in boiling water for 3 hours, or until tender.
2. Remove chicken pieces and strain broth.
3. Add onions, celery, and corn cut from the cob to the broth.
4. Remove chicken from bones; dice.
5. Add cubes to soup.
6. Cook until vegetables are tender.
7. Mix flour with egg and milk.
8. Rub mixture with a fork until it crumbles.
9. Slowly drop crumbs into soup.
10. Cook, covered, over low heat for 15 minutes without stirring.
11. Just before serving, add hard-cooked eggs; salt and pepper to taste.

Yield: 6 servings

BROCCOLI-CHICKEN SOUP

2 (6-3/4-ounce) cans chunk-style chicken
3 tablespoons butter or margarine
1/4 cup chopped onion
1/4 cup all-purpose flour
1 teaspoon dry mustard
1/4 teaspoon salt
1/4 teaspoon dried thyme, crushed
1/8 teaspoon pepper
1-3/4 cups milk
1 (14-1/2-ounce) can chicken broth
1/2 of a 20-ounce package (2 cups) frozen mixed broccoli, cauliflower,
    and carrots

1. Drain chicken, reserving liquid.
2. Chop chicken; set aside.
3. In a 3-quart saucepan, melt butter or margarine; add onion; cook
until tender but not browned.
4. Stir in flour, dry mustard, salt, thyme, and pepper.
5. Stir in milk and chicken broth all at once.
6. Cook and stir over medium heat until slightly thickened and bubbly.
7. Stir in vegetables, chicken, and chicken liquid.
8. Cook and stir for 4 to 6 minutes more or until vegetables are tender
and soup is heated through.

Yield: 4 to 6 servings

CHICKEN NOODLE SOUP

Note: This recipe is our favorite Chicken and Rice Soup. We substitute 1 cup of uncooked rice for the 2-1/2 cups of homemade noodles. Either way you try it, the soup is delicious.

The noodles may be refrigerated for as long as a week, or frozen.

Soup
10 cups water
1 frying chicken, cut up
1 carrot, peeled and cut into chunks
1 medium onion, cut into chunks
1 rib celery, cut into chunks
1 bay leaf

1 cup finely diced celery
1 cup finely diced carrots
1 cup finely diced onion
1 tablespoon chicken stock base
2 teaspoons salt
1 teaspoon onion salt
1/2 teaspoon pepper
2-1/2 cups homemade noodles (see recipe below)
Fresh parsley sprigs

Homemade Noodles
4 eggs
2-1/3 to 2-2/3 cups sifted flour
1 teaspoon salt

For Soup
1. Combine chicken, carrot, onion, celery, and bay leaf with water in large suacepan.
2. Cover; simmer 1 hour or until chicken and vegetables are tender. Cool.
3. Remove chicken from skin and bones; cut into bite-sized pieces; set aside.
4. Discard skin and bones.
5. Reserve and strain liquid for stock.
6. Combine celery, carrots, onion, chicken stock base, salt, onion salt, and pepper with reserved stock in large pot.
7. Cover; cook over medium heat for 30 to 45 minutes, or until vegetables are tender.
8. Add noodles and reserved chicken for last 20 minutes of cooking time.
9. Garnish each serving with a parsley sprig.

Homemade Noodles
1. Beat eggs in large bowl.
2. Stir in salt and enough of the flour to make a stiff dough.
3. Turn out on lightly floured board.
4. Knead for 3 to 5 minutes.
5. Roll out very thin.
6. Cover with towel and let rest for 20 minutes.
7. Cut into strips.

Yield: 10 servings

CHICKEN CHOWDER

4 chicken breast halves, skinned
4 cups water
1/2 teaspoon salt
2 medium potatoes, peeled and cubed
2 medium carrots, coarsely chopped
1 (17-ounce) can cream-style corn
1 (15-ounce) can tomato sauce with tomato bits
1/4 teaspoon pepper

1. Combine first 3 ingredients in a Dutch oven; bring to a boil.
2. Cover; reduce heat; simmer 30 to 45 minutes or until chicken is tender.
3. Remove chicken from broth, reserving 3 cups broth in Dutch oven.
4. Remove the meat from the bones; cut into bite-sized pieces; set aside.
5. Add potatoes and carrots to broth; bring to a boil.
6. Cover; reduce heat; simmer 10 to 12 minutes.
7. Add chicken, corn, tomato sauce, and pepper; cover; simmer 15 minutes or until vegetables are tender, stirring occasionally.

Yield: 2 quarts

TURKEY VEGETABLE SOUP

1/4 cup (1/2 stick) butter or margarine
2 medium onions, chopped
2 tablespoons all-purpose flour
1 teaspoon curry powder
3 cups chicken broth
1 cup chopped potatoes
1/2 cup thinly sliced carrots
1/2 cup sliced celery
2 tablespoons chopped, fresh parsley
1/2 teaspoon sage or poultry seasoning
2 cups cubed cooked turkey
1-1/2 cups half-and-half cream
1 (10-ounce) package frozen chopped spinach
Salt and freshly ground pepper

1. Melt butter in large saucepan over medium-high heat.
2. Add onions; saute until translucent - about 10 minutes.
3. Stir in flour and curry powder; cook 2 to 3 minutes.
4. Add broth, potatoes, carrots, celery, parsley, and sage; bring to boil.
5. Reduce heat to low; cover; simmer 10 minutes.
6. Add turkey, half-and-half, and spinach.
7. Cover and continue simmering until heated through - about 7 minutes.
8. Season with salt and pepper.
9. Serve hot.

Yield: 6 to 8 servings

BEEF AND BARLEY SOUP

Note: Serve with French bread and a big green salad for a very hearty meal.

3 pounds lean beef short ribs
2 large onions, chopped
1/4 cup parsley, chopped
3 cloves garlic, minced or pressed
3/4 cup split peas
3/4 cup dried baby lima beans
8 cups water
3 beef bouillon cubes
1 tablespoon dill weed
1/4 pound mushrooms, sliced
1/2 cup pearl barley
8 large carrots, cut into 1-inch slices
Salt and pepper to taste

1. In a 6- to 8-quart kettle, brown meat on all sides.
2. Add onion; saute until limp.
3. Stir in parsley, garlic, split peas, limas, water, and bouillon cubes.
4. Cover; simmer 2 hours or until meat is tender when pierced.
5. Lift out meat; skim and discard fat from broth.
6. Whirl broth and vegetables a small amount at a time in blender until pureed.
7. Return to kettle; stir in dill, mushrooms, barley, and carrots.
8. Discard bones and break meat into bite-sized pieces.
9. Stir into soup.
10. Add salt and pepper to taste.
11. Cover; simmer about 45 minutes or until barley is tender.

Yield: 6 to 8 servings

FRESH VEGETABLE BEEF SOUP

2 pounds beef shank, cut into pieces
3 quarts water
1 large onion, diced
1 tablespoon salt
1/2 teaspoon dried thyme, crumbled
1/2 cup dried split peas
5 medium carrots, cut into 1-inch slices
3 large celery stalks, cut into 1/2-inch pieces
3 medium tomatoes, peeled, seeded, and coarsely chopped
1-1/2 cups fresh corn kernels
1 large potato, peeled and diced
1 large green bell pepper, cored, seeded, and diced
1 cup shelled fresh peas
1 cup shelled fresh lima beans
1 cup fresh green beans, broken into small pieces
1 cup chopped fresh spinach leaves
1 cup catsup
2 tablespoons chopped fresh parsley leaves
Salt and freshly ground pepper

1. Cover beef with water in large stockpot.
2. Add onion, salt, and thyme; bring to a boil, skimming fat from surface.
3. When foam subsides, add split peas.
4. Cover; simmer over low heat 4 hours.
5. Remove shank bones.
6. Cut off meat; return to soup; discard bones.
7. Let soup cool; refrigerate.
8. Discard fat from surface.
9. Add all remaining ingredients except salt and pepper.
10. Cover; simmer until vegetables are tender - about 1 hour.
11. Season with salt and pepper.
12. Serve hot.

Yield: 6 quarts

BEEF AND BARLEY IN BRANDY BROTH

Note: I love the flavor of barley, especially when it is cooked with beef. This makes a perfect dinner for a winter evening.

3 pounds beef chuck, cut into 1-1/2-inch cubes
Salt and freshly ground black pepper
6 tablespoons butter
1 (6x1-inch) strip orange zest
12 to 15 small boiling onions, peeled
2/3 cup very strong beef stock or undiluted condensed beef broth
1/2 cup brandy
1 large pressed garlic clove
2 tablespoons butter
2/3 cup barley
6 carrots, peeled and cut into 2x1/4-inch strips
4 teaspoons grated fresh lemon peel
4 tablespoons finely chopped fresh parsley

1. Blot meat with paper towels.
2. Season with salt and pepper. Be generous with the pepper.
3. Heat butter in larger heavy kettle or Dutch oven over medium heat until it bubbles and begins to brown.
4. Add meat, turning to coat each piece with butter.
5. Add orange zest.
6. Arrange onions over meat.
7. Stir together stock, 1/4 cup brandy, and garlic. Add to meat.
8. Cover; cook without stirring over low heat about 2-1/2 hours or until meat is tender.
9. Saute barley in 2 tablespoons butter. Add to soup; simmer 30 more minutes.
10. Add carrots, tucking them beneath liquid. Cover; simmer just until tender - about 30 minutes.
11. Gently stir in lemon peel, remaining 1/4 cup brandy, and 2 tablespoons parsley.
12. Taste; add more salt, if necessary.
13. Ladle into shallow soup plates.
14. Sprinkle with remaining parsley.

Yield: 5 to 6 servings

BEAN AND BACON SOUP

1 pound dried navy beans
6 cups water
2 teaspoons salt
1/4 teaspoon pepper
2 cloves garlic, minced
1 bay leaf
4 slices bacon
2 medium onions, finely chopped
1 small green pepper, finely chopped
1/2 cup finely chopped carrots
1 (8-ounce) can tomato sauce
1 teaspoon minced fresh parsley

1. Sort and wash beans; place in a large Dutch oven.
2. Cover with water 2 inches above beans; let soak overnight.
3. Drain beans; cover with 6 cups water.
4. Add salt, pepper, garlic, and bay leaf.
5. Cook bacon until crisp; remove bacon, reserving drippings.
6. Crumble bacon; set aside.
7. Add onion and green pepper to drippings; saute until tender.
8. Add onion, green pepper, and carrots to beans.
9. Bring to boil; cover; reduce heat; simmer 1 hour.
10. Add tomato sauce and parsley to soup; cover; simmer an additional 30 minutes.
11. Remove bay leaf.
12. Ladle into serving bowls, and sprinkle with reserved bacon.

Yield: 3 quarts

OLD-FASHIONED HAMBURGER CHOWDER

2 pounds ground beef
2 cups coarsely chopped cabbage
2 carrots, cut into chunks
1 large onion, sliced
1 celery stalk, sliced
1-1/2 cups water
1 (13-3/4-ounce) can chicken broth
1 (10-1/2-ounce) can condensed beef broth
Dash pepper
1 (8-1/2-ounce) can Green Giant Sweet Peas, drained
1 (7-ounce) can Green Giant Mexicorn Golden Whole Kernel Corn with
   Sweet Peppers, drained

1. In large saucepan or Dutch oven, brown ground beef; drain.
2. Add ramaining ingredients except peas and corn.
3. Bring to a boil; simmer 20 minutes or until vegetables are tender.
4. Add peas and corn; heat thoroughly.

Yield: 6 servings

CRAB SOUP

1 tablespoon butter
1 tablespoon all-purpose white flour
2 hard-cooked eggs, whites and yolks separated
1 (10-3/4-ounce) can condensed cream of celery soup
1 cup light cream
1 cup milk
1 tablespoon chopped fresh parsley
1 clove garlic, minced
1/2 pound flaked crab meat
1 tablespoon grated lemon rind
2 tablespoons dry sherry

1. In top of double boiler, melt butter; blend in flour.
2. Press the egg yolks through a coarse sieve; add to the butter and
flour.
3. Blend in the soup, cream, milk, parsley, and garlic.
4. Cook, stirring constantly, until mixture is smooth and very hot.
5. Add crab; heat gently.
6. Just before serving, press the egg whites through a coarse sieve;
add them along with the lemon rind and sherry.
7. Reheat but do not boil.

Yield: 4 servings

SHRIMP AND SPINACH SOUP

6-8 ounces fresh or frozen spinach, chopped
10 ounces or so small shrimp pieces
1/2 tablespoon granulated garlic
1 teaspoon salt
1 teaspoon black pepper
1/2 teaspoon ground ginger
3 medium onions, chopped, to make about 2-1/4 cups
1 gallon chicken stock

1. Put everything into a pot.
2. Bring to a boil and simmer at least 1 hour.

Yield: 1 gallon

SHRIMP-VEGETABLE BISQUE

1 pound zucchini, thinly sliced
1 cup thinly sliced carrots
1/2 cup chopped celery
1/2 cup sliced green onion
1/2 cup chicken broth
1-3/4 cups skim milk
1/2 cup water
1 (10-3/4-ounce) can cream of mushroom soup, undiluted
1/2 cup plain yogurt
1 (4-1/2-ounce) can small shrimp, drained and rinsed
1 tablespoon dry white wine

1. Combine vegetables and chicken broth in a Dutch oven; cover and
simmer 15 to 20 minutes or until vegetables are tender.
2. Spoon half of vegetable mixture into container of electric blender;
process until smooth.
3. Repeat procedure with remaining mixture.
4. Return vegetable mixture to Dutch oven; stir in remaining ingredients.
5. Cook over low heat, stirring constantly, until thoroughly heated.

Yield: 10 cups

Breads

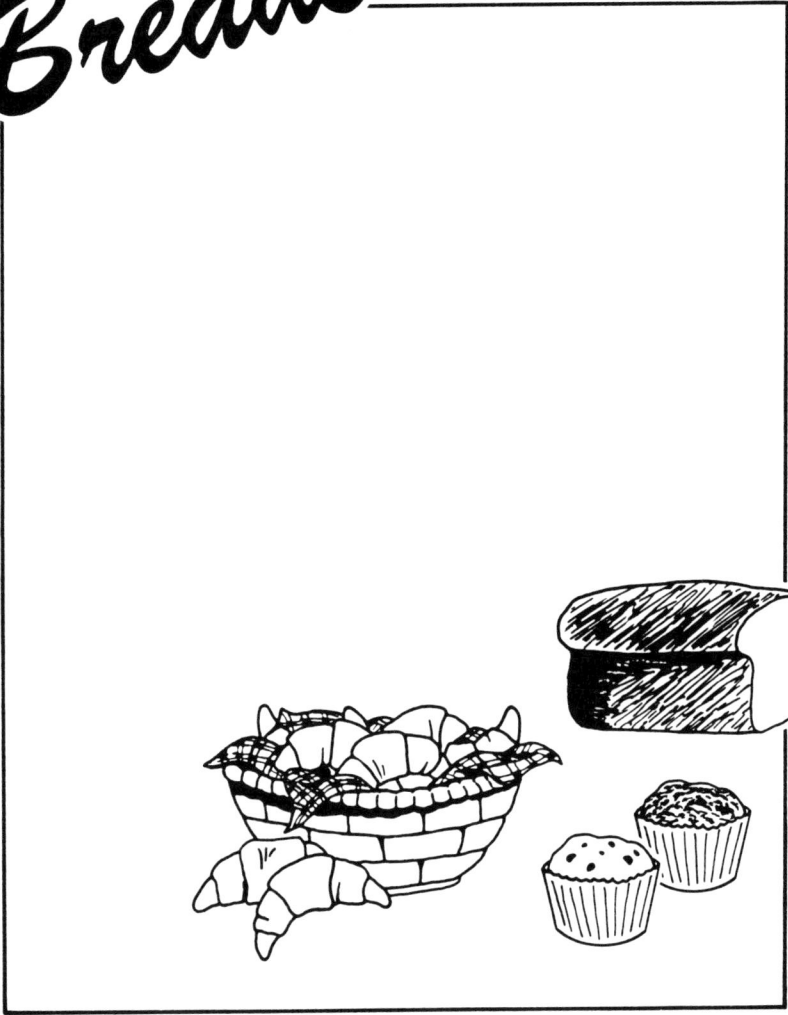

SWEDISH CHEESE BREAD

Note: A former neighbor of mine brought a loaf of this over one day and then was kind enough to share the recipe with me. The first time we served it as a Friday Morning Goodie, it was an immediate success. Once you try it you'll see why. We use a little more filling per roll than the recipe calls for; you can vary it as you like.

Dough
1 cup dairy sour cream
1/2 cup sugar
1 teaspoon salt
1/2 cup melted butter
2 packages yeast
1/2 cup warm water
2 eggs, beaten
4 cups flour

Filling
1-1/2 to 2 (8-ounce) packages cream cheese
3/4 cup sugar
1 egg, beaten
1/8 teaspoon salt
2 teaspoons vanilla

Glaze
2 cups powdered sugar
4 tablespoons milk

For Dough
1. Heat the sour cream, sugar, salt, and butter to lukewarm; let cool.
2. Dissolve the yeast in the warm water; add to the sour cream mixture.
3. Add eggs and flour and mix well.
4. Cover tightly and refrigerate overnight.
5. Divide dough into four equal parts.
6. Roll in rectangles and spread with filling.
7. Roll up in jelly roll fashion, pinch ends and edges together, and slit at 2-inch intervals.
8. Cover and let rise 1 hour or doubled.
9. Bake at 375F for 20 minutes.
10. Glaze while warm.

For Filling
1. Cream together cream cheese and sugar.
2. Add egg and beat well.
3. Add remaining ingredients.

For Glaze
1. Combine ingredients. For a thinner consistency, add a few drops of milk; for a thicker consistency, add a little more sugar.

Yield: 4 rolls

WHOLE WHEAT STICKY BUNS

Note: Perhaps the whole wheat flour will make you feel virtuous!
If you don't have any whole wheat flour, you can use unbleached.
These really are the sticky, gooey kind of sticky buns. What a way
to start a perfect morning!

Dough
1/2 cup milk
1/2 cup butter
1/4 cup sugar
1 teaspoon salt
1 package (1 tablespoon) yeast
1/2 cup warm water
2 large eggs, beaten
2-1/2 cups whole wheat flour
3 cups unbleached flour
1 teaspoon lemon peel
1/2 teaspoon ground ginger

Filling
3 tablespoons butter, softened
1/4 cup brown sugar
1 tablespoon cinnamon
3/4 cup raisins

Topping
1/2 cup brown sugar
1/4 cup butter
2 tablespoons dark corn syrup
1 tablespoon water
Chopped nuts

For Dough
1. Scald milk. To scald milk, place milk in heavy bottomed pot. Heat
on medium/high heat without stirring just until small bubbles appear
around the edges of the pot. Remove from the heat. Add butter, sugar,
and salt; cool.
2. Sprinkle yeast over warm water.
3. Combine milk mixture with eggs. Add yeast and seasonings; mix well.
4. Gradually add flours until dough forms a ball.
5. Cover with a damp cloth; let rest 10 minutes.
6. Knead for 10 minutes until dough is very elastic.
7. Place dough in a large greased bowl, turning once to grease surface
of dough.
8. Let dough rise in a warm place for 2 hours.
9. Punch down dough; knead 1 or 2 times; let rise again for 40
minutes.
10. While dough is rising, prepare filling and topping.

For Filling
1. Combine all filling ingredients (except raisins) in a mixing bowl or
food processor.
2. Mix well. (Raisins will be sprinkled in filling during assembly.)

For Topping
1. Combine all topping ingredients (except nuts) in a mixing bowl or food processor.
2. Mix well. (Nuts will be placed during assembly.)

To Assemble
1. When dough is ready, punch down; divide it in half.
2. Roll 1/2 of dough into a 10x18-inch rectangle.
3. Spread half of filling over rectangle.
4. Sprinkle with 1/2 of the raisins.
5. Starting at the long edge, roll up dough in jelly roll fashion.
6. Cut into 3/4-inch slices.
7. Repeat procedure with other 1/2 of the dough.
8. Spread topping on the bottom of a baking sheet.
9. Sprinkle with nuts.
10. Place dough slices (cut side down) in pan about 1-inch apart.
11. Cover with damp cloth; let rise in warm place for about 30 minutes.
12. Bake at 325F for about 20 minutes or until nicely browned.
13. Remove from oven; immediately invert baking pan on a pan or plate the same size or larger than the first. The bottom of the buns is now the top. Be sure to scrape out any of the goo that remains in the pan, that's the best part.
14. Serve warm.

Yield: 16 to 20 buns

MORAVIAN SUGAR CAKE

Note: Sugar cakes freeze very well. To serve, thaw and warm gently.

1 cup hot mashed potatoes*
1 cup hot potato water
3/4 cup butter or shortening
7/8 cup granulated sugar
2 slightly beaten eggs
2 envelopes dry yeast dissolved in 1/2 cup lukewarm water
2 teaspoons salt
4-5 cups flour
Butter
Light brown sugar
Cinnamon

1. Cook peeled potatoes in unsalted water.
2. Drain; reserve 1 cup cooking water.
3. Mash potatoes, adding nothing.
4. Mix well the 1 cup potatoes, reserved water, butter, sugar, and salt; cool to lukewarm.
5. Add eggs and dissolved yeast.
6. Stir in flour until dough resembles heavy muffin batter.
7. Cover; let rise in warm place until doubled.
8. Punch down; spread in five 9-inch greased layer pans (or greased foil pans).
9. Cover; let rise to top of pans.
10. When risen, punch surface with holes.
11. Fill holes with bits of butter.
12. Cover tops with light brown sugar; dust lightly with cinnamon.
13. Bake at 375F for 20 minutes or until brown.

*If using instant potatoes: Prepare instant mashed potatoes to make 1 cup using all water (no milk or seasonings). Use 1 cup hot water for potato water in above recipe. Proceed as above.

Yield: 5 9-inch cakes

WAFFLES WITH FRESH FRUIT

Note: This is a truly beautiful luncheon or brunch dish. The first time we served it in the Cafe, my husband was appalled at the idea. He came for lunch that day, saw how pretty and tasty it was, and has been a big fan of it ever since!

2 cups sifted flour
3 teaspoons baking powder
1 teaspoon salt
2 tablespoons sugar
2 eggs, separated
1-1/2 cups milk
6 tablespoons melted butter or salad oil
Sliced fresh seasonal fruit such as raspberries, strawberries, blue-
    berries, peaches, bananas, or grapes
Maple syrup
Whipped butter

1. Sift together the flour, baking powder, salt, and sugar.
2. Beat egg yolks; add milk and melted shortening. Pour into flour mixture; stir just enough to moisten dry ingredients. Do not overmix; you do not want to develop the gluten in the flour or your waffles will be tough.
3. Beat egg whites until stiff, but not dry. Fold into batter.
4. Grease a hot waffle iron if necessary; pour batter until it flows one inch from the edge. Bake four to five minutes. Waffles should be golden brown.
5. Top with prepared fruit. When selecting the fruits, be mindful of their color and flavor compatibility, and compliment.
6. Place a scoop of whipped butter in center and drizzle Maple syrup over all. You may wish to add the syrup to the butter when you are whipping it.

Yield: 4 to 6 waffles

Variation:
You may wish to add 1/2 cup finely chopped pecans to the batter.

CINNAMON CRISPS

Note: This is a variation on the earlier sticky buns. The extra step is well worth the effort.

3-1/2 cups sifted flour, divided
1 package dry yeast
1-1/4 cups milk
1-3/4 cup sugar, divided
1/4 cup shortening
1 teaspoon salt
1 egg
8 tablespoons butter, melted, divided
1/2 cup pecans, chopped
1/2 cup brown sugar
1-1/2 teaspoons cinnamon, divided

1. In a large bowl, combine 2 cups flour and yeast.
2. Heat milk, 1/4 cup sugar, shortening, and salt just until shortening melts.
3. Add to dry ingredients; add egg; beat at low speed until mixed.
4. Beat 3 minutes on high, then stir in by hand enough of the remaining flour to make a moderately stiff dough.
5. Place in a greased bowl, turning once to grease surface.
6. Cover and let rise in a warm place until double - about 1-1/2 to 2 hours.
7. Turn out onto a lightly floured surface; divide in half.
8. Roll out one portion of dough at a time into a 12-inch square.
9. Combine 4 tablespoons of butter, brown sugar, 1/2 cup sugar, and 1/2 teaspoon cinnamon. Spread half of this over the dough.
10. Roll up in jelly roll fashion; pinch the edges to seal.
11. Cut into 12 pieces and place on a greased baking sheet.
12. Flatten each to about 3-inch diameter.
13. Repeat with other half of dough.
14. Let rise about 30 minutes.
15. Cover with waxed paper; flatten again.
16. Remove paper; brush with 4 tablespoons butter.
17. Combine 1 cup sugar, 1/2 cup pecans, and 1 teaspoon cinnamon; sprinkle over rolls.
18. Cover with paper; flatten.
19. Bake at 400F for 10 to 12 minutes.
20. Remove immediately from baking sheets. Serve warm.

Yield: 24 rolls

LEMON MUFFINS

1 cup butter
1 cup sugar
4 eggs, separated
2 cups flour
2 teaspoon baking powder
1 teaspoon salt
1/2 cup fresh lemon juice
2 teaspoons lemon peel, grated

1. Cream butter and sugar until smooth.
2. Add egg yolks; beat until light.
3. Sift flour with baking powder and salt; add alternately with lemon juice, mixing thoroughly after each addition. Do not overmix.
4. Fold in stiffly beaten egg whites and grated lemon peel.
5. Fill buttered muffin tins 3/4 full.
6. Bake at 375 for about 20 minutes.

Yield: 12 to 16 servings

FUNNEL CAKE

Note: The first time I had funnel cake was at the Kutztown Fair. Kutztown is in the Pennsylvania Dutch Country, and the fair is an old-fashioned festival. The only rides they have are the buggy rides around the horsetrack. All the people exhibit the crafts they have been working on during the year. The food served, in addition to the funnel cake, includes Shoo Fly Pie and corn-on-the-cob on a stick.

2 cups milk
2 eggs, beaten
2 cups flour
1 teaspoon baking powder
1/2 teaspoon salt

1. Combine milk and eggs.
2. In separate bowl, sift together flour, baking powder, and salt.
3. Add eggs and milk to dry ingredients; mix thoroughly.
4. Test for texture. Add flour if too thin, milk if too thick.
5. Pour into hot fat in a spiral pattern. Turn and brown the other side.
6. Top with powdered sugar or cinnamon sugar while still warm.

Yield: 4 to 6 servings

SUPER NUT ROLL

Note: This was one of those recipes that we kept losing. I
hope that you never do because it is sure to become a family favorite.

Sometimes we add cinnamon, nutmeg, and/or cocoa to the nut mixture.

1 cake of yeast or 2 packages yeast
1/2 pint or 1 cup dairy sour cream
3-1/2 cups flour
1/4 teaspoon salt
2 tablespoons sugar
2 sticks of butter
4 egg yolks

Nut Mixture
3 cups ground nuts
1 cup brown or white sugar (whichever you prefer)

1. Mix butter and egg yolks together.
2. Add the salt and sugar.
3. Add flour; mix until crumbly like corn meal.
4. Make a hole in the center of the mixture.
5. Mix yeast and sour cream; add to the flour mixture.
6. Knead until dough pulls away from the bowl.
7. Divide into four parts.
8. Let stand for 8 hours in the refrigerator.
9. Roll dough into a 1/4 inch thick rectangle.
10. Spread nut mixture over the dough; roll up like a jelly roll.
11. Place on a cookie sheet; let stand for 1 or 2 hours.
12. Bake at 350F until lightly brown.

Yield: 4 rolls

SOUR CREAM COFFEE CAKE

Note: Be sure to put enough of the filling inside the cake. This is so moist and delicious. It is one of the favorite Friday Morning Goodies.

1/2 cup butter or margarine
1 cup sugar
2 eggs
2 cups sifted flour
1 teaspoon baking soda
1 teaspoon baking powder
1/2 teaspoon salt
1 teaspoon vanilla
1 cup dairy sour cream

Topping
1 cup pecans, chopped
3/4 cup brown sugar
1/4 cup white sugar
1 teaspoon cinnamon (We always use more.)
Melted butter to glaze finished cake, about 1/2-3/4 cup

1. Combine topping ingredients; set aside.
2. Cream together shortening and sugar.
3. Add eggs one at a time; mix well.
4. Add dry ingredients, sour cream, and vanilla.
5. Pour half in lightly greased 9x13-inch pan.
6. Cover with half of the topping mix.
7. Pour on the rest of the batter, then the rest of the topping.
8. Bake for 40 minutes at 325F.
9. Brush with melted butter while still hot.

Yield: 16 servings

CHOCOLATE PECAN MUFFINS

Note: Why not?

1/2 pound butter
2 cups chocolate syrup
1-1/2 cups milk
3 eggs
3/4 tablespoon vanilla
4 cups flour
1-1/2 cups sugar
1 tablespoon salt
2 tablespoons baking powder

Topping
1/2 cup pecans, finely chopped
1/4 cup brown sugar
1 tablespoon butter, melted

1. Beat butter; blend with chocolate syrup, milk, eggs, and vanilla.
2. Add dry ingredients, beating as little as possible to mix well.
3. Pour into greased or lined muffin tins.
4. Mix ingredients for topping by hand; put a thin layer on top of each muffin.
5. Bake at 350F for 20-25 minutes or until top springs back when pressed.

Yield: 3 dozen

VANILLA MUFFINS

4 tablespoons butter, melted
1 cup sugar
1 cup milk
1 egg, beaten
1-1/2 teaspoons vanilla
2 cups flour
2 tablespoons baking powder

1. Preheat oven to 375F.
2. In small bowl, mix butter, sugar, milk, egg, and vanilla together.
3. In medium-sized bowl, mix flour and baking powder together.
4. Add liquid mixture all at once to flour.
5. Mix well.
6. Spoon into greased, hot muffin tins.
7. Bake 375F for 15 minutes.

Yield: 12 muffins

OATMEAL MUFFINS

Note: To make 1 cup sour milk, combine 1 tablespoon vinegar plus enough sweet milk to equal 1 cup.

1 cup Quick Oats
1 cup buttermilk or sour milk (see note)
1 egg
1/2 cup brown sugar
1 cup flour
1/2 teaspoon salt
1 teaspoon baking powder
1/2 teaspoon soda
1/2 cup margarine, melted

1. Soak oatmeal in milk for 1 hour; add egg and beat well.
2. Add sugar and mix.
3. Add flour sifted with salt, baking powder, and soda.
4. Add cooled shortening.
5. Bake in greased muffin tins at 400F for 15-20 minutes.

Yield: 1 dozen

LEMON BREAD

Note: This bread can be done ahead of time and can be frozen. It makes a wonderful breakfast bread to have on hand.

1 cup margarine
2 cups sugar
4 eggs
3 cups sifted flour
1/2 teaspoon salt
1/2 teaspoon soda
1 cup buttermilk
Grated rind of 1 lemon
1 cup chopped nuts
Juice of 3 lemons
1 cup confectioner's sugar

1. Cream together margarine and sugar.
2. Add eggs one at a time; blend well.
3. Sift together flour, salt, and soda.
4. Add alternately with buttermilk, lemon rind, and chopped nuts.
5. Pour into 2 greased loaf pans.
6. Bake 1 hour at 350F.
7. While bread bakes, combine lemon juice and confectioner's sugar.
8. When bread is baked, pour lemon syrup over hot bread.

Yield: 2 loaves

SPICED ZUCCHINI BREAD

Note: Zucchini is such a versatile vegetable. Here it adds its dictinctive flavor to a moist, quick bread.

3 cups flour
2 teaspoons baking soda
1 teaspoon salt
1/2 teaspoon baking powder
1-1/2 teaspoon ground cinnamon
3/4 cup finely chopped walnuts
3 eggs
2 cups sugar
1 cup vegetable oil
2 teaspoons vanilla
2 cups coarsely shredded zucchini
1 (8-ounce) can crushed pineapple

1. Combine flour, soda, salt, baking powder, cinnamon, and nuts; set aside.
2. Beat egg lightly in a large bowl, add sugar, oil, and vanilla; beat until creamy.
3. Stir in zucchini and pineapple.
4. Add dry ingredients, stirring only until dry ingredients are moistened.
5. Spoon batter into 2 well greased and floured 9x5x3-inch loaf pans.
6. Bake 350F for 1 hour or until done.
7. Cool 10 minutes before removing from pans; turn out on rack and cool completely.

Yield: 2 loaves

BANANA NUT BREAD

Note: This is our favorite Banana Nut Bread. It's nicely moist
and nutty. I usually use 2 bananas per recipe.

1/2 cup butter
1 cup sugar
2 eggs
2 cups flour
1 teaspoon baking soda
1/2 teaspoon salt
1 cup mashed ripe banana
1/2 cup chopped walnuts

1. Preheat oven to moderate (350F).
2. Cream butter and sugar together until light.
3. Beat in eggs.
4. Sift together flour, baking soda, and salt.
5. Stir into butter-sugar mixture, blending well.
6. Stir in bananas and walnuts.
7. Spoon batter into a well buttered, 2-pound bread tin (9-1/2x5-1/2x
2-3/4); bake in the moderate oven for 1 hour, or until loaf tests
done.
8. Cool for 5 minutes; turn out on rack to cool completely.

Yield: 1 loaf

FRENCH BEER BREAD

Note: This is another one of Jean's wonderful bread recipes. It must be made ahead.

2/3 cup beer
2 cups warm water
1-1/3 tablespoons yeast
3 tablespoons wheat flour
2 cups all-purpose flour
1 tablespoon salt
1 cup flour

1. Mix beer and warm water 24 hours in advance.
2. Stir in the yeast.
3. Add wheat flour and all-purpose flour. Continue to add flour until the mixture has a thick sludge consistency.
4. A few hours before serving, stir the mixture.
5. Add the salt and 1 cup flour. Continue to add flour until the dough is no longer sticky.
6. Knead 10-15 minutes by hand or knead 40 seconds in a food processor.
7. Shape into 2 loaves.
8. Let rise until double in bulk.
9. Bake at 400F for 40-50 minutes or until done.

Yield: 2 loaves

HERB BUTTER FOR BREAD

Note: The lemon juice adds a surprising tang to this recipe. It will make the most ordinary loaf of grocery store French bread come alive. If you have a favorite French bread recipe, try this variation: when shaping your bread, spread dough out into a rectangle about 1 inch thick. Instead of melting the butter in the recipe, simply cream the ingredients and spread on the dough. Roll up jelly-roll fashion and seal well. Bake as usual.

1/2 cup butter or margarine
1/4 cup parsley
2 teaspoons lemon juice
1 teaspoon basil
1 teaspoon marjoram or oregano
1 clove garlic

1. Melt butter.
2. Add remaining ingredients.
3. Spread or brush on bread.

Yield: 1/2 cup

GREEN ONION FLAT BREAD

Note: Bread can be arranged on a baking sheet and reheated in 300F oven for 10 to 12 minutes.

1-2/3 cups unbleached all-purpose flour
1/4 cup plus 1 tablespoon bread flour
1 teaspoon salt, divided
1 cup boiling water
1-1/4-inch slice fresh ginger, peeled
6 large green onions, including green tops, cut into thirds
1 teaspoon peanut oil
Peanut oil

1. Combine flours and 3/4 teaspoon salt in work bowl of food processor.
2. With machine running, pour water through feed tube; continue mixing until dough is smooth and elastic - about 40 seconds.
3. Transfer dough to plastic bag; seal tightly.
4. Let rest at room temperature 30 minutes.
5. Mince ginger by dropping through feed tube of food processor with machine running. Leave in work bowl.
6. Arrange green onions vertically in feed tube; slice, using light pressure.
7. Heat 1 teaspoon peanut oil in 6-inch skillet over high heat.
8. Add green onion mixture and remaining salt; saute until onion is tender - about 2 minutes.
9. Remove from heat and cool.
10. Turn dough out onto well-floured surface; roll into 14x16-inch rectangle.
11. Spoon green onion mixture over dough, spreading evenly.
12. Roll dough up from short side in jelly roll fashion.
13. Cut cylinder into fourteen 1-inch slices.
14. Pressing firmly with palms of hands, flatten each slice on well floured surface.
15. Generously flour slices.
16. Roll each into 5-inch circle between 2 sheets of waxed paper while working with remaining dough.
17. Pour oil into 2-quart saucepan to depth of 1 inch.
18. Heat over high heat to 350F (or when pea-size piece of dough added to oil sizzles and pops up immediately).
19. Add 1 circle of dough; fry until crisp and golden - about 40 seconds per side.
20. Drain on paper towels.
21. Repeat with remaining dough.
22. Cut into wedges using kitchen shears.
23. Serve warm.

Yield: 14 rounds

FRENCH BREAD

Note: This recipe was contributed by Jean McCoy, who came to work in the cafe in August 1983. I would have hired her just for this recipe, but fortunately for me she has many other talents in the kitchen.

1 package dry yeast
1 cup warm water
1 teaspoon sugar
2 to 3 cups bread flour
1 teaspoon salt

1. Dissolve yeast and sugar in warm water.
2. Place 2 cups flour and salt in work bowl of food processor on steel blade. Process until just combined.
3. Add yeast/water/sugar mixture.
4. Process until dough forms a ball, adding flour as necessary until stickiness almost disappears. Continue to process for about 1 minute or until dough is well-kneaded.
5. Remove dough from bowl. Cover; allow to rise until double in bulk - about 1 hour.
6. Punch down; shape into three long, thin loaves; place in French bread pan or on cookie sheet.
7. Let rise again until double - about 30 minutes.
8. Brush loaves with melted butter; bake in preheated 375F oven for 30 minutes. Brush with melted butter two or three times during baking period.
9. Cool slightly before slicing to serve.

Yield: 3 loaves

PIZZA CACIA NANZA

Note: When I was in Italy this past spring, I saw this bread
that reminded me of Moravian Sugar Cake. Shortly after our return,
I found this recipe and was so happy to learn how to make this
wonderful bread. It is terrific with any Italian-type dish or with
lamb. It's not that difficult and is easy to serve.

2-1/2 cups all-purpose flour
1/2 teaspoon salt
3/4 teaspoon active dry yeast
1 cup warm water (100 to 115 degrees, approximately)
2 cloves garlic, thinly sliced
2 tablespoons rosemary
3 tablespoons olive oil
Salt and freshly ground black pepper to taste

1. Preheat oven to 400F.
2. Combine the flour, salt, yeast, and water in a mixing bowl.
3. Blend well; turn the dough onto a lightly floured board.
4. Knead well for about 15 minutes; shape the dough into a ball.
5. Place it in a lightly greased mixing bowl. Cover with a towel;
let rise in a warm place until double its size - about 1 to 1-1/2 hours.
6. Turn the dough onto the board and knead once more. Put it back into
the bowl and let rise again.
7. Punch down the dough and turn it onto a lightly floured board.
8. Roll it out to 1/2-inch thickness.
9. Rub the surface of a baking sheet with oil.
10. Transfer the round of dough to the baking sheet.
11. Make indentations over the surface of the dough; insert a thin
sliver of garlic and a bit of rosemary into each indentation.
12. Pour the olive oil over the pizza and rub gently with your hands.
13. Sprinkle with salt and pepper; bake 15 minutes or until golden
brown.
14. Remove the garlic before serving.

Yield: 1 round loaf; serves 4 to 6 people

NINETY-MINUTE BEER BREAD

Note: This is a great bread. We have used the dough to form
dinner rolls and hot dog rolls.

3-1/2 to 4 cups bread flour*
3-1/2 cups rye flour
2 cups beer, room temperature
1/4 cup honey
2 tablespoons butter or margarine
1/2 cup warm water
2 packages active dry yeast
4 teaspoons salt
2 teaspoons caraway seed
1 teaspoon garlic powder

1. Grease two 8- or 9-inch round cake pans.
2. Combine 3 cups bread flour and all of the rye flour; set aside.
3. In medium saucepan, heat beer, honey, and butter until warm (105 to
115 degrees).
4. In small bowl, dissolve yeast in warm water (105 to 115 degrees).
Let stand 3 minutes.
5. In large bowl, combine 3 cups flour mixture, warm liquid, yeast mixture, salt, caraway seed, and garlic powder.
6. Blend at low speed until moistened; beat 2 minutes at medium speed.
7. Stir in remaining flour mixture and 1/4 to 1/2 cup bread flour until
dough pulls cleanly away from sides of bowl.
8. On floured surface, knead in 1/4 to 1/2 cup bread flour until dough
is smooth and elastic - about 10 minutes.
9. Allow to rest on counter covered with inverted bowl for 15 minutes.
10. Divide dough in half and shape into balls. Place in prepared pans.
Flatten slightly to fit pans. Cover.
11. Place loaves in cold oven; put a pan of hot water on shelf below.
Let rise about 35 minutes.
12. Recover loaves and remove pan of water. Leave loaves in oven.
13. Set oven to 375F and bake for 35 to 40 minutes or until loaves
sound hollow when lightly tapped.
14. Remove from pans immediately; cool on wire racks.

*All-purpose or unbleached flour can be substituted for bread flour.
Decrease kneading time to 5 minutes and omit resting period.

Yield: Two 24-ounce loaves

CUBAN BREAD

Note: This is my standard bread recipe. I can't tell you how many times I have made it. It has never failed me even when I used different flours and the oven temperature was messed up. The only direction you must follow exactly is that the oven must be cold; otherwise, bread will not rise and it will burn.

1 package yeast
2 cups lukewarm water
1-1/4 tablespoons salt
1 tablespoon sugar
6 to 7 cups sifted flour

1. Dissolve the yeast in the water; add the salt and sugar, stirring thoroughly.
2. Add the flour, one cup at a time, beating it in with a wooden spoon or the dough hook on an electric mixer at low speed. Add enough flour to make a fairly stiff dough.
3. When the dough is thoroughly mixed, shape it into a ball and place it in a greased bowl. Grease the top of the dough.
4. Cover with a towel; let stand in a warm place (80 to 85 degrees) until doubled in bulk.
5. Turn the dough out onto a lightly floured board; shape into two long, French-style loaves or round, Italian-style loaves.
6. Arrange on a baking sheet heavily sprinkled with cornmeal; allow to rise 5 minutes.
7. Slash the tops of the loaves in two or three places with a knife or scissors.
8. Brush the loaves with water; place them in a cold oven.
9. Set the oven to 400F; place a pan of boiling water on the bottom of the oven.
10. Bake the loaves until they are crusty and done - about 40 to 45 minutes.

Yield: 2 loaves

Sandwiches

GYROS (GREEK SPICED SANDWICHES WITH YOGURT DILL SAUCE)

Sauce
1 large egg yolk
1/4 cup vegetable oil
1 tablespoon white wine vinegar
1-1/2 teaspoons sugar
1/4 teaspoon salt
1 tablespoon Dijon-style mustard
1/2 cup snipped fresh dill weed
1/4 teaspoon Tabasco sauce
1/4 cup plain yogurt

3/4 pound ground lamb
1/4 pound ground beef
1 cup fresh bread crumbs
3 tablespoons minced fresh parsley leaves
1 large egg, beaten lightly
1 garlic clove, minced
1/2 teaspoon cumin
4 6-inch pita loaves, halved horizontally to form 8 rounds, stacked, and
   wrapped in foil
12 Greek olives, chopped
4 scallions, sliced thin

1. In a blender or food processor, blend the egg yolk, oil, vinegar, sugar, salt, and mustard until the mixture is thickened; blend in the dill and the Tabasco.
2. Transfer the mixture to bowl; stir in the yogurt; chill for 30 minutes.
3. In a bowl, combine the lamb, beef, bread crumbs, parsley, egg, garlic, and cumin; salt and pepper to taste.
4. Form the mixture into eight 4-inch logs; bake the logs in a baking pan in a preheated 375F oven for 15 minutes, or until they are cooked through.
5. Heat the pita rounds in the foil in the oven for the last 5 minutes.
6. Unwrap the pita rounds; arrange a meat log on each round.
7. Spoon some of the dill sauce over the meat; divide the olives and the scallions among the gyros; wrap the pita around the filling to enclose it.
8. Serve the gyros wrapped in foil.

Yield: 8 servings

MONTE CRISTO SANDWICH

2 slices white bread
Butter
1 thin slice baked or boiled ham
1 thin slice Swiss cheese
1 thin slice baked or boiled turkey
1 thin slice American cheese
1 egg
Dash of salt and pepper
1 tablespoon cold water
1 tablespoon salad oil
Butter and oil for frying

1. Spread both bread slices with butter.
2. Place ham on one slice; top with Swiss cheese; add turkey, then American cheese.
3. Cover with second slice of bread.
4. Press sandwich firmly together.
5. Wrap prepared sandwich in damp, cold towel.
6. Refrigerate until well chilled or until ready to cook.
7. Combine egg, salt, pepper, cold water, and salad oil.
8. Blend well with wire whisk.
9. Holding sandwich firmly together, dip it in the egg mixture on both sides.
10. Fry sandwich in a heavy skillet in 2 parts oil and 1 part butter, enough mixture to cover bottom of skillet to 1/8-inch.
11. When brown on both sides, transfer to a shallow baking dish.
12. Place in preheated 350F oven for 8 to 10 minutes.
13. Allow sandwich to cool; drain briefly on paper towels.

Yield: 1 sandwich

GARDEN POCKET SANDWICHES

White or whole-wheat pita bread
Carrots, grated
Tomatoes, sliced
Mushrooms, sliced
Cucumbers, sliced
Lettuce, shredded
Muenster cheese, sliced
Alfalfa sprouts
Lemon Tahini Dressing (see recipe)

1. Combine carrots, tomatoes, mushrooms, cucumbers, and lettuce.
2. Add Lemon Tahini Dressing.
3. Assemble by putting one slice of cheese, some of the vegetable mixture, and alfalfa sprouts in each half of a pita.
4. Serve two halves to each person.

HOT DOGS

Note: My husband grew up in San Juan, where there were several hot dog shops that prepared their hot dogs this way. I love these hot dogs; hopefully, you will, too.

If you are going to be cooking your hot dogs on the grill, soak them in the undiluted beer for several hours before you place them on the grill. They will puff up to twice their normal size and be so delicious. Go on, try it!

1 package all-beef hot dogs
1 bottle of beer
1 bottle of water

Combine water and beer in pot. Add hot dogs; steam 10-15 minutes.

HOT BROWNS

Sauce
2 tablespoons butter
1/4 cup flour
2 cups milk
1/4 teaspoon salt
1/2 teaspoon Worcestershire sauce
1/4 cup sharp cheddar cheese, grated
1/4 cup Parmesan cheese

1 pound turkey, thinly sliced
8 slices trimmed toast
4 slices tomato
8 strips bacon, partially cooked
4 ounces Parmesan cheese

For Sauce
1. Melt butter in saucepan.
2. Add flour; stir well.
3. Gradually add milk, stirring to make a smooth sauce.
4. Cook, stirring constantly, until mixture thickens.
5. Add cheeses and seasonings; cook until cheeses melt.

To Assemble
1. Cut toast into triangles; place on baking sheet.
2. Arrange turkey slices on toast; cover with hot cheese sauce.
3. Top with tomato slices and bacon strips.
4. Sprinkle with Parmesan cheese.
5. Bake at 425F until bubbly.

Yield: 4 servings

PHILADELPHIA CHEESE STEAK

Note: Growing up in Philadelphia, I quickly learned that no matter which restaurant I was patronizing, there would be some version of the Philadelphia Steak Sandwich on their menu. My husband's brother-in-law, also a Philadelphiaite, tells the following story. He had been away from home for several years. He walked into a new restaurant, sat down, did not look at the menu. When his order was requested, he said, "Give me a cheese steak." The reply was "With or without onions?" After tasting this sandwich, I am sure that you will understand its strong appeal.

Perhaps one of the most critical factors in a cheese steak is the roll. The bread should be tender with a chewy crust. The best rolls are baked by the Amorosos Bakery. They are so good that a restaurant in Wilmington, N.C. flies them in; beleive me, they do make a difference. Just find the best roll you can and enjoy!

1 pound lean rib-eye steak, sliced wafer thin
2 tablespoons butter
1 (8-ounce) can tomato sauce
1 teaspoon Italian seasoning
1/2 green pepper, chopped
1/2 onion, sliced
1 clove garlic, mashed
4 ounces mozzarella or provelone cheese
4 good hard rolls

1. Saute the onion, green pepper, and garlic in the butter. Onion should be soft and transparent. Add the Italian seasoning and the can of tomato sauce. Simmer for 15-20 minutes. Taste for seasoning; adjust if necessary.
2. Brown the steak in a saucepan; you may wish to add a little butter to the pan. Just before the meat is done, break it up with the end of your spatula.
3. Divide the meat into 4 equal piles in the saucepan. Spoon equal amounts of the sauce onto each pile. Top each with the cheese.
4. Split the roll and place on top of each pile. Allow to rest for 60 seconds. With a large spatula, lift the entire pile of meat, sauce cheese, and roll. Arrange beef inside roll with aid of spatula edge. Serve immediately. If you cannot serve immediately, wrap tightly in foil and place in a very low oven until you are ready for the sandwiches.

Yield: 4 sandwiches

STEAK SANDWICH II

Note: When I lived in Winston-Salem, there was a small Greek restaurant, the proverbial dive, that prepared its steak sandwiches this way. Even I, a Philadelphia girl through and through, have to say that this is a wonderful way to prepare steak sandwiches.

1 pound rib-eye steak, sliced wafer thin
2 tablespoons butter
2 onions, sliced
1 teaspoon freshly ground black pepper
Mayonnaise
4 sandwich buns
4 ounces mozzarella cheese, sliced

1. Melt the butter in a skillet; saute the onion with the black pepper until the onion is soft. Remove from the pan.
2. Place the meat in the pan; saute until barely pink. Break the meat up with the end of a spatula; continue cooking until it is done to your preference.
3. Divide the meat into four sections within the pan. On top of each section, place 1/4th of the sauteed onions and 1 slice of the mozzarella cheese.
4. Spread mayonnaise on each sandwich bun top.
5. Lift the meat and cheese from the pan with a spatula and place on the sandwich bun. Serve immediately.

Yield: 4 sandwiches

SLOPPY JOES

Note: This was a favorite family supper when we were growing up. Much better than a Manwich!

1 pound hamburger
2 teaspoons salt
Pepper
1 medium onion, chopped
1 teaspoon vinegar
1 teaspoon mustard
Chopped celery
1/2 cup catsup
1/2 teaspoon Worcestershire sauce

1. Brown ground beef; pour off the fat.
2. Add all other ingredients; bring to a boil.
3. Simmer, covered, for 45 minutes.
4. Serve on a hamburger bun.

Yield: 4 sandwiches

CATTLE COUNTRY STUFFED HAMBURGERS

2 pounds ground beef
1/4 cup grated Parmesan cheese
1/2 teaspoon pepper
1/4 teaspoon garlic powder
2 tablespoons steak sauce

1. In large bowl, combine all ingredients.
2. Shape into twelve 4-inch patties.
3. Place 6 patties on waxed paper.
4. Top each with a portion of either Mushroom-Bacon, Reuben, or Blue Cheese Stuffing.
5. Place remaining patties over stuffing; press edges to seal.
6. When ready to barbecue, place patties on grill 3 to 4 inches from hot coals.
7. Cook until browned on both sides and of desired doneness.
8. If topping with cheese, place on pattie during last few minutes of cooking; heat until cheese begins to melt.
9. Serve on buns that have been toasted on grill, if desired.

Yield: 6 servings

Mushroom-Bacon Stuffing
4 slices bacon
1/4 cup thinly sliced celery
1/4 cup chopped onion
1 (4-ounce) can mushroom pieces and stems, drained

1. In small skillet, fry bacon until crisp.
2. Remove bacon from pan; crumble and set aside.
3. Drain all but 2 tablespoons bacon drippings; add celery and onion, cooking until tender.
4. Stir in mushrooms and crumbled bacon.
5. Divide into 6 portions.

Yield: 1-1/4 cups

Reuben Stuffing
4 ounces (1 cup) shredded Swiss cheese or 6 slices Swiss cheese
6 tablespoons sauerkraut

1. Divide cheese and sauerkraut evenly into 6 portions. (Cheese slices can be used either as part of filling or as topping.)

Yield: 1-1/3 cups

Blue Cheese Stuffing
2 ounces (1/2 cup) crumbled blue cheese
1/4 cup dairy sour cream
1/4 cup chopped sweet pickles, if desired

1. In small bowl, combine all ingredients.
2. Divide into 6 portions.

Yield: 2/3 cup

Chicken

POLLO ALA ROMANA

Tarragon Cream Sauce

1 tablespoon butter or clarified butter
2 tablespoons finely chopped shallots
1 cup dry white wine
2 cups chicken broth (preferably homemade)
2 cups whipping cream
1 tablespoon chopped fresh tarragon, or to taste
Salt and freshly ground white pepper

Stuffed Chicken Breasts

6 large chicken breast halves, boned and flattened to even thickness (do
  not skin)
2 medium carrots, cut into fine julienne
1 medium leek, trimmed and cut into fine julienne

4 cups chicken broth
6 tablespoons (3/4 stick) unsalted butter, cut into 3 pieces

For Cream Sauce

1. Melt butter in heavy large saucepan over medium heat.
2. Add shallots and stir until soft but not browned - about 3 minutes.
3. Add wine, increase heat to high; boil until reduced to glaze
(about 2 tablespoons).
4. Stir in broth; boil until reduced to 1/2 cup.
5. Add cream and tarragon; continue boiling until sauce is thickened
to desired consistency.
6. Season with salt and white pepper; set aside.

For Stuffed Chicken Breasts

1. Place 1 flattened chicken breast half, skin side down, on piece of
plastic wrap, leaving a margin of several inches at each side.
2. Season with salt and white pepper.
3. Arrange 1/6 of carrot and 1/6 of leek near 1 edge of chicken.
4. Using plastic as aid, roll chicken up tightly to enclose vegetables.
5. Twist ends of plastic tightly to secure.
6. Repeat with remaining chicken and vegetables.
7. Bring broth to simmer in large saucepan (liquid should be barely
shaking).
8. Add chicken breasts and poach until cooked through - about 16
minutes; do not overcook.
9. Remove chicken from broth, using slotted spoon.
10. Discard plastic.
11. Cut each breast diagonally into 6 to 8 slices.
12. Arrange on heated platter and keep warm.
13. Return sauce to boil; remove from heat; whisk in butter 1 piece
at a time.
14. Spoon sauce around chicken.
15. Serve immediately.

Yield: 6 servings

POULET A LA BONNE FEMME

Note: This is not necessarily a feminine dish - the men love it too!

4 whole chicken breasts, halved, patted dry
8 chicken legs, patted dry
8 large baking potatoes, unpeeled, each cut lengthwise into 1/2-inch
  thick slices, patted dry
Salt and pepper
1 pound sliced bacon
1/4 cup all-purpose flour
4 cups chicken stock
1 teaspoon salt
1 tablespoon fresh thyme or 1 teaspoon dried, crumbled
1 tablespoon fresh marjoram or 1 teaspoon dried, crumbled
1-1/2 teaspoons fresh sage or 1/2 teaspoon dried, crumbled
1-1/2 teaspoons fresh rosemary or 1/2 teaspoon dried, crumbled
1/2 teaspoon freshly ground pepper
1/2 teaspoon ground red pepper
1/4 teaspoon freshly grated nutmeg
5 onions, halved and thinly sliced
1 bunch green onions, sliced
1/4 cup minced fresh parsley

1. Season chicken with salt and pepper.
2. Season potatoes with salt and pepper.
3. Cook bacon in heavy large skillet over medium-high heat until crisp.
4. Drain on paper towels.
5. Add chicken to same skillet in batches in single layer and brown in hot bacon drippings until golden - 2 to 3 minutes per side.
6. Drain on paper towels.
7. Arrange potato slices in single layer in same skillet over medium heat and cook until well browned - about 4 minutes per side - turning carefully.
8. Drain on paper towels.
9. Discard all but 4 tablespoons bacon drippings from skillet.
10. Reheat remainder over medium heat.
11. Remove from heat; stir in flour.
12. Return to heat; stir until flour begins to brown - 4 to 5 minutes.
13. Stir in stock.
14. Increase heat; bring to boil.
15. Reduce heat to low; simmer until thickened.
16. Preheat oven to 350F.
17. Blend seasonings in small bowl.
18. Arrange 4 chicken breasts and 4 drumsticks alternately in 10-inch baking dish.
19. Cover with layer of browned potato slices.
20. Cover with half of sliced onions.
21. Sprinkle with half of seasoning mixture.
22. Add layer of bacon.
23. Repeat layering with remaining chicken, potato slices, onions, seasoning mixture, and bacon.
24. Sprinkle with green onions and parsley.
25. Pour reserved sauce into dish.

26. Cover; bake 30 minutes.
27. Uncover; continue baking 15 minutes.
28. Serve immediately.

Yield: 8 servings

CHICKEN JACQUELINE

1/4 cup (1/2 stick) butter
1 pound mushrooms, sliced
2 tablespoons dry white wine
6 chicken breast halves, skinned, boned, and pounded 1/8-inch thick
1 garlic clove, minced
Salt and freshly ground pepper
3 ounces Monterey Jack cheese, cut into 6 sticks about 3x1/2x3/8-inches
3 ounces Swiss cheese, cut into 6 sticks about 3x1/2x3/8-inches
1/2 cup (1 stick) butter cut into 6 sticks about 3 inches long, frozen
1/4 cup (about) all-purpose flour
2 eggs, lightly beaten
1/2 cup (about) fine cracker meal
Oil for deep frying
Bearnaise Sauce

1. Melt 1/4 cup butter in heavy skillet over medium-high heat.
2. Add mushrooms and wine; saute until mushrooms are tender and juices have evaporated - about 5 minutes. Remove from heat and set aside.
3. Season chicken breasts with garlic, salt, and pepper.
4. Spoon mushroom mixture into center of each chicken breast, dividing evenly.
5. Top mushrooms with 1 stick each Monterey Jack cheese, Swiss cheese, and frozen butter.
6. Fold chicken breasts in half to enclose filling, pressing edges together to seal.
7. Roll in flour, dip in egg to coat well, then roll in cracker meal, covering completely.
8. Refrigerate at least 30 minutes, or freeze 10 minutes.
9. Heat oil in wok or deep fryer to 400F.
10. Preheat oven to 450F.
11. Deep-fry chicken (in batches if necessary) until light golden brown - about 5 minutes.
12. Drain on paper towels.
13. Transfer to baking sheet; bake 15 minutes.
14. Serve immediately, accompanied by Bearnaise Sauce.

Yield: 6 servings

COQ AU VIN

Brown Sauce
1/2 cup unsalted butter
1/2 cup minced pared carrot
1/2 cup minced celery
2/3 cup minced onion
2/3 cup dry red wine
1/2 cup plus 1 tablespoon all-purpose flour
3 quarts rich veal stock
1 tablespoon tomato paste
Scant 1/2 teaspoon whole peppercorns, crushed
Pinch of dried thyme, crumbled
Small piece of bay leaf

Coq au Vin
2 cups brown sauce
4 slices firm, white home-style bread
4 slices bacon, cut into 1/2-inch dices
40 pearl onions, as small as possible, peeled
1/2 cup finely diced carrot
1/2 cup finely diced celery
8 boneless, skinless chicken breasts (about 6 ounces each), trimmed
Salt
Freshly ground pepper
2 teaspoons dried rosemary, crumbled
2 teaspoons dried thyme, crumbled
1/4 cup clarified butter
2-1/2 ounces fresh mushrooms, wiped clean with dampened paper toweling,
    quartered
1-1/4 cups dry red wine, preferably Beaujolais
Chopped fresh parsley

For Brown Sauce
1. Melt butter; add minced vegetables; saute until softened but not browned.
2. Add wine; cook uncovered until wine is almost evaporated - 3-4 minutes.
3. Add flour; cook, stirring constantly until flour is hazelnut brown - 6 to 10 minutes.
4. Add veal stock and tomato paste.
5. Heat to boiling; simmer, uncovered, skimming occasionally but not stirring, until liquid is reduced to 6 cups - about 40 minutes.
6. Halfway through cooking time, add peppercorns, thyme, and bay leaf.
7. Strain sauce pressing vegetables to extract as much flavor as possible.
8. Degrease before using.

For Coq au Vin

1. Make brown sauce.
2. Toast bread; while still warm, remove crusts and cut each slice in half on the diagonal to make 8 triangular croutons. Set aside.
3. Scatter bacon, onions, carrot, and celery over bottom of large, heavy, noncorrodible Dutch oven. Cook until bacon is transparent.
4. Season chicken breasts with salt, pepper, rosemary, and thyme; place in one layer on top of bacon and vegetables.
5. Pour clarified butter over chicken; cook uncovered over high heat until lightly browned on undersides - about 5 minutes.
6. Turn breast; cook on second side until lightly browned - another 5 minutes.
7. Add mushrooms to Dutch oven; cook, covered, until they begin to soften - about 3 minutes.
8. Add wine to pan, scraping up browned bits from bottom of pan with wooden spoon; simmer 1 minute.
9. Transfer chicken to deep serving bowl; keep warm, covered, in oven set at lowest setting.
10. Add 2 cups brown sauce to Dutch oven; heat to boiling, stirring.
11. Cook, uncovered, until sauce is slightly reduced - about 5 minutes.
12. Remove from heat; taste for seasoning, adjusting if necessary.
13. Pour sauce over chicken; serve immediately, surrounded by croutons and sprinkled with chopped parsley.

Yield: 8 servings

CHAMPAGNE CHICKEN

Note: You can't lose with this one.

4 ounces butter
1 cup onion, minced
4 cloves garlic, minced
1 pound mushroom caps
4 chicken breast fillets
1 can artichoke hearts (10 to 12 count)
6 tablespoons champagne (use the rest on you or your guests)
1-1/2 cups chicken stock
Pinch thyme
Beurre Manie (4 tablespoons butter and 4 tablespoons flour combined
    to make paste)
Salt and pepper

1. Saute onions in butter until limp and glossy.
2. Add garlic and mushrooms, then chicken, cooking and turning the chicken over medium heat until done on both sides.
3. Add artichoke hearts; splash with the champagne.
4. Add 1-1/2 cups of stock and the thyme; bring to a boil.
5. Thicken with Beurre Manie, using only as much as you need; season with salt and pepper; serve immediately.

Yield: 4 servings

CHICKEN SOONG

1/2 pound skinless, boneless chicken breast, partially frozen
1 egg white
2 tablespoons medium-dry sherry
1-1/2 teaspoon water chestnut powder* or cornstarch
1/2 ounce dried Chinese mushrooms* (about 4)
2 tablespoons hoisin sauce*
1 tablespoon dark soy sauce*
1/4 teaspoon freshly ground pepper
2 cups peanut oil
1/3 cup minced shallots
1/4 cup diced (1/4-inch) carrots
1 medium garlic clove, minced
1 teaspoon minced fresh gingerroot
1/4 cup diced (1/4-inch) red bell pepper
1/2 cup diced (1/4-inch) water chestnuts, preferably fresh*
1/2 cup diced (1/4-inch) snow peas (strings removed)
1 teaspoon oriental sesame oil
1/4 cup pine nuts (pignoli), lightly toasted
1 head of iceberg lettuce, cored and cut in half, with individual leaves
    loosened

*Available at Oriental grocery stores

1. Cut the chicken into diced pieces.
2. In a medium bowl, combine the chicken with the egg white, 1/2 tablespoon of the sherry, and the water chestnut powder. Stir to coat.
3. Cover and refrigerate for at least 1 hour, or up to 12 hours.
4. Rinse the mushrooms under cold running water.
5. Put them in a bowl and cover them with 2 cups of cold water.
6. Soak until soft, about 1 hour.
7. Squeeze the excess moisture out of the mushrooms.
8. Remove the stems and discard.
9. Cut the mushrom caps into 1/4-inch diced pieces.
10. In small bowl, combine the remaining 1-1/2 tablespoons sherry, the hoisin sauce, soy sauce, and pepper. Blend well.
11. Place a wok over high heat for about 1-1/2 minutes.
12. Pour in the oil; heat to 325F.
13. Stir the marinated chicken; carefully add it to the hot oil.
14. Cook, stirring constantly, until the chicken turns opaque - about 1 minute. Turn off the heat.
15. Pour the chicken and the oil into a colander set over a large bowl.
16. Shake to drain off as much oil as possible.
17. Reserve 1 tablespoon of the oil.
18. Put the wok over moderate heat and add the 1 tablespoon reserved oil along with the shallots, carrots, and mushrooms.
19. Stir-fry for 1 minute.
20. Add the garlic and ginger; stir-fry for 1 minute longer.
21. Increase the heat to high; add the bell pepper, water chestnuts, and snow peas.
22. Stir-fry for 1 minute; then remove the vegetables from the wok.
23. Return the wok to high heat.
24. Stir the seasoning sauce; add it to the wok.
25. Cook, stirring, for 30 seconds.

26. Return the cooked chicken to the wok.
27. Stir-fry for about 30 seconds.
28. Add the cooked vegetable mixture to the wok; stir-fry for 30 seconds until all the ingredients are heated through.
29. Turn off the heat; add the sesame oil. Stir to blend.
30. Transfer the mixture to a heated platter.
31. Sprinkle the pine nuts on top.
32. Serve hot with the lettuce leaves.

Yield: 6 servings

CHICKEN WITH ARTICHOKES

4 chicken breasts
Salt and pepper to taste
1/2 teaspoon poultry seasoning
1 jar marinated artichoke hearts*
1 cup white wine
1/2 cup basic chicken stock**
1/2 pound fresh mushroom caps
1 tablespoon cornstarch
1/4 cup water

1. Remove the skin and bones from the chicken breasts, then sprinkle the breasts with salt, pepper, and poultry seasoning.
2. Drain the artichoke hearts; reserve 3 tablespoons oil.
3. Heat the reserved oil in a frying pan.
4. Place the chicken breasts in the oil; cook until brown.
5. Add 1/2 cup wine and chicken stock, then cover tightly.
6. Simmer for 35 to 45 minutes or until the chicken is almost tender.
7. Add the mushroom caps, artichoke hearts, and remaining wine; simmer for 15 to 20 minutes longer.
8. Remove the chicken to a platter and keep warm.
9. Mix the cornstarch with 1/4 cup water; stir into the liquid in the frypan.
10. Cook until thickened, stirring constantly; pour over the chicken.
11. Serve immediately. Delicious served with wild rice.

*One package frozen artichokes and 3 tablespoons butter may be used instead of the marinated artichokes.

**Canned chicken broth may be substituted for the basic chicken stock.

Yield: 4 servings

CHICKEN DIVAN

2 (10-ounce) packages frozen broccoli
6 boned chicken breasts, cooked
Garlic salt
Butter
1/4 cup American cheese, grated
Toasted slivered almonds
1 can cream of chicken soup
1 cup dairy sour cream
3 tablespoons milk
2 cups cheddar cheese, grated
3 tablespoons sherry
Paprika

1. Cook broccoli according to package directions.
2. Place a layer of broccoli and a layer of chicken pieces in casserole, sprinkle all over with garlic salt and chunks of butter.
3. Cover lightly with 1/4 cup grated cheese and sprinkle with almonds.
4. Mix soup, sour cream, milk, 1 cup of grated cheese, and sherry together in a saucepan and heat.
5. Pour over chicken and broccoli.
6. Sprinkle with more almonds and paprika.
7. Bake at 375F for 45 minutes.

Yield: 6 servings

POULET CHAMPIGNON

2 tablespoons butter
1 medium onion, minced
4 whole chicken breast fillets
2 cups fresh mushroom caps
1 cup dry white wine (drink the rest)
4 tablespoons grated Swiss cheese
2 tablespoons heavy cream (optional)
Chicken stock
Beurre Manie (2 tablespoons butter combined with 2 tablespoons flour)

1. Saute the onions in butter until limp.
2. Add mushrooms, chicken breasts, and cream, turning the chicken until
white and opague - about 3 to 5 minutes.
3. Add white wine and bring to boil for 1 minute; stir in Beurre Manie
to thicken.
4. Place Swiss cheese on chicken and broil until lightly browned.

Yield: 4 servings

ORANGE-FLAVORED CHICKEN KEBOBS

4 whole chicken breasts, halved, boned, and skinned

Marinade
1 cup orange marmalade
1/2 cup soy sauce
1/3 cup fresh lemon juice
1/2 teaspoon powdered ginger
Rind of 1/2 orange, coarsely grated
Freshly ground black pepper, to taste

2 green peppers, seeded and cut into chunks
2 sweet red peppers, seeded and cut into chunks
16 small white onions, blanched in boiling water 3-5 minutes, or
    just until tender
16 large mushrooms, stems removed

Fresh pineapple, cut into spears, for garnish (optional)

1. In a ceramic or glass dish just large enough to hold the chicken in
one layer, combine the marinade ingredients.
2. Add the chicken; let marinate for 2-3 hours, turning it once
or twice.
3. Remove the chicken from the marinade and save the marinade; cut the
chicken into chunks.
4. Thread skewers, starting with a mushroom, alternating the chicken
with the vegetables and finishing each skewer with a mushroom.
5. Have the coals glowing.
6. Grill the kebobs for 10-15 minutes in all, depending upon the heat
of the coals, basting them with the reserved marinade and turning them.
7. Transfer the kebobs to heated plates; garnish with the pineapple
spears, if desired.
8. Serve immediately.

Yield: 8 servings

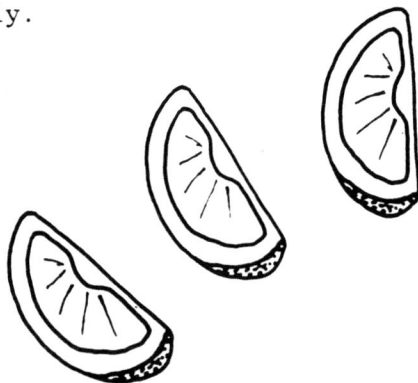

BROILED CHICKEN WITH GARLIC PESTO

Garlic Pesto Butter Sauce
1/2 cup (1 stick) butter, room temperature
1 medium-sized green onion, chopped
2 teaspoons Garlic Pesto*
1 teaspoon lemon juice
1 teaspoon sage
1/4 teaspoon freshly ground pepper
Pinch of salt

2 whole chicken breasts, boned and halved
For Sauce
1. Mix all ingredients in processor; sauce will be thick.
2. Preheat broiler.
3. Top chicken with sauce.
4. Broil until chicken is tender, 5 minutes on each side, basting occasionally with sauce.
5. Serve immediately.

Yield: 4 servings

*Garlic Pesto
1/2 cup unpeeled garlic cloves (about 24 medium-sized)
1/2 cup safflower oil

1. Soak garlic in warm water to loosen skin - about 5 minutes; peel.
2. Puree in food processor.
3. With machine running, add oil through feed tube in slow, steady stream.
4. Spoon paste into jar with tight-fitting lid.
5. Store pesto in freezer.

Yield: 3/4 cup

BAKED CHICKEN SUPREME

6 whole chicken breasts
1 (16-ounce) carton (2 cups) dairy sour cream
3 tablespoons lemon juice
4 teaspoons Worcestershire sauce
4 teaspoons celery salt
2 teaspoons paprika
1 teaspoon salt
1/2 teaspoon pepper
4 garlic cloves, minced
1-3/4 cups dry bread crumbs
1/3 cup margarine or butter
1/3 cup shortening

1. Cut chicken breast in half.
2. Rinse in cold water; pat dry.
3. In large bowl, combine sour cream, lemon juice, Worcestershire sauce, celery salt, paprika, salt, pepper, and garlic; mix well.
4. Add chicken to sour cream marinade, covering each piece well.
5. Cover bowl and refrigerate overnight.
6. Lightly grease two 15x10-inch jelly roll pans or two 13x9-inch pans.
7. Heat oven to 350F.
8. Remove chicken from sour cream marinade; roll chicken in bread crumbs.
9. Arrange in single layer in prepared pan.
10. Discard marinade.
11. In small saucepan, melt margarine and shortening; spoon 1/3 cup evenly over chicken.
12. Bake, uncovered, at 350F for 45 to 50 minutes.
13. Spoon remaining margarine mixture over chicken.
14. Bake an additional 15 to 20 minutes or until chicken is tender and golden brown.

Yield: 12 servings

COUNTRY CAPTAIN CHICKEN

Curry Mixture
4 bay leaves, coarsely crumbled
2 tablespoons cumin seed
2 tablespoons coriander seed
1 cinnamon stick, broken into pieces
1 tablespoon black peppercorns
1 teaspoon fennel seed
1 teaspoon ground tumeric
1/2 teaspoon whole allspice

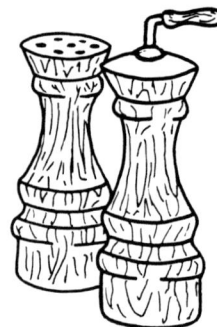

1 (3- to 3-1/2-pound) chicken

Salt and freshly ground pepper
3 tablespoons peanut oil

1/4 cup dry white wine
3/4 cup (or more) chicken stock, preferably homemade
2 medium-sized green bell peppers, cut into matchstick julienne
2 medium-sized red bell peppers, cut into matchstick julienne
2 medium-sized tomatoes, peeled, seeded and diced
1 medium-sized onion, halved and very thinly sliced
3 medium-sized green onions, thinly sliced
2 tablespoons chutney

Freshly cooked white or brown rice
Toasted slivered almonds
Currants

1. For curry mixture, grind all spices to powder.
2. Remove wings and back from chicken; reserve for another use.
3. Cut remaining chicken into 2 legs, 2 thighs, and 2 breasts.
4. Trim excess skin and fat.
5. Preheat oven to 400F.
6. Pat chicken dry. Season with salt and pepper.
7. Heat oil in heavy skillet over medium-high heat.
8. Add chicken in single layer, skin side down; brown lightly - about 5 minutes.
9. Turn and brown other side.
10. Transfer chicken to shallow baking dish, using slotted spoon.
11. Bake until just cooked through - 10 to 15 minutes.
12. Debone breast pieces.
13. Pour excess fat from skillet.
14. Set over low heat.
15. Stir in 1 teaspoon curry mixture (reserve remainder for another use).
16. Add wine, scraping up browned bits.
17. Boil until wine is reduced by half.
18. Add 3/4 cup stock and reduce by half.
19. Stir in red and green bell peppers, tomatoes, and onion.
20. Reduce heat, cover and simmer until peppers are tender - about 5 minutes.
21. Adjust sauce consistency, if necessary, by boiling if too thin or adding 2 to 3 tablespoons more stock if too thick.

22. Blend in half of green onion and 2 tablespoons chutney.
23. Mix chicken into sauce.
24. Simmer until heated through.
25. Mound rice on platter.
26. Top with chicken.
27. Spoon sauce over.
28. Garnish with remaining green onion.
29. Sprinkle with nuts and currants; serve.

Yield: 2 to 4 servings

DONBURI

4 cups of rice (wash 2 to 3 times until clean)
Whole chicken cut into pieces or 4 chicken breasts
4 eggs beaten
Cornstarch - 1 tablespoon combined with 1 tablespoon water
Green beans or snow peas

Kijiyaki-Donburi Sauce
1/4 cup soy sauce
1 tablespoon sugar
1/4 cup water

1. Debone chicken.
2. Brown chicken directly over flame. Should be quite brown.
3. Put Kijiyaki-Donburi Sauce and chicken into a skillet; cover.
4. Boil until sauce is reduced by half.
5. Beat eggs, add salt, 1 tablespoon water, and 1 tablespoon cornstarch.
6. Make very thin omelets, about the thickness of a crepe skin. Roll as you remove them from from pan. Cut roll into julienne. It should resemble yellow spaghetti.
7. Put rice in a bowl; then pour sauce over rice.
8. Top with eggs, then chicken.
9. Steam beans or snow peas, then slice into thin strips and put on top of chicken. You now have an attractive stack of white rice, chicken, yellow eggs and green vegetable.
10. May be served hot or cold.

Yield: 4 servings

CHICKEN FLORENTINE

Note: This is always a popular dish. It is so easy and yet elegant. I often use it when entertaining.

Once I made this dish for a catering job and there was a lot left over. My poor husband ate Chicken Florentine for three or four nights. He was so pleased that we were going to friend's house for dinner on Saturday night and he would get a reprieve. Of course, you know what she served: Chicken Florentine! However, she had not taken the time to thicken the sauce and hers was not as good as mine; my husband pointed that out, since he was now an expert on the dish!

8 chicken breasts, boned or not
Salt and freshly ground black pepper to taste
6 tablespoons of butter, divided
3 tablespoons of flour
1 1/2 cup milk
Pepper to taste
1 (10-ounce) box frozen chopped spinach
1/4 teaspoon nutmeg
1 cup freshly grated Parmesan cheese

1. Season the chicken with salt and pepper. In a saucepan, melt 3 tablespoons of the butter. Add the chicken pieces; cook until lightly browned on each side. When chicken is pierced, the juices should be clear.
2. In a second saucepan, melt the remaining 3 tablespoons of butter; add the flour; stir with a whisk until well blended. Cook an additional minute or two to cook the flour. If you don't do this, the sauce will taste of flour.
3. Slowly add the milk, incorporating well. Sauce should be thick and smooth. Please take enough time to do this step properly: if the sauce is not thick enough or has lumps in it, the dish will not be nearly as good. Sauce should be the consistency of cake batter.
4. Add 1/2 cup of the Parmesan cheese; stir well.
5. Cook the spinach; squeeze to drain and dry well. Add 1/2 cup of the sauce.
6. Put a dab of the sauce on the bottom of a flat, ovenproof dish. Top with the spinach. Sprinkle some of the grated Parmesan on the spinach. Arrange the chicken breasts on top.
7. Spoon the remaining sauce over the chicken breasts; sprinkle with the remaining cheese.
8. Bake at 350F for 30 minutes or until edges are bubbling and top is lightly browned.

Yield: 8 servings

CHICKEN WITH CASHEWS

3 single chicken breasts, skinned, boned and cut into 1/2-inch cubes
1 tablespoon cornstarch
2 tablespoons sherry
1 tablespoon soy sauce
1/2 teaspoon sugar
1/2 teaspoon salt
1/2 medium-sized onion, finely chopped
2 slices fresh ginger root, minced
1 clove garlic, crushed
3 tablespoons soy sauce
1-1/2 tablespoons sherry
1 teaspoon sesame oil
1 teaspoon sugar
1/4 cup chicken broth
3 tablespoons oil, divided
1/3 cup roasted cashew nuts
1 teaspoon cornstarch dissolved in 1 tablespoon water

1. Place the chicken cubes, cornstarch, sherry, soy sauce, sugar, and salt in a bowl; mix thoroughly.
2. Combine the onion, ginger root, and garlic in a bowl and set aside.
3. In a small bowl, mix the soy sauce, sherry, sesame oil, sugar, and broth; set aside.
4. Heat two tablespoons oil in a wok or large skillet.
5. Add the chicken; stir-fry two or three minutes until lightly browned.
6. Remove the chicken from the pan.
7. Add the remaining oil; heat until very hot.
8. Add the onion mixture; stir-fry one minute.
9. Add the cashew nuts; stir to coat with oil.
10. Return the chicken to the pan; add the soy sauce mixture.
11. Bring to a boil; stir in the cornstarch mixture to thicken.

Yield: 4 servings

NORMA'S CHICKEN AND DUMPLINGS

The only way to get Norma's chicken and dumplings is to call Norma and invite her down for a visit. I would not even try to give you the recipe for it - it couldn't come close!

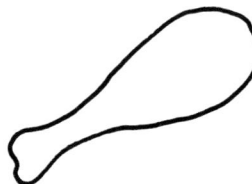

ACAPULCO CHICKEN

4 whole chicken breasts
1 teaspoon salt
1/2 teaspoon pepper
1/2 teaspoon oregano
1 can cream of chicken soup
1 can cream of mushroom soup
1/2 cup milk
1 small onion, chopped
1/2 (4-ounce) can green chilies, chopped (optional)
1 (7-ounce) bottle green taco sauce or red taco sauce
12 or more corn tortillas, cut in half
3/4 pound grated cheddar cheese

1. Preheat oven to 400F.
2. Season chicken breasts with salt, pepper, and oregano.
3. Place in roasting pan.
4. Wrap securely with foil.
5. Bake 1 hour.
6. Cool; cut into chunks.
7. Reserve 1 cup liquid from pan.
8. Combine reserved liquid, soups, milk, onion, green chilies, and taco sauce.
9. Butter a 3-quart casserole.
10. Layer tortillas, chicken, and sauce in 2 or 3 layers.
11. Top with grated cheese.
12. Refrigerate for at least 2 hours before heating.
13. Bake at 350F for 1 hour.

Yield: 8 to 10 servings

TARRAGON CHICKEN

Note: This is one dish you can enjoy while you are on a diet and still feel virtuous. If you serve it to your family or guests, they won't know that it's a diet dish!

6-8 chicken breasts, skinned
2 teaspoons dried tarragon or 1/4 cup fresh tarragon
2 lemons, thinly sliced
1 tablespoon margarine
1/2 cup white wine or chicken stock

1. Arrange chicken breasts in bottom of ovenproof casserole. Casserole should be large enough to accommodate all of the breasts without too much overlapping.
2. Sprinkle heavily with the tarragon
3. Arrange sliced lemons on top of the chicken. There should be enough lemon slices to lightly cover the breasts.
4. Dot with the butter. This is not enough butter to throw your diet, but if you want to be really good, you can omit it.
5. Drizzle the wine all around the breasts.
6. Tightly seal with foil. If this dish is not sealed tightly enough, it will dry out and be flavorless. Most lids will not provide a tight enough seal.
7. Bake at 375F for 1 hour.

Yield: 6-8 servings
Variation:
To make this meal-in-one casserole, you could put 1 cup of rice and 2 cups of water or chicken stock in the casserole before the chicken breasts.

CHICKEN WITH SAUSAGE AND MUSHROOMS

1 chicken, boiled and cut into large pieces
1 pound Neese's hot sausage, cooked and drained
1 small box Uncle Ben's Long Grained and Wild Rice, cooked
1 (10-3/4-ounce) can cream of mushroom soup
1 (6-ounce) can mushrooms, sliced (do not drain)

1. Mix all ingredients in a shallow, 2-3 quart casserole.
2. Bake at 350F for 30 minutes.
3. Serve immediately.

Yield: 6 to 8 servings

POLLO ALLA BARTOLUCCI (CHICKEN WITH SPINACH AND RICOTTA)

Note: The spinach and ricotta cheese topping would also be good on veal. The blending of these flavors is wonderful - a perfect company dish, but your family will love it, too.

Sauce
2/3 cup veal stock
2/3 cup chicken stock
1/4 cup (1/2 stick) butter
6 tablespoons all-purpose flour
3 tablespoons tomato sauce
1/4 cup white wine

Spinach Ricotta Topping
1 tablespoon olive oil
1 medium garlic clove
3 ounces cooked spinach, finely chopped
Salt and freshly ground pepper

1 cup plus 3 tablespoons ricotta cheese
1/2 cup grated romano cheese

Chicken
6 servings chicken
All-purpose flour
3 tablespoons olive oil
3 eggs, beaten to blend

1 cup grated mozzarella cheese

For Sauce
1. Bring stock to boil in medium-sized saucepan over high heat.
2. Melt butter in another medium-sized saucepan over low heat.
3. Blend flour into butter and whisk until mixture foams - about 2 minutes; do not brown. Remove from heat.
4. Gradually whisk in hot stock.
5. Return to low heat.
6. Whisk in tomato sauce. Bring sauce to boil over medium-high heat, whisking constantly. Let boil 1 minute.
7. Reduce heat to medium; simmer 20 minutes.
8. Whisk in wine; simmer 10 minutes longer.
9. Strain sauce into bowl or another saucepan.
10. Keep warm over very low heat or in water bath.

For Spinach Ricotta Topping
1. Heat 1 tablespoon olive oil in heavy medium skillet over medium heat.
2. Add garlic; stir until brown.
3. Discard garlic.
4. Add cooked spinach to skillet.
5. Season with salt and pepper; toss to coat with oil.
6. Remove with slotted spoon; cool.
7. Combine cooled spinach with ricotta and romano cheeses in large

bowl.
8. Add salt and pepper.

For Chicken
1. Season chicken lightly with salt and pepper.
2. Coat lightly with flour, shaking off excess.
3. Heat 3 tablespoons each butter and olive oil in large, heavy skillet over medium heat.
4. Dip chicken in egg.
5. Add to skillet; brown on both sides.
6. Drain on paper towels.

To Assemble
1. Preheat oven to 375F.
2. Spoon thin layer of sauce into 1-1/2- to 2-quart, broiler-proof baking dish.
3. Arrange chicken in dish.
4. Spread 4 tablespoons topping onto each piece of chicken.
5. Cover with remaining sauce.
6. Sprinkle with grated mozzarella.
7. Bake 5 minutes.
8. Set oven at broil.
9. Place chicken under broiler until topping is golden brown - approximately 5 minutes.
10. Serve immediately.

Yield: 6 servings

CHICKEN BONNE FEMME

1 fryer, cut in pieces
1-1/2 teaspoons salt
1/2 teaspoon pepper
1/2 cups oil
2 large baking potatoes, thinly sliced
2 tablespoons butter
1 large white onion, thinly sliced
1/2 pound mushrooms, sliced
1 tablespoon grated Parmesan cheese
1 teaspoon chopped fresh parsley

1. Dry chicken thoroughly; season with 1/2 teaspoon salt and 1/4 teaspoon pepper.
2. Heat oil in large skillet; fry chicken until cooked.
3. Remove from skillet, drain on paper towels; keep warm.
4. Fry potatoes in hot oil until brown. Drain and keep warm.
5. Pour oil out of skillet.
6. Add butter; saute onions and mushrooms until onions are soft. Remove and drain.
7. Assemble chicken on a heated platter.
8. Arrange potatoes around chicken.
9. Spread mushrooms and onions over chicken; season with 1 teaspoon salt and 1/4 teaspoon pepper.
10. Sprinkle with cheese and parsley.

Yield: 4 servings

CHICKEN PARMESAN

1 cup crushed herb-seasoned stuffing mix
2/3 cup grated Parmesan cheese
1/4 cup chopped, fresh parsley
3/4 cup butter
1 large clove garlic, crushed
1 (3-pound) frying chicken, cut up

1. Pre-heat oven to 375F.
2. Mix crumbs, cheese, and parsley together in small bowl.
3. Melt butter in small skillet.
4. Add garlic while butter is melting, so flavors can blend.
5. Dip chicken in butter.
6. Roll in crumbs.
7. Place in baking dish.
8. Sprinkle remaining crumbs and butter over chicken.
9. Bake at 375F for 45 minutes, or until chicken is done. May be re-frigerated several hours before baking.

Yield: 4 servings

PHILIPPINE LUMPIA

Filling
1/2 cup finely chopped onion
1 clove garlic, crushed
2 tablespoons cooking oil
3/4 cup finely chopped cooked pork or chicken
1/4 cup finely chopped cooked shrimp
1-1/2 cups finely shredded cabbage
1/2 of a 9-ounce package frozen French-style green beans, thawed and
    finely chopped
1 cup bean sprouts
1/2 cup carrots, shredded
2 tablespoons soy sauce

10 egg roll skins
10 romaine lettuce leaves, ribs removed

Dipping Sauce
3 tablespoons brown sugar
2 tablespoons cornstarch
1 cup chicken broth
1/2 cup water
2 tablespoons soy sauce

For Filling
1. In skillet, stir-fry onion and garlic in the 2 tablespoons oil
until tender but not brown.
2. Add meat and shrimp; stir-fry about 2 minutes.
3. Add the cabbage, green beans, bean sprouts, carrots, and soy
sauce.
4. Stir-fry 2 to 3 minutes or until vegetables are crisp-tender.
5. Remove from heat; cool to room temperature.

To Assemble
1. Brush a little cooking oil in a large, shallow skillet.
2. Cook one egg roll skin, on one side only, for about 1 minute or
until lightly browned.
3. Turn out onto paper towel.
4. Repeat with remaining skins; add more oil as needed.
5. Place one egg roll skin, unbrowned side up, with one corner facing
you.
6. Top with one lettuce leaf.
7. Spoon about 1/3 cup filling onto lettuce.
8. Roll up, folding in one side of egg roll skin and lettuce and
leaving other end open.
9. Serve at room temperature with Dipping Sauce.

For Dipping Sauce
1. Cook and stir till thickened and bubbly.
2. Cook and stir 1 to 2 minutes longer.
3. Cover surface with clear plastic wrap.
4. Cool to room temperature.

Yield: 10 rolls

CHICKEN POT PIE

2 broiler-fryers (2-1/2 to 3 pounds each)
2 ribs of celery, chopped
1 medium onion, sliced
1 bay leaf
1 teaspoon salt
1/2 teaspoon white pepper
1/2 cup butter
1/2 cup all-purpose flour
1 (10-ounce) package frozen peas, cooked
4 ribs of celery, diced and cooked
4 carrots, sliced and cooked
1-3/4 cups potatoes, diced and cooked
1 egg
2 tablespoons milk
Pastry crust mix as needed

1. Preheat oven to 375F 10 minutes before pies are to go in the oven.
2. Put chicken on to cook in a large saucepan with enough water to cover.
3. Add chopped celery, onion, bay leaf, salt, and pepper.
4. Bring water to a boil; reduce to a simmer; cook until chicken is done.
5. Remove fat; strain stock.
6. Discard skin and bones; cut chicken into large pieces.
7. Melt butter; stir in flour.
8. Cook 5 minutes, stirring constantly.
9. Add enough chicken stock, stirring constantly, to achieve sauce consistency desired.
10. Simmer 5 minutes.
11. Salt and pepper to taste.
12. Divide chicken and cooked vegetables equally into 6 or 8 individual casseroles.
13. Add sauce to amount desired, gently lifting chicken and vegetables so that sauce will flow down and around.
14. Mix egg and milk together to make egg wash.
15. Cover each casserole with pastry; brush with egg wash; puncture pastry with a fork in several places to allow steam to escape.
16. Bake at 375F until crust is golden brown.
17. Serve piping hot.

Yield: 6 to 8 servings

CHICKEN AND FLUFFY DUMPLINGS

2 (3-pound) frying chickens, cut into serving pieces
4 to 4-1/2 cups water
5 stalks celery with leaves, cut into 1-inch pieces
1 cup sliced carrots
3 sprigs parsley, if desired
1 bay leaf
4 peppercorns or 1/2 teaspoon pepper
2 teaspoons salt

Dumplings
1-1/2 cups all-purpose flour
1 tablespoon minced parsley
2 teaspoons baking powder
1/2 teaspoon salt
1/8 teaspoon nutmeg or mace, if desired
2/3 cup milk
2 tablespoons oil or melted shortening
1 egg, slightly beaten

Gravy
1 cup water
1/2 cup flour
1 teaspoon salt
1/4 teaspoon pepper

1. Combine chicken, water, celery, carrots, parsley, bay leaf, peppercorns, and salt; heat to boiling.
2. Simmer, covered, 1 to 1-1/2 hours or until chicken is tender.
3. Skim off fat.
4. To prepare dumplings, combine flour, parsley, baking powder, salt,
and nutmeg in medium bowl.
5. Stir in remaining ingredients just until dry ingredients are moistened.
6. Drop dough by tablespoons into hot chicken and boiling stock.
7. Cover tightly; return to boiling.
8. Reduce heat; do not lift cover.
9. Simmer 12 to 15 minutes or until dumplings are fluffy and dry.
10. Arrange dumplings and chicken on serving platter; keep hot.
11. Strain broth; reserve.
12. To prepare gravy, combine water and flour; blend until smooth.
13. In medium saucepan, bring 4 cups reserved broth to boiling; add
flour mixture.
14. Bring to a boil; cook until thickened.
15. Add salt and pepper.
16. Pour over chicken and dumplings.

Yield: 8 servings

MARYLAND CHICKEN AND COUNTRY HAM

Note: The Cafe puts it together in layers: stuffing/ham/stuffing /chicken/sauce/stuffing.

1 (3- to 3-1/2-pound) broiler-fryer, quartered
1 medium onion
2 cloves garlic
2 stalks celery
3 or 4 sprigs fresh parsley
1 teaspoon salt
2 cups soft breadcrumbs
1 small onion, minced
2 tablespoons chopped fresh parsley
1 teaspoon dried whole savory
Dash of pepper
6 thin slices lean country ham
2 tablespoons butter or margarine
2 tablespoons all-purpose flour
1 cup half-and-half cream
Dash of ground nutmeg

1. Combine first 6 ingredients and water to cover in a Dutch oven; bring to boil.
2. Cover; reduce heat; simmer 1 hour or until chicken is tender.
3. Remove chicken from broth; cool.
4. Strain broth, reserving 2/3 cup.
5. Discard vegetables.
6. Bone chicken and chop meat.
7. Place chopped chicken in a 12x8x2-inch baking dish.
8. Combine breadcrumbs, onion, chopped parsley, savory, and pepper in a small mixing bowl.
9. Stir in reserved broth; mix well.
10. Set aside 3 tablespoons stuffing mixture.
11. Spoon remaining stuffing in center of each slice of ham; roll up tightly.
12 Arrange ham rolls, seam side down, around chicken in baking dish.
13 Melt butter in a heavy saucepan over low heat; add flour, stirring until smooth.
14 Cook 1 minute, stirring constantly.
15. Gradually add half-and-half; cook over medium heat, stirring constantly, until thickened and bubbly.
16. Stir in nutmeg.
17. Spoon sauce over chicken and ham rolls; sprinkle with reserved stuffing.
18. Bake, covered, at 350F for 15 mintues.
19. Uncover and bake an additional 15 minutes.

Yield: 6 servings

CHICKEN CHASSEUR

2 broilers, quartered, or 16 pieces of frying chicken
4 tablespoons cooking oil
2-1/2 cups chopped onions
2 tablespoons flour
5 tablespoons tomato paste
3 medium tomatoes, peeled, seeded, and chopped
2 cloves garlic, pressed
2 bay leaves
1 teaspoon thyme
1 teaspoon salt
1 teaspoon pepper
3/4 cup consomme
2/3 cup dry white wine
3/4 pound mushrooms, sliced
2 tablespoons butter
3 tablepsoons chopped parsley
8 slices French bread (1/2-inch thick), fried in batter

1. Dry chicken thoroughly; brown in oil; place in a large, covered pot to keep warm.
2. Brown onions in same oil; sprinkle flour over onions; continue cooking for 3 to 5 minutes, stirring constantly.
3. Stir in tomato paste, tomatoes, garlic, bay leaves, thyme, salt, pepper, consomme, and wine.
4. Bring to a boil; pour over chicken.
5. Cover tightly and bake in a 350F oven until tender - about 30 to 45 minutes.
6. In original pan, saute mushrooms over low flame, adding butter if necessary.
7. When chicken is tender, transfer to serving dish, using a slotted spoon.
8. Add mushrooms to gravy; pour over chicken.
9. Garnish with parsley; border dish with French bread.
10. Remove bay leaves before serving.

Yield: 8 to 10 servings

ROAST CHICKEN A LA NIVERNAISE

1 (4-1/2-pound) roasting chicken with giblets (neck, gizzard, liver)
2 cups chicken stock
Salt and pepper
1 large pinch dried tarragon or thyme
1 tablespoon shallots or scallions, finely minced
1 tablespoon butter
1 tablespoon or so fresh olive oil or peanut oil
2/3 cup each sliced carrots and onion to roast with the chicken
1/2 cup or so dry white wine or dry white French vermouth (optional)
2 tablespoons flour, blended in a small bowl with 2 tablespoons stock
12 to 18 fresh carrots, depending on size
2 tablespoons shallots or scallions, minced
A handful of fresh parsley, chopped

1. While preparing the rest of the ingredients, simmer the chicken neck
and gizzard in the chicken stock, plus water to cover, for 1-1/2 hours;
strain, degrease, and reserve for the sauce later. You should have
about 1 cup strong chicken essence.
2. Pull out and discard loose fat from inside the chicken; cut off wing
nubbins at elbows, and (if you wish, for easier carving) cut out wish-
bone from inside neck end. Add those to your stock.
3. Wash chicken inside and out under the cold water faucet, and dry
thoroughly in paper towels.
4. Season cavity with a sprinkling of salt, pepper, herbs, and the
minced shallots or scallions; insert the tablespoon of butter and the
liver (which will cook inside the chicken and can be served with it).
5. Truss the chicken; rub outside with oil.
6. Set it breast up in a shallow roasting pan. (May be prepared in
advance; cover and refrigerate.)
7. When you are ready to roast, set chicken, still breast up, in the
middle level of a preheated 425F oven for 5 minutes.
8. Baste with accumulated fat (use a basting or pastry brush).
9. Turn on its other side; roast another 5 minutes.
10. Turn oven thermostat down to 350F; stew the sliced vegetables
in the pan.
11. Baste chicken and vegetables with the accumulated fat; continue
roasting, basting again in 15 minutes.
12. After a total roasting time of 45 minutes, baste again, salt the
chicken lightly on its upturned side; turn it on its other side.
13. Continue roasting for another 30 minutes, basting once.
14. Finally, salt the chicken on this side, and turn it breast up for
the final minutes of roasting. Chicken is done when its legs move
easily in their sockets and feel tender when pressed; when chicken is
lifted and drained, the last drops to fall from its vent should be clear
yellow, with no trace of rosy color.
15. Remove chicken to another pan; keep it warm, uncovered, in
turned-off oven with the door ajar.
16. Thoroughly degrease cooking juices, leaving the vegetables in the
pan.
17. Return juices to the pan; add the reserved chicken stock along
with the optional wine or vermouth. Boil rapidly, scraping up any
coagulated roasting juices into liquid.
18. At the same time, skim off any fat from surface; continue boiling

for several minutes, until juices have reduced to about 1-1/2 cups
and are full of flavor.
19. Remove from heat, and whisk in the flour mixture; return to heat,
and simmer for 2 to 3 minutes.
20. Sauce should be slightly thickened; taste; correct seasoning;
strain into a saucepan, pressing juices out of vegetables.
21. Set aside; reheat to the simmer before using.
22. While the chicken is roasting, trim and peel the carrots.
23. Cut carrots into 2-inch crosswise pieces, and then into lengthwise
halves, thirds or quarters to make pieces all of approximately the same
size.
24. Place in a rather wide saucepan, to make about two layers; add
water to come halfway up, a little salt, and the minced shallots or
scallions.
25. Bring to the boil; cover; boil slowly for about 8 minutes, or
until almost tender.
26. Uncover; boil off any remaining liquid. (May be done in advance
--do not overcook.)
27. Carve the chicken into serving pieces; arrange on a hot platter
leaving space in the center for the carrots.
28. Toss the carrots with a spoonful or so of the sauce to enrobe them;
then toss with the parsley; turn into the center of the platter.
29. Spoon a little sauce over each piece of chicken; pass any of
the remainder in a warm sauce bowl.

Yield: 6 servings

BAKED HONEY CHICKEN

1 (3-pound) chicken, cut up
3 tablespoons finely chopped onion
2 tablespoons honey
2 tablespoons dark soy sauce
1 tablespoon minced ginger
1 teaspoon garlic
1/4 cup thinly sliced green onion, green part only

1. Arrange chicken in 9x13 baking dish.
2. Combine onion, honey, soy sauce, ginger, and garlic in small bowl
and spoon over chicken.
3. Marinate for 1 hour, turning chicken once.
4. Preheat oven to 425F.
5. Bake chicken 30 minutes.
6. Turn pieces over; sprinkle with green onion.
7. Continue to bake until chicken is tender - 10-15 minutes.
8. Serve immediately.

Yield: 6 servings

PASTA-STUFFED ROAST CHICKEN

Note: You can also make this recipe using chicken pieces. Just put the stuffing down in a casserole and place the pieces on top. You could even use boneless chicken breasts if you wanted to be fancy.

6 ounces pasta
2 small bunches scallions, sliced
2/3 cup chopped Italian parsley
2 tablespoons pignoli
1 cup Pesto
4- to 5-pound roasting chicken
2 tablespoons butter
4 slices bacon

1. Cook and drain the pasta.
2. Combine the pasta, scallions, parsley, pignoli, and pesto in a mixing bowl.
3. Stuff the chicken with the dressing and close the opening by placing a slice of bread over it.
4. Truss the chicken and rub it lightly with the butter.
5. Place the bird on its side on a rack in a shallow roasting pan.
6. Cover with the bacon slices.
7. Roast for 25 minutes at 425F.
8. Remove the bacon; turn the bird onto its other side; cover with the same strips of bacon.
9. Roast another 25 minutes.
10. Place the chicken breast up; discard the bacon.
11. Roast for 20 to 25 minutes longer, basting with the pan juices. At this point, if the thigh joint moves easily--if you can "shake hands with the bird"--it's too late: the chicken is overcooked and dry! A better test is to insert a meat thermometer into the thigh, avoiding the bone. It should register 160F when the bird is done.
12. Take it out of the oven, place it on a hot platter, and let it sit for a few minutes before you carve it.

Yield: 4 servings

CHICKEN CORDON BLEU CASSEROLE

Note: This can be frozen before baking.

3 cups cooked, cubed chicken
1 cup slivered, cooked ham
2 cups fine noodles
6 tablespoons butter
1 medium onion, sliced
1 cup fresh, sliced mushrooms
3 tablespoons flour
2 cups milk, heated
1/3 cup sherry
2 cups grated Swiss cheese

1. Cook noodles according to package directions; drain and rinse.
2. Cook onion and mushrooms in butter until soft.
3. Blend in flour; add hot milk; stir until thickened.
4. Add sherry.
5. Fold in cheese, reserving about 3 tablespoons.
6. Add noodles, chicken, and ham.
7. Pour into greased, 9x13-inch baking dish; sprinkle reserved cheese on top.
8. Bake at 350F for about 45 minutes.

Yield: 8 servings

CHICKEN QUICHE ALMANDINE

1 unbaked 9-inch pie shell
1/2 cup diced, cooked chicken
3 tablespoons sliced almonds
1-1/2 cups Swiss cheese, shredded
3 eggs, slightly beaten
1-1/2 cups milk
1/4 teaspoon mace
1/8 teaspoon pepper
2 tablespoons Parmesan cheese

1. Bake pie shell at 400F oven for 10 minutes.
2. Place diced chicken in bottom of pie shell, top with Swiss cheese and almonds.
3. Mix together eggs, milk, mace, and pepper.
4. Pour into pie shell.
5. Sprinkle top with Parmesan cheese.
6. Bake at 375F for 30 to 35 minutes.
7. Let stand 10 minutes before serving.

Yield: 5 or 6 servings

CHICKEN BROCCOLI CRESCENT BAKE

Note: In the Cafe, we used puff pastry instead of crescent rolls.

1 (3-ounce) package cream cheese, softened
1 (10-3/4-ounce) can condensed cream of chicken soup
2 cups cubed, cooked chicken
1 (9-ounce) package frozen cut broccoli, cooked, well drained
3 tablespoons chopped ripe olives
1 tablespoon chopped onion
1/2 teaspoon salt, if desired
Dash pepper
2 (8-ounce) cans Pillsbury Refrigerated Quick Crescent Dinner Rolls
2 ounces (1/2 cup) Kraft sharp natural cheddar cheese, shredded

1. Heat oven to 350F.
2. In large bowl, blend cream cheese and soup until smooth; stir in chicken, broccoli, olives, onion, salt, and pepper.
3. Unroll 1 can of dough into 2 long rectangles.
4. Place rectangles on ungreased large cookie sheet 2-inches apart; firmly press perforations to seal.
5. Place half of chicken mixture over each rectangle to within 1 inch of edges.
6. Sprinkle 1/4 cup cheese over each.
7. Unroll second can; press or roll each to form 13x5-inch rectangle; place over cheese.
8. Press edges with fork to seal.
9. Bake at 350F for 22 to 28 minutes or until deep golden brown.
10. Cool 5 minutes; slice to serve.

Yield: 8 to 10 servings

Tip: To reheat, wrap loosely in foil; heat at 350F for 20 to 25 minutes or until warm.

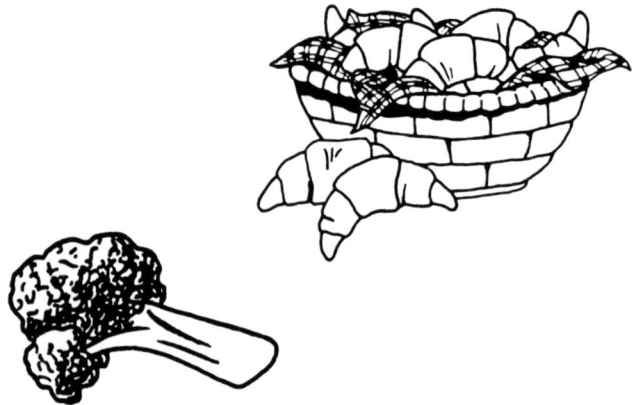

RUIDOSO CHICKEN

Note: This can be made the night before and refrigerated, then baked at 325F for 1 hour.

1 (8-ounce) package green spinach noodles
1/4 cup butter
1/4 cup flour
1 cup milk
1 cup chicken stock
1 pint dairy sour cream
1/3 to 1/2 cup lemon juice
1 (6-ounce) can mushroom pieces and juice
2 teaspoons seasoned salt
1/2 teaspoon nutmeg
1 teaspoon paprika
2 teaspoons pepper
1/2 teaspoon cayenne pepper (optional)
1 tablespoon parsley flakes
4 cups cooked chicken
1/2 cup toasted bread crumbs
Parmesan cheese

1. Cook noodles; drain.
2. Melt butter in a large saucepan.
3. Stir in flour, slowly add milk and chicken stock.
4. Cook over low heat, stirring constantly until sauce thickens.
5. To the cream sauce, add sour cream, lemon juice, mushrooms, seasoned salt, nutmeg, paprika, pepper, and parsley flakes. Mix well.
6. Cut chicken into large, bite-sized pieces (4 cups).
7. Butter a 3-quart casserole.
8. Place 1/2 drained noodles in casserole.
9. Add layer of chicken.
10. Pour some sauce over chicken.
11. Sprinkle with bread crumbs and Parmesan cheese.
12. Repeat layers, ending with cheese on top.
13. Heat in 350F oven until bubbly - about 25 minutes.

Yield: 8 to 10 servings

TOMATO AND CHICKEN CREPES

Filling
2 large fresh tomatoes
2 cups cooked diced chicken or turkey
1/2 cup tomato sauce
2 tablespoons minced onion
2 tablespoons chopped raisins
2 tablespoons chopped almonds
2 tablespoons pepitas*, excess salt wiped off
1/4 teaspoon ground cumin
Salt and freshly ground pepper

Sauce
2 tablespoons oil
1 medium onion, minced
1 (28-ounce) can Italian plum tomatoes, drained and chopped
1 (8-ounce) can tomato sauce or marinara sauce
3/4 pound fresh tomatoes, chopped
1/4 to 1/2 teaspoon crushed red pepper
1/2 green pepper, seeded and chopped
2 tablespoons fresh snipped cilantro
1/2 teaspoon oregano, or more to taste
Salt and freshly ground pepper

16 (8-inch) crepes
1 pint dairy sour cream
1 cup grated Monterey Jack, Mozzarella, Parmesan, or cheddar cheese

For Filling
Combine all ingredients in medium bowl; toss gently to blend.
(May be refrigerated, covered with plastic wrap, for up to 2 days.)

For Sauce
1. Heat oil in large saucepan over medium-high heat.
2. Add onion and cook until softened.
3. Add remaining ingredients, reduce heat; simmer, uncovered, 40 to
50 minutes, or until reduced to about 2 cups, stirring occasionally.
(Sauce may be frozen and defrosted prior to use.)

To Assemble
1. Preheat oven to 325F.
2. Butter a shallow, 3-quart baking dish.
3. Place about 3 tablespoons filling in center of each crepe and fold
or roll envelope-style.
4. Place seam side down in prepared dish and cover with sauce.
5. Dollop with sour cream and sprinkle with cheese.
6. Bake 15 to 20 minutes, or until hot.
7. Serve immediately.

*If unavailable, substitute hulled, unsalted pumpkin seeds available in
specialty and health food stores.

Yield: 5 to 6 servings

CARIBBEAN CHICKEN DELIGHT

1 (3- to 3-1/2-pound) whole chicken
1 pound medium-sized onions, peeled and halved
2 bay leaves
1 (8-1/2-ounce) can green peas, drained
4 tablespoons butter
1/4 cup dry sherry
1 (4-ounce) can pimientos

1. Season chicken; refrigerate overnight.
2. Arrange onions in bottom of a pot with a heavy lid.
3. Add bay leaves.
4. Place chicken in breast down; cover pot; and cook over moderate heat for 5 minutes.
5. Turn heat to low, cover, and cook about 2 hours or until done. (Drumstick will feel soft when pressed, and when pierced with a cooking fork, renders no liquid.)
6. Remove chicken and bay leaves from pot.
7. Cut chicken into pieces; separate meat from bones.
8. Shred meat into large chunks; add to pot.
9. Add peas, butter, and sherry; mix; cook, uncovered, over moderate heat, until butter melts.
10. Heat pimientos in their juice, drain, cut in strips; garnish.
11. Serve in a deep dish.

Yield: 4 servings

Beef

CARBONNADE OF BEEF

Note: The first time I made this, I served it to my in-laws and they loved it! It really is a delicious, easy company meal.

3 pounds boneless chuck, cut into 1-1/2-to-2-inch cubes
1/4 cup flour
2 tablespoons oil
4 tablespoons butter, divided
3 cloves garlic, minced
1 cup beef stock
1-1/2 cups dark beer
2 tablespoons brown sugar
2 teaspoons salt
1 Bouquet Garni of parsley, bay leaf, and thyme
25 pearl onions, peeled (could use canned)
6 to 8 medium carrots, peeled and cut into 1-1/2 inch lengths
1/2 pound mushrooms, cleaned and quartered
Salt and freshly ground pepper

1. Coat beef cubes lightly in flour; reserve any leftover flour. If there is too much flour on the beef, the meat will be difficult to brown, and the sauce will be too thick and will taste of flour.
2. Heat oil and 2 tablespoons of the butter in Dutch oven.
3. Brown beef cubes, a few at a time. If you add too many at one time, they will brown too slowly.
4. Remove beef from pan with a slotted spoon; keep warm.
5. Add minced garlic to Dutch oven; cook about 1 minute.
6. Stir in reserved flour; cook for 1 minute.
7. Add beef stock to Dutch oven; stir over medium heat to deglaze.
To deglaze a pan, add liquid and stir, scraping the pan drippings from the bottom and incorporating them into the sauce. This is the time to make sure that you will not have any lumps in your sauce. Add the stock, slowly smoothing out any lumps as you go.
8. Add beer, sugar, salt, and Bouquet Garni; heat to a simmer.
9. Add browned beef to Dutch oven; let mixture return to a simmer.
10. Reduce heat; cover; cook at a low simmer for 1 hour. Meat should be tender and flavorful. If it is not tender, cook longer.
Adjust seasonings and continue simmering until their flavor is also incorporated.
11. In a separate skillet, melt remaining 2 tablespoons of butter. Add the pearl onions and carrots; saute for 5 minutes. Remove vegetables from the skillet with a slotted spoon; set aside.
13. Add mushrooms to skillet; saute about 5 minutes; remove and set aside.
14. When the beef is tender and flavorful, add the sauteed vegetables to the Dutch Oven; cover; cook for an additional 15 minutes.
15. Stir in sauteed mushrooms; cover; cook for another 15 minutes.
16. Adjust seasonings; remove Bouquet Garni; skim off excess fat; serve.

Yield: 6 to 8 servings

INCREDIBLE INDOOR BARBEQUE

Note: Generally I do not approve of the concept of liquid smoke, so we tried making the dish without liquid smoke and the flavor was not nearly as good. So go ahead, live a little!

This recipe can be prepared up to 3 days ahead, covered and refrigerated, or up to one month ahead and frozen.

10 pounds boneless beef brisket
1 cup liquid smoke
4 cups diced onion
2 tablespoons minced garlic
2 (12-ounce) cans tomato paste
5 to 6 cups beer
1 (28-ounce) can plum tomatoes with liquid
1 cup firmly packed dark brown sugar
2/3 cup red wine vinegar
1/2 cup Worcestershire sauce
3 to 4 tablespoons chili powder
2 tablespoons molasses
4 teaspoons ground cumin
2 teaspoons salt
1/4 teaspoon ground cloves
Red and green bell pepper strips and sliced green onion (optional)

1. Preheat oven to 325F.
2. Set rack in bottom of 1 large or 2 small roasting pans.
3. Arrange meat in single layer on rack.
4. Add liquid smoke to pan (meat should not touch liquid; if necessary, raise rack with small cans or metal cups).
5. Cover; bake, turning once, until meat is very tender - 4 to 5 hours. (Your kitchen will smell like a barbeque pit.)
6. Refrigerate on rack in pan overnight.
7. Set meat aside; reserve 1/4 cup fat from surface and all pan liquid.
8. Melt fat in large Dutch oven over low heat.
9. Add onion and garlic; cover; cook until soft, stirring occasionally - about 10 minutes.
10. Mix in tomato paste.
11. Measure reserved pan liquid. Add enough beer to make 5-1/2 cups liquid total. Blend into onion mixture.
12. Add all remaining ingredients except meat and the garnish; bring to a rolling boil.
13. Reduce heat to low; simmer sauce for 30 minutes, stirring occasionally.
14. Pull and cut meat into 1-inch chunks or shred meat.
15. Add meat to sauce; cover; simmer for 1 hour, stirring occassionally. If sauce seems too thin, uncover pan and increase heat. Boil until sauce is thick enough. If sauce is too thick, add more beer.
17. Garnish with red and green bell pepper strips and sliced green onion, if desired.
18. Serve hot.

Yield: 24 to 30 servings

POT ROAST

Note: Pot Roast is always a favorite. Out of all of the ones that we have tried over the years, this is our favorite. Try serving Pot Roast the next time you entertain. A mellow, cordial evening is all but guaranteed!

3-1/2 pounds beef shoulder or cross-rib roast, rolled and tied
1 teaspoon freshly ground black pepper, to taste
3 tablespoons olive oil
1-1/2 to 2 cups beef stock
2 cups dry red wine
1 bunch of parsley, finely chopped, plus more, unchopped, for garnish
1 teaspoon salt
7 whole cloves
2-1/2 cups coarsely chopped yellow onions
2 cups peeled carrot chunks (1-inch chunks)
8 medium-sized potatoes, scrubbed and cut into thirds
2 cups canned Italian plum tomatoes, with juice
1 cup diced celery

1. Preheat oven to 350F.
2. Rub roast with black pepper.
3. Heat olive oil in a heavy, flameproof casserole or Dutch oven and sear roast for several minutes on each side, browning well.
4. Pour in stock and wine. Add parsley, 1 teaspoon salt, 1 teaspoon black pepper, and the whole cloves.
5. Stir in onions, carrots, potatoes, tomatoes, and celery. Liquid in casserole should just cover vegetables. Add additional beef stock if necessary.
6. Bring to a simmer on top of the stove. Cover and place in center of the oven to cook for 2 1/2 hours.
7. Uncover and cook longer, until meat is tender - about 1-1/2 hours; baste frequently.
8. Transfer roast to a deep serving platter and arrange vegetables around it.
9. Spoon a bit of sauce over all and garnish the platter with parsley. Pass additional sauce in a gravy boat.

Yield: 6 servings

BEEF STEW PROVENCAL

Note: As the name Provencal indicates, this is a stew with plenty of tomatoes and garlic. It's a nice variation on the standard stew.

3 pounds boneless beef chuck

Marinade
1 navel orange
1-1/2 cups dry red wine
1-1/2 tablespoons dried thyme leaves

1/2 cup all-purpose flour
Salt
1/4 teaspoon pepper
1 leek (8 ounces), washed
1/4 cup butter or margarine
2 tablespoons olive or salad oil
10 small white onions (3/4 pound), peeled
1 clove garlic, crushed
2 bay leaves
1 can (1 pound, 12 ounces) tomatoes, drained
10 small new potatoes (1-1/2 pounds), scrubbed
4 zucchini (1-1/2 pounds), washed
12 ripe olives
Chopped parsley

1. Wipe beef with damp paper towels. With sharp knife, cut into 1-1/2 inch cubes.
2. With parer, cut strip of orange peel 1-inch wide, 3-inches long.
3. In large bowl, combine orange peel, red wine, and thyme. Mix well.
4. Add beef; toss to coat well.
5. Refrigerate, tightly covered, 2 to 3 hours.
6. Drain well; reserve marinade and peel.
7. On waxed paper, coat beef cubes with flour mixed with 1 tablespoon salt and the pepper; reserve remaining flour mixture.
8. Trim leek. Cut off root, tips, and most of dark green. With sharp knife, slice leek crosswise, 1/8-inch thick (this should make 1 cup).
9. In 6-quart Dutch oven, heat butter and oil over high heat.
10. Add beef cubes in single layer (do not overcrowd).
11. Saute beef over medium heat, turning to brown on all sides.
12. With tongs, remove beef to bowl as it browns. Continue browning rest (takes 1/2 hour in all).
13. Add leek, onions, and garlic to drippings; cook, stirring until golden, for 10 minutes. Remove.
14. Return beef to Dutch oven.
15. Add bay leaves, tomatoes, and marinade. Stir until well combined.
16. Bring to boiling; reduce heat; simmer, covered (place sheet of waxed paper on top, under lid, to catch any liquid), for 1 hour.
17. Pare strip of peel around potatoes.
18. Slice zucchini 1-inch thick.
19. Add onions, leek, and potatoes to beef. Cook 40 minutes, covered.
20. Add zucchini and olives; cook 20 minutes, or until beef and vege-

tables are tender.
21. Stir the flour into 1/4 cup water until smooth.
22. Stir into beef. Simmer, uncovered, 10 minutes; stir occasionally.
23. Add peel and parsley.

Yield: 8 servings

SESAME STEAKS

Note: We also cut the beef into 1/2x1-inch pieces and stir-fry
it after it's been marinated.

1 pound sirloin steak, cut 1/2-inch thick
1 teaspoon lemon juice
1 tablespoon salad oil
1/4 cup soy sauce
1 tablespoon brown sugar
1 teaspoon onion powder
1/4 teaspoon black pepper
1/4 teaspoon garlic salt
1/4 teaspoon ginger
1 tablespoon sesame seed

1. Cut steak into 3 or 4 serving-size pieces; place in flat baking
dish.
2. Combine remaining ingredients; pour over steak, being sure to coat
all sides.
3. Let stand 1 hour or longer, turning once or twice.
4. Broil 3-inches from heat a few minutes on each side to desired
degree of doneness.
5. Serve with rice.
Yield: 2 to 3 servings

PERFECT POT ROAST

4-to-5 pound beef rump roast
2 tablespoons salad oil
2 tablespoons butter or regular margarine
1 small onion, sliced
1 clove garlic, crushed
1 teaspoon dried thyme leaves
1 teaspoon dried marjoram leaves
1 bay leaf, crumbled
8 whole black peppers
1 teaspoon salt
1 (10-1/2-ounce) can condensed beef broth, undiluted (1-1/3 cups)
8 halved, pared carrots (1 pound)
12 small white onions, peeled
1 sprig parsley
3 tablespoons flour

1. Whip pot roast with damp paper towels.
2. In hot oil and butter in 5-quart Dutch oven or heavy kettle, over medium heat, brown roast along with sliced onion (onion browns and gives a good dark color and rich flavor to pan drippings), turning roast with two wooden spoons, until well browned on all sides - 25 minutes in all. Slow browning gives the meat and gravy a better flavor and color.
3. To drippings in Dutch oven, add garlic, thyme, marjoram, bay leaf, black peppers, and salt; stir 1/2 minute (this restores flavor to herbs, and meat absorbs seasonings).
4. Add beef broth (you may substitute tomato juice, stewed tomatoes, beer, or red wine to vary the flavor).
5. Bring to boiling; reduce heat to simmer (cook just below the boiling point), covered, for 2-1/2 hours. Turn meat occasionally so that it will cook evenly.
6. Add carrots, onions, and parsley; simmer, covered, 30 minutes, or until vegetables and meat are tender.
7. Remove meat and vegetables from Dutch oven to a warm platter; keep in a warm place, covered loosely with foil.
8. Make a gravy by pouring 1/4 cup water into measuring cup; add flour; mix with fork until smooth. (If flour is added to the water, it will dissolve more easily.)
9. Strain liquid remaining in Dutch oven. If necessary, add water to measure 2 cups. Return to Dutch oven.
10. Stir flour mixture into liquid in Dutch oven; bring to boiling, stirring.
11. Reduce heat; simmer 3 minutes. Taste; add salt if desired.
12. Spoon a little of the gravy over meat; then pass with vegetables. Nice with boiled potatoes.

Yield: 10 servings

SOPHISTICATED STEW

3 pounds lean beef stew meat
1/2 cup flour
Salt and pepper
6 pieces bacon
2 cloves garlic, minced
1 ounce brandy, warmed
12 small whole mushrooms
1 cup condensed beef bouillon
1-1/2 cups dry red wine
12 small whole onions
12 small carrots, sliced
6 peppercorns, slightly bruised
4 whole cloves
1 bay leaf, crumbled
2 tablespoons chopped fresh parsley
1/4 teaspoon dried marjoram
1/4 teaspoon thyme

1. Shake beef a few at a time in paper bag with salt, pepper, and flour.
2. In large iron skillet, fry bacon until it browns but is not crisp.
3. Cut bacon in 1-inch pieces after cooking. Place in a heavy earthenware baking dish.
4. Cook the garlic in bacon fat.
5. Add beef cubes; brown quickly on all sides.
6. Pour brandy into skillet; light it; when flame dies out, remove the meat and garlic and put them into casserole.
7. Put mushrooms in skillet; brown lightly; add them to casserole.
8. Put bouillon and 1 cup of red wine in skillet.
9. Bring to a boil; stir bottom to loosen particles. Pour liquid into casserole.
10. Add onions, carrots, peppercorns, cloves, bay leaf, parsley, marjoram, and thyme to casserole.
11. Pour remaining 1/2 cup red wine over casserole.
12. Cover casserole; bake at 300F for 2 hours.
13. Cool; place in refrigerator, covered.
14. When ready to use next day, spoon liquid from bottom of casserole over meat; cook in 300F oven covered for 1 hour or until piping hot.

Yield: 8 to 10 servings

BEEF BOURGUIGNONNE

Note: The mushrooms in the broth really enrich the flavor.
Please use fresh mushrooms and don't skimp.

1/4 pound salt pork, diced
1/4 cup cognac
1/8 teaspoon freshly ground pepper
1/2 cup flour
1-1/2 teaspoons salt
1/2 teaspoon pepper
Dash cayenne pepper
1/4 cup chopped fresh parsley
1 pound fresh mushrooms
3 pounds bottom round, cut in 1-1/2-inch pieces
1/4 pound butter
4 medium onions, chopped
2 cups beef stock or as needed
1/2 teaspoon dried thyme
1/2 teaspoon dried marjoram
1-1/2 cups burgundy wine
16 small white onions, peeled
Fresh, chopped parsley for garnish

1. Marinate salt pork in cognac, parsley, and 1/8 teaspoon pepper for 2 to 3 hours.
2. Combine flour, salt, pepper, and cayenne. Dredge beef in seasoned flour.
3. Melt half the butter in a heavy skillet; brown meat on all sides.
4. Add chopped onions and brown.
5. Transfer beef and onions to a 3-quart casserole with a tight-fitting lid.
6. Drain salt pork, reserving marinade; brown it in 1 teaspoon butter. Add to beef.
7. Deglaze skillet with marinade and 1/4 cup beef stock. Pour over meat.
8. Add wine, thyme, marjoram, and enough stock to cover meat.
9. Cover; bake in a preheated 375F oven for 2 hours.
10. Saute mushrooms in 2 tablespoons butter until just barely cooked. Add sauteed mushrooms and fresh parsley to meat.
11. Parboil white onions for 3 minutes; drain well; saute in remaining butter to brown lightly.
12. Add to meat, replace cover; continue cooking for 1 more hour.
13. Add more wine or stock if needed.
14. Adjust seasonings; serve sprinkled with fresh, chopped parsley.

Yield: 8 servings

CARBONNADES A LA FLAMANDE

Note: Carbonnades a la Flamande is probably Belgium's most famous dish. It is the one beef stew which, traditionally, is made with beer. Serve with plenty of cold beer.

Flour for dredging
Salt and freshly ground black pepper to taste
2 pounds boneless chuck, cut into 1-inch cubes
1/4 cup salad oil
6 medium onions, sliced
1 clove garlic, finely chopped
1 12 ounce bottle or can of beer
1 tablespoon chopped parsley
1 bay leaf
1/4 teaspoon thyme

1. Combine flour, salt, and pepper.
2. Dredge the meat in the seasoned flour.
3. Heat oil in a skillet.
4. Add onion slices and garlic; cook until tender, but not brown.
5. Remove the onions from the skillet.
6. Add the meat; brown on all sides, adding a little more oil if necessary.
7. Return the onions to the skillet.
8. Add the remaining ingredients.
9. Cover; cook over low heat until meat is tender - about 1-1/4 hours.
10. Serve hot with boiled potatoes.

Yield: 4 to 6 servings

CLUB 302 CHILI

Note: The Scotch enriches the flavor. Go ahead! Try it, you'll like it!

2 pounds stew beef
Chili powder
Cumin
Garlic
Salt and pepper
Brown sugar
3 cans of beer
2 green peppers
2 large onions
1 jigger Scotch (optional)

1. Trim all the fat from the beef; cut the meat into 1/2-inch chunks.
2. Brown the beef; put it in a pot with the beer. Bring to a simmer.
3. Cut the peppers and onions into large chunks; saute with the garlic. When done, add to the pot.
4. As the chili heats, add the spices. Start with at least half of tin of chili powder (go on, you can do it!) and take it from there. Add about half that much cumin. Start with 4 tablespoons of brown sugar and, oh yes, don't forget the Scotch! It really adds a nice twist.
5. Simmer uncovered until there's very little liquid left. This can take as long as 12 hours over low heat. I'd suggest putting it on Saturday, refrigrerating it overnight, and putting it on again for a Sunday night dinner.

Yield: 8 servings

ROULADEN

Note: This is a wonderful German recipe. You can serve it either as a main dish or as an hor d'ouerve.

Round steak, cut in 4 (1/2-ounce) pieces
Onion, minced
Grainy mustard
Kosher dill pickles, quartered
1 tablespoon arrowroot, or cornstarch

1. Pound round steak pieces to about 1/8-inch thickness; brush one side with about 2 teaspoons of grainy mustard. A little horseradish may be stirred into the mustard.
2. Sprinkle about 1 tablespoon of onion on top of the mustard.
3. Place a pickle spear in the center and roll the steak around it. Secure with toothpicks.
4. Salt and pepper each roll; dredge it in flour.
5. Lightly brown each roll on all sides in a small amount of vegetable oil.
6. Place rolls in a baking pan; reserve juices from browning pan for gravy.
7. Bake in a 350F oven for 10-15 minutes.
8. Make a gravy from the pan juices by adding 1 tablespoon of arrowroot or cornstarch that has been dissolved in 1/4 cup of water.
9. Simmer gravy on top of the stove; stir until thick.
10. Spoon over steak rolls.

Yield: 4 servings

BEEF STROGANOFF

Note: I never liked beef stroganoff until I tried this recipe.
This one is very light and flavorful.

When I served this to my parents, I made a batch of crepe skins, put
the meat inside, and the sauce on top. I placed the filled crepes in
the center of an ovenproof platter, encircled them with broccoli spears
and put shredded Swiss cheese on top. Just before dinner I ran the
platter under the broiler to brown the cheese. Very elegant, very easy,
and very delicious.

1-1/2 pounds beef fillet, sirloin, or porterhouse steak
Salt and freshly ground black pepper to taste
3 tablespoons butter, divided
1 tablespoon flour
1 cup beef broth or canned consomme
1 teaspoon prepared mustard
1 onion, sliced
3 tablespoons dairy sour cream, room temperature

1. Remove all the fat and gristle from the meat. Cut into narrow
strips about 2 inches long and 1/2-inch thick.
2. Season the strips with salt and pepper; refrigerate two hours.
3. In a saucepan, melt 1-1/2 tablespoons of butter; add the flour;
stir with a wire whisk until blended.
4. Meanwhile, bring the consomme to a boil; add all at once to the
butter-flour mixture, stirring vigorously with the whisk until the sauce
is thickened and smooth.
5. Stir in the mustard.
6. In a separate pan, heat the remaining butter; add the meat and
sliced onion; brown quickly on both sides.
7. Remove the meat to a hot platter. You may wish to remove the onions
and discard them. I think they add a nice flavor but for some they are
too strong.
8. Add the sour cream to the mustard sauce; heat over a brisk flame
for three minutes.
9. Pour sauce over meat; serve at once or keep warm.

Yield: 6 servings

REUBEN QUICHE

Note: This unusual combination is quite tasty. If you cut it into little pieces, it makes a great hor d'ouerve.

This recipe can be made ahead and reheated.

1 recipe for pie crust
4 ounces corned beef, finely chopped
1 small can sauerkraut, well drained
12 ounces Swiss cheese, shredded
1/4 cup Thousand Island Dressing (or 2 tablespoons each of mayonnaise,
    catsup, and sweet pickle relish)
1 teaspoon caraway seeds
1 tablespoon good-quality mustard
3 eggs beaten
1 cup milk

1. Prepare pie crust. Line either a deep dish pie plate if you plan on serving this as an entree, or a jelly roll pan if you plan on using this for an hor d'ouevre with the rolled out crust.
2. Pierce crust with the tines of a fork to let air escape while you bake the crust at 350F for 10 minutes.
3. Evenly cover the bottom of the crust with the corned beef.
4. Place a layer of the sauerkraut on the corned beef. You may not wish to use the entire can of sauerkraut.
5. Amply fill the crust with the Swiss cheese.
6. Combine the salad dressing, caraway seeds, mustard, eggs, and milk; beat to blend well. Pour over the cheese.
7. Bake at 375F for 40 minutes or until the top is set. Let the quiche sit for 15 minutes before cutting. Serve warm.

PEPPER STEAK

Note: This recipe was given to us by the wife of one of our employees. It is her favorite recipe for Pepper Steak, and we agree with her!

1-1/2 pounds top round steak, 1/2-inch thick
1/2 teaspoons salt
2 medium onions, cut into rings
2 beef bouillon cubes in 3 cups water
3 tablespoons Worcestershire sauce
2 green peppers, cut into 1-inch pieces (or 1 green and 1 red)
2 tablespoons cornstarch mixed in 1/4 cup cold water
2 tomatoes, peeled and cut into eighths
1/4 stick butter
2 tablespoons sherry or white wine

1. Cut meat into bite-sized pieces.
2. Grease large skillet with oil.
3. Brown meat thoroughly on both sides.
4. While meat is browning, saute onions and pepper in butter with 1/4 cup water.
5. Reduce heat from steak; add onions, peppers, beef broth, Worcestershire sauce and sherry.
6. Simmer 15 minutes or until meat is tender.
7. Add cornstarch mixture. Stir and mix well.
8. Add tomatoes; simmer 5 minutes, uncovered.
9. Serve over rice.

Yield: 4 servings

FLANK STEAK

Note: Whenever we serve flank steak, we can never cook it fast enough. It really is a simple dish and so good. It is even better if you can cook it on the grill.

One of our favorite company meals is to have flank steak, broccoli spears, Caesar salad, and cheese souffle. WOW!

1. Prepare one package of garlic or Italian dressing, using wine vinegar and olive oil.
2. Marinate flank steak in dressing for about 24 hours. The longer you marinate the steak, the better it is.
3. Broil about 5 minutes a side.

Yield: 4 to 6 servings

THIN PAN-BROILED STEAKS WITH TOMATOES AND OLIVES

1/2 medium yellow onion, sliced thin
Olive oil, sufficient to come 1/4-inch up the side of the pan
2 medium cloves garlic, peeled and diced
2/3 cup canned Italian tomatoes, roughly chopped, with their juice
1 dozen black Greek olives, pitted and quartered
1/4 teaspoon oregano
Salt to taste
Freshly ground pepper, 6 to 8 twists of the mill
1 pound beef steaks, preferably chuck or chicken steaks, sliced 1/4-inch
    thick, pounded, and edges notched to keep from curling

1. In a good-sized skillet (the broader the skillet, the faster the
sauce will thicken), slowly saute the sliced onion in the olive oil,
letting it wilt gradually.
2. As it takes on a pale gold color, add the diced garlic.
3. Continue sauteing until the garlic has colored lightly; add the
tomatoes, olives, oregano, salt, and pepper.
4. Stir and cook at a lively simmer until the tomatoes and oil separate
- about 15 minutes or more. (The sauce may be prepared ahead of time
up to this point.)
5. Turn the heat down, keeping the sauce at the barest simmer.
6. Heat up a heavy iron skillet until it is smoking hot.
7. Quickly grease the bottom with an oil-soaked cloth or paper towel.
8. Put in the beef slices; cook just long enough to brown the meat
well on both sides.
9. As you turn the meat, season it with salt and pepper. (Do not overcook or the thinly sliced steaks will become tough.)
10. Transfer the browned meat first to the simmering sauce, turning it
quickly and basting it with sauce, then to a hot platter, pouring the
sauce over the meat.
11. Serve immediately.

Yield: 4 servings

CARNE ASADA (STEAK SLICES IN STEAMED TORTILLAS)

Note: This is a terrific Mexican dish. Rather than being
spicy hot, it is richly flavorful.

1-1/2 pound top round steak or boneless chuck steak, cut 1-1/2-inches
   thick*

Marinade
1/4 cup red wine vinegar
2 tablespoons oil
1 teaspoon sage leaves
1 teaspoon summer savory, if desired
1/2 teaspoon salt
1/2 teaspoon dry mustard
1/2 teaspoon paprika

2 tablespoons steak sauce
12 flour tortillas, 5 to 8 inches in diameter
2 medium onions, sliced paper thin or chopped
1 4-ounce can whole green chilies, cut into strips
Softened butter or margarine
Salsa, if desired
Guacamole, if desired

1. Place steak in plastic bag or non-metal baking dish.
2. In a small bowl, combine marinade ingredients. Pour over steak,
turning to coat.
3. Seal bag or cover dish; marinate at least 6 hours or overnight in
refrigerator, turning once or twice.
4. When ready to barbeque, drain meat, reserving marinade by placing in
small saucepan.
5. Add steak sauce to marinade; blend well. Heat on grill.
6. Place steak 4 to 6 inches from medium-hot coals.
7. Cook 30 to 40 minutes, turning once, or until desired doneness,
brushing occasionally with marinade.
8. Meanwhile, heat foil-wrapped tortillas on grill until thoroughly
heated and steaming;** wrap in cloth napkin or towel to keep warm.
9. To serve, cut steak across grain into thin slices.
10. Spoon any remaining marinade over slices.
11. Arrange steak, warmed tortillas, onions, chilies, butter, salsa, and
guacamole on large platter.
12. Spread butter on tortillas; top with meat and any combination of
vegetables or sauces. Roll up to eat.

*Sirloin steak, cut 1-1/2 inches thick, can be substituted for round or
chuck steak. Omit marinating step. Cook over hot coals for 15 to 20
minutes, turning once, or until desired doneness. Season with butter
and steak sauce, if desired, when removed from grill. Sprinkle with
salt and pepper to taste. Steak can be broiled, as directed, in
oven.

**Foil-wrapped tortillas can be heated in oven at 425F for 15 minutes or place in two stacks between paper towels and microwave on high for 45 seconds.

Yield: 6 servings

Salsa
1 (28-ounce) can tomato wedges or tomatoes, drained and chopped*
1/2 cup thinly sliced green onions
1 (4-ounce) can green chilies, seeded and chopped**
1 teaspoon grated lemon peel, if desired
1/2 teaspoon salt
1/2 teaspoon oregano leaves
1/8 teaspoon pepper
2 to 3 tablespoons lemon juice
2 tablespoons oil

1. In large bowl, combine all ingredients; mix well.
2. Cover; refrigerate to blend flavors.
*Two cups (2-3 medium) chopped, peeled tomatoes can be substituted for canned tomatoes.

**One or two fresh jalapeno peppers, seeded and finely chopped, can be used for green chilies.

Yield: 2-1/2 cups

TOMATO BEEF CURRY (GA LEI FON KARE GNOW YUKE)

Note: You really need to have pretty tomatoes for this dish.
If you can't find nice tomatoes in the store, buy a good grade of
canned tomato wedges and marinate them.

This recipe is a winner, even for people that say they do not like
curry. The secret with any curry recipe is to not add too much curry.
Otherwise, the curry overpowers the recipe.

1 pound flank steak

Meat Marinade
1 tablespoon cornstarch
1 tablespoon light soy sauce
1 tablespoon sherry

2 medium tomatoes, cut in wedges
1 tablespoon brown sugar
1 medium onion, cut into 1-inch chunks
1 medium green pepper, cut in wedges
2 tablespoons curry powder
1 teaspoon salt
4 tablespoons catsup
1 tablespoon oyster sauce
3 tablespoons oil

1. Slice flank steak 1/8-inch thick across the grain.
2. Marinate for 15 minutes.
3. Sprinkle brown sugar over tomato wedges.
4. Heat wok. Add 1 tablespoon oil and heat.
5. Stir-fry onion with green pepper for 1/2 minute.
6. Add 1 tablespoon water; cover for 1/2 minute; uncover; stir until
water has evaporated. Set aside.
7. Pour 2 tablespoons oil into wok and stir in the curry powder. Let
the flavor release (a few seconds).
8. Add beef and salt; stir-fry until 3/4 done - about 1 minute.
9. Add tomato wedges; stir until just heated through.
10. Add catsup and heat until sauce bubbles.
11. Add all other vegetables and oyster sauce. Mix well.

Yield: 4 servings

PICADILLO

3 cups water
1 pound stew beef, cut into cubes
2 teaspoons oil
3/4 cup chopped onion
2 cloves garlic, minced
2 tablespoons raisins
8 small stuffed olives, sliced
1/2 teaspoon allspice
1/2 teaspoon salt
1/4 teaspoon cinnamon
1/8 teaspoon cayenne pepper

1. In medium saucepan, bring the water to the boil over medium-high heat.
2. Add beef; cover; simmer 1-1/2 hours, or until beef is tender.
3. Shred the beef; reserve 1/2 cup of the poaching broth.
4. In a large, non-stick skillet, heat the oil over medium heat.
5. Add the onion and garlic; saute until the onion is transparent.
6. Stir in the remaining ingredients and the reserved beef broth.
7. Simmer, uncovered, until the sauce thickens.

Yield: 4 servings

LASAGNE

Note: The raisins add a natural sweetness to this recipe. If the thought of raisins bothers you, try adding some shredded carrots instead.

Tomato Sauce
1-1/2 pounds lean beef
1-1/2 pounds lean pork
18 fresh parsley sprigs, leaves only
2 large garlic cloves, mashed
1/4 cup olive oil
1/2 cup grated Parmesan cheese
2 ounces salt pork or bacon, diced
3/4 pounds onions, peeled and diced
1-1/2 teaspoons freshly ground black pepper
1-1/2 pounds canned peeled plum tomatoes, chopped or sieved
1 small green pepper (2 to 3 ounces), diced
3 tablespoons tomato paste
1/2 cup raisins

1. Grind beef and pork together.
2. Chop parsley and garlic together.
3. Combine olive oil and salt pork in a skillet; heat.
4. Add onions; saute to medium brown.
5. Add ground meat; brown. Stir well.
6. Add parsley, garlic, and pepper, and cook for 20 minutes.
7. Add tomatoes, green pepper, raisins, and Parmesan cheese. Taste for salt and add if desired.
8. Cook slowly for 1-1/2 hours.
9. When cooked, add tomato paste; stir well. Taste again for seasoning. (I always add a healthy portion of basil and a little bit of sugar.)

Sauce for Top of Lasagne

Note: I usually double this.

2 tablespoons butter, melted
2 tablespoons heavy cream
3/4 cup tomato sauce (the sauce you just made)
2 tablespoons all-purpose flour

1. Combine butter, cream, and tomato sauce in a saucepan; heat.
2. Stir and add flour.

Assembling Lasagne
Tomato Sauce
Cooked lasagne noodles, about 1/2-3/4 pounds
2 pounds ricotta cheese
1-1/2 cups of grated Parmesan cheese
Sauce for Top of Lasagne

1. Pour a thin layer of tomato sauce into the bottom of a rectangular baking pan; cover with a layer of noodles (three noodles).
2. Spread a thin layer of ricotta over the noodles.

3. Sprinkle with some of the Parmesan cheese.
4. Repeat the layers until you run out of noodles; reserve some of the Parmesan for the top of the lasagne.
5. Spread on the Sauce for the Top of the Lasagne and sprinkle with reserved Parmesan.
6. Bake at 350F for 30 to 40 minutes.
7. Let sit for 10 minutes before serving.

Yield: 8 to 10 servings

ROMA MEATLOAF

Note: Before I was married, a good friend of my mother's, Mrs. Smith, gave me a bridal shower. This recipe was attached to one of the gifts. Just after we were married, I served it to my husband's boss. He loved it, and so has everyone else ever since.

This recipe can be prepared ahead.

2 pounds lean ground beef
2 eggs
3/4 cup cracker crumbs
1/2 cup finely chopped onion
16 ounces tomato sauce with cheese
1 teaspoon salt
1/2 teaspoon oregano
1/8 teaspoon pepper
2 cups shredded mozzarella cheese

1. Combine everything except cheese and use only 1/3 cup of the tomato sauce. Mix well.
2. Shape meat mixture into a flat rectangle on wax paper.
3. Sprinkle cheese evenly over meat mixture.
4. Roll up like a jelly roll; press ends of roll to seal.
5. Place in loaf pan. Bake for one hour at 350. Pour off excess fat.
6. Pour remaining tomato sauce on top; bake a few minutes longer to set and lightly brown the tomato sauce.

Yield: 6 servings

CHILI FOR A CROWD

1/2 cup best-quality olive oil
1-3/4 pounds yellow onions, coarsely chopped
2 pounds sweet Italian sausage meat, removed from casings
8 pounds beef chuck, ground
1-1/2 tablespoons freshly ground black pepper
2 (12-ounce) cans tomato paste
3 tablespoons fresh garlic, minced
3 ounces ground cuminseed
4 ounces plain chili powder
1/2 cup prepared Dijon-style mustard
4 tablespoons salt
4 tablespoons dried basil
4 tablespoons dried oregano
6 pounds canned Italian plum tomatoes, drained (about 5 cans, each 2
    pounds, 3 ounces before draining)
1/2 cup burgundy wine
1/4 cup lemon juice
1 tablespoon dill weed
1/2 cup chopped Italian parsley
3 (16-ounce) cans dark red kidney beans, drained
4 (5-1/5-ounce) cans pitted black olives, drained

1. Heat olive oil in a very large soup kettle.
2. Add onions; cook over low heat, covered, until tender and translucent - about 10 minutes.
3. Crumble the sausage meat and ground chuck into kettle; cook over
medium-high heat, stirring often, until meats are well browned.
4. Spoon out as much excess fat as possible.
5. Over low heat, stir in black pepper, tomato paste, garlic, cuminseed, chili powder, mustard, salt, basil, and oregano.
6. Add drained tomatoes, burgundy wine, lemon juice, dill, parsley,
and drained kidney beans.
7. Stir well; simmer, uncovered, for another 15 minutes.
8. Taste and correct seasonings.
9. Add olives; simmer for another 5 minutes to heat through; serve
immediately.

Yield: 35 to 40 servings

DAVID RUSSO'S MEAT SAUCE

Note: Many people think the only way to make a tomato sauce is with lots of oregano. David insisted that oregano was not as important as the basil, and he was right! As with many tomato sauces, the secret is to let it simmer for several hours.

1-1/2 pounds ground beef
Garlic powder
1/2 large onion
1 can paste
Basil
Salt
Pepper
1 large can tomato puree
Water

1. Brown beef in skillet.
2. Add salt, pepper, and garlic powder to taste.
3. Remove beef; drain grease.
4. Brown chopped onion.
5. Mix beef and onion in saucepan.
6. Add puree and 1/2 can of water.
7. Add paste and 2 cans of water.
8. Add pinch of pepper, 1 tablespoon of basil, and salt to taste.
9. Bring to boil.
10. Reduce heat; slow boil with lid slightly ajar for 1-1/2 hours. Stir slowly from time to time.

Yield: 6 to 8 servings

Variations:
1. Brown sausage, hot or mild and add to recipe, or brown boneless pork (chops or cubes) and add.
2. Serve over spaghetti or macaroni of any kind.

TACO MEAT

2 tablespoons oil*
1 large onion, chopped
1 pound ground beef
2 medium tomatoes, peeled and chopped, or 1 cup canned tomatoes
1 clove garlic, pressed
1 or more tablespoons green chili relish or taco sauce
1 teaspoon oregano, rubbed between hands
1 teaspoon vinegar
Salt to taste
1/2 cup slivered almonds (optional)

1. Brown beef and onions with oil in large skillet.
2. Pour off fat.
3. Add remaining ingredients.
4. Simmer for 15 minutes.

*Use only if you have very lean meat.

Yield: 6 to 12 servings

GREEN ONION CASSEROLE

Note: This casserole can be made ahead of time and frozen.

2 pounds ground chuck
3 teaspoons salt
4 teaspoons sugar
1/2 teaspoon pepper
2 (16-ounce) cans tomatoes
2 (8-ounce) cans tomato sauce
4 cloves garlic, chopped
1 (10-ounce) package thin egg noodles
8 ounces cream cheese
2 cups dairy sour cream
12 green onions, chopped with tops
2 cups grated sharp cheddar cheese

1. Combine meat, salt, sugar, pepper, tomatoes, sauce, and garlic; simmer 10 minutes.
2. Cook egg noodles; drain.
3. Combine hot noodles with cream cheese.
4. Add sour cream and green onions.
5. In a 4-quart casserole, layer noodles, meat mixture, and top with grated cheese.
6. Bake at 325F for 30 minutes.

Yield: 8 to 10 servings

ENCHILADA CASSEROLE

Note: This is a wonderful recipe. It's easy and really delicious.
It is always a big seller when we serve it. It is one of the few things
that we have served more than once.

This recipe is best if made ahead of time and refrigerated or frozen.

2 pounds ground meat
1 large onion, chopped
1 (10-ounce) package frozen chopped spinach (optional)
1 (16-ounce) can tomatoes
1 (10-ounce) can Ro-Tel tomatoes and green chilies
1 teaspoon salt
1/2 teaspoon pepper
1 can cream of mushroom soup
1 can golden mushroom soup
1 (8-ounce) carton dairy sour cream
1/4 cup milk
1/4 teaspoon garlic powder
16 to 20 corn tortillas
1 (4-ounce) can chopped green chilies
1/2 pound cheddar cheese, grated

1. Cook and drain meat.
2. In separate skillet, cook onion until transparent; add to meat.
3. Cook and drain spinach.
4. Mix with tomatoes, Ro-Tel, salt, and pepper.
5. Combine with meat; simmer until thickened.
6. Mix soup, sour cream, milk, and garlic powder.
7. Place tortillas on the bottom and sides of a 3-quart casserole.
8. Spoon the meat mixture into the casserole.
9. Scatter green chilies on top.
10. Next, layer some grated cheese.
11. Place a layer of tortillas on the cheese and cover with soup
mixture.
12. Sprinkle with more cheese.
13. Bake at 350F for about 35-40 minutes.

Yield: 8 to 10 servings

CANNELLONI (MEAT-STUFFED PASTA ROLLS)

Bechamel Sauce
2 cups milk
1/4 cup butter
3 tablespoons all-purpose flour
1/4 teaspoon salt

Stuffing
1-1/2 tablespoons finely chopped yellow onion
2 tablespoons olive oil
6 ounces lean ground beef
Salt
1/2 cup chopped mortadella or unsmoked ham
1 egg yolk
1/2 teaspoon nutmeg
1-1/2 cups freshly grated Parmesan cheese
1-1/4 cups fresh ricotta cheese

Meat Sauce
1 tablespoon finely chopped yellow onion
2 tablespoons olive oil
6 ounces lean ground beef
1 teaspoon salt
1/2 cup canned Italian tomatoes, chopped, with their juice

Pasta Dough
1 sheet of homemade pasta dough, using 2 eggs and 1-1/2 cups flour, or
   good store-bought pasta
1 tablespoon salt
1/3 cup freshly grated Parmesan cheese
1/4 cup butter

For Bechamel Sauce
1. In small pan, heat the milk until it comes to the very edge of a boil.
2. While you are heating the milk, melt the butter over low heat in a heavy, enameled iron saucepan of 4 to 6 cups capacity.
3. When the butter is melted, add all the flour, stirring constantly with a wooden spoon.
4. Let the flour and butter bubble for 2 minutes; continue stirring. Do not let the flour become colored.
5. Turn off the heat; add the hot milk 2 tablespoons at a time, stirring it constantly into the flour/butter mixture.
6. As soon as the first 2 tablespoons have been incorporated into the mixture, add another 2 tablespoons, always stirring with your trusty spoon.
7. When you have added 1/2 cup of milk to the mixture, you can start adding 1/4 cup at a time, until you have added it all. (Never add more than 1/4 cup at one time.)
8. When all the milk has been incorporated, turn on the heat to low, add the salt; stir-cook until the sauce is as dense as thick cream. If you need it thicker, cook and stir a little longer. If you need it thinner, cook a little less.
9. Make sure the sauce is warm when you get ready to use it.

For Stuffing

1. Put the chopped onion in a saucepan or a skillet with the olive oil; cook over medium heat until translucent but not colored.
2. Add the ground beef; turn the heat down to medium low; cook it without letting it brown. Crumble the meat with a fork as it cooks.
3. When it loses its raw red color, cook it for 1 minute more without browning.
4. Transfer the meat with a perforated ladle or colander to a mixing bowl, carrying with it as little of the cooking fat as possible.
5. Add 1-1/2 teaspoons salt, chopped mortadella, egg yolk, nutmeg, grated cheese, ricotta, and 1/4 cup of the Bechamel Sauce. Mix thoroughly.
6. Taste and correct for salt and set aside.

For Meat Sauce

1. Put the chopped onion in a saucepan with the olive oil; saute over medium heat until very pale gold in color.
2. Add the meat; turn the heat down to medium low; cook it without browning, exactly as you did for the stuffing.
3. Add the salt, the chopped tomatoes, and their juice; cook at the barest simmer for 45 minutes. Set aside.

For Pasta Dough

1. Prepare the pasta dough, making it as thin as possible.
2. Cut the pasta into 3x4-inch rectangles. Do not allow it to dry longer than it takes to bring 4 quarts of water to a boil.
3. While the water is coming to a boil, lay one or more clean, dry towels open flat on the work counter, and set a bowl of cold water not far from the stove.
4. When the water comes to a boil, add the salt; drop in 5 of the pasta strips. Stir with a wooden spoon.
5. When the water returns to a boil, wait 20 seconds, then retrieve the pasta with a large slotted spoon, dip it and rinse it in the cold water, then spread it on the dry towel.
6. Cook all the pasta strips, no more than 5 at a time, in the same manner.
7. When all the pasta is laid out on the towel, pat it dry with another towel.

To Assemble

1. Preheat the oven to 400F.
2. Butter the bottom of a 9x14-inch bake-and-serve pan.
3. To stuff the pasta, lay a pasta strip flat and spread a tablespoon of stuffing on it, covering the whole strip except for a 1/2-inch border all around.
4. Roll the strip up on its narrow side, keeping it somewhat loose.
5. Lay it in the baking pan with its folded-over edge facing down.
6. Proceed until you've used up either all the pasta or all the stuffing. (Somehow it's hard to make them come out exactly even.)
7. Squeeze the cannelloni in tightly, if you have to, but don't overlay them.
8. Spread the meat sauce over the cannelloni, coating them evenly with sauce.
9. Spread the Bechamel Sauce over this.
10. Sprinkle with the grated cheese; dot with butter.

11. Bake on the next-to-highest rack in the oven for 15 minutes, or until a very light, golden crust forms. (Do not in any case exceed 20 minutes, or it will be over-cooked.)
12. Allow to settle for about 10 to 15 minutes, then serve.
13. Although the cannelloni are already richly seasoned, you might have some extra grated cheese available at the table.

Yield: 6 servings

GRECO

Note: This is really good served in a deep pot. I like to add extra cheese. If you like a more moist casserole, you may add juice from tomatoes to suit.

1 (8-ounce) package large seashell noodles
2 onions, diced
1 green pepper, diced
1 large can tomatoes
2 cans corn (1 regular, 1 creamed), drained
1/2 pound white sharp cheddar cheese, grated
1 pound ground round
1 can pitted black olives

1. Fry onions and green pepper until transparent.
2. Brown meat; drain.
3. Cook noodles until tender.
4. Combine noodles, meat, green peppers, and onion.
5. Cut up tomatoes; add to mixture.
6. Add corn.
7. Stir in half of the cheese.
8. Put olives on top; sprinkle with the rest of the cheese. Can be refrigerated or frozen at this point if made in advance.
9. Bring casserole to room temperature.
10. Bake at 300F for 1 hour.

Yield: 8 servings

Pork

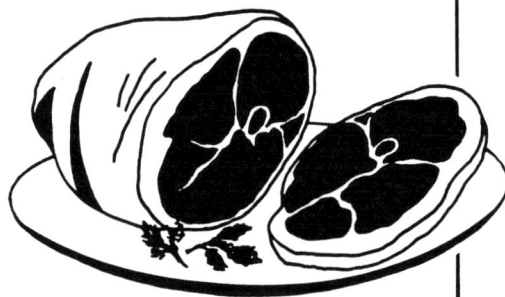

HAM AND CHEESE CREPES (MADEIRA)

12 (1-ounce each) slices boiled ham
2 pounds fresh asparagus, cleaned and trimmed
12 slices Swiss cheese
12 crepes

Mushroom Madeira Sauce
8 ounces fresh mushrooms, sliced
3 tablespoons butter
3 tablespoons flour
3/4 cup chicken broth
1/4 cup Madeira wine
1 tablespoons chopped chives
1 teaspoon horseradish (go easy; taste)
1/4 cup cream

1. Steam asparagus 10 to 15 minutes until crisp-tender.
2. Place 1 ham slice, 1 cheese slice, and 3 or 4 asparagus spears on each crepe; fold crepe to enclose filling, place in large shallow baking dish, seam side down.
3. In medium-sized saucepan, saute mushrooms in butter until tender.
4. Stir in flour.
5. Add chicken broth, wine, chives, and horseradish.
6. Cook over medium heat, stirring constantly, until thickened.
7. Stir in cream.
8. Spoon sauce over crepes.
9. Bake in preheated 350F oven for 20-30 minutes.

Yield: 6 servings

BAKED HAM

Ham
Whole cloves
Molasses
Dry mustard
1 cup brown sugar
1 bottle of beer

1. Score the top of the ham; stud it with cloves.
2. Pour molasses over top; sprinkle with dry mustard and brown sugar.
3. Pour beer over top; bake until heated through.

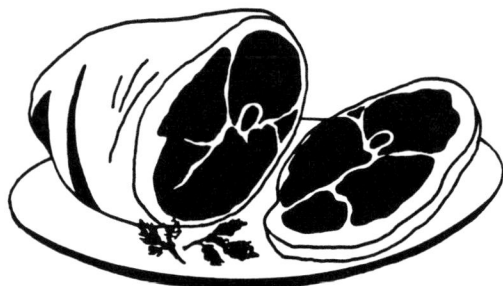

FETTUCCINE WITH THREE CHEESES

8 ounces plain egg fettuccine and 8 ounces spinach fettuccine,
   preferably fresh
1/2 cup coarsely chopped walnuts
2 cups heavy cream, room temperature
8 ounces whole-milk mozzarella, preferably fresh unsalted, shredded
6 ounces sweet Gorgonzola, crumbled*
3 tablespoons freshly grated Parmesan cheese, plus additional for
   serving
3 tablespoons finely chopped Italian (flat leaf) parsley
2 tablespoons finely chopped fresh basil
1 tablespoon finely chopped fresh oregano or 1/2 teaspoon dried
1 tablespoon finely chopped fresh chives

1. Heat 3 quarts salted water in large heavy saucepan over high heat
to boiling.
2. Stir fettuccine into boiling water; cover.
3. Heat to rapid boil; uncover and stir.
4. Cook, uncovered, until tender but still slightly firm to the bite
- 2 to 4 minutes for fresh, 5 to 8 minutes for dried.
5. While fettuccine is cooking, heat dry, small, heavy skillet over
medium heat until hot enough to evaporate a bead of water on contact
- about 1 minute.
6. Add walnuts to skillet; toast, stirring constantly, until fragrant
- about 2 minutes.
7. Remove from heat; reserve.
8. When fettuccine is cooked, drain in large colander; shake colander
to release excess moisture.
9. Pour cream into saucepan in which fettuccine was cooked; heat over
high heat to boiling.
10. Adjusting heat to maintain steady boil; boil cream 1 minute.
11. Add fettuccine, mozzarella, Gorgonzola, 3 tablespoons grated
Parmesan, the parsley, basil, oregano, and chives; heat, stirring
occasionally, until sauce is well blended and slightly thickened
- about 2 minutes.
12. Pour mixture onto warmed large platter; sprinkle with walnuts and
additional Parmesan to taste.
13. Serve immediately.

*Sweet Gorgonzola, young and unaged, is milder than the aged variety.
If it is unavailable, 4 ounces aged Gorgonzola can be substituted.

Yield: 4 servings

ORANGE PORK CHOPS

4 (1-inch thick) pork chops
Freshly ground pepper
2/3 cup chicken broth
1/3 cup sugar
1 tablespoon cornstarch
1 cup fresh orange juice
1 teaspoon grated orange peel
1/8 to 1/4 teaspoon cinnamon
1/8 teaspoon ground cloves
Salt
1 medium orange, thinly sliced

1. Lightly grease large skillet.
2. Season pork chops with pepper.
3. Add chops to skillet; cook over medium-high heat until well browned - 5 to 6 minutes on each side.
4. Remove; keep warm.
5. Add chicken broth to skillet; bring to boil, scraping up any browned bits.
6. Reduce heat; simmer until broth is reduced to 1/2 cup - about 5 minutes.
7. Dissolve sugar and cornstarch in orange juice; add to skillet.
8. Mix in orange peel, cinnamon, and cloves.
9. Season with salt.
10. Stir over medium heat until thickened - 3 to 4 minutes.
11. Reduce heat to low; return chops to skillet; spoon sauce over.
12. Cover skillet and simmer until chops are tender and cooked through - about 10 minutes.
13. Add orange slices to skillet; heat through.
14. Transfer chops to platter.
15. Spoon some of sauce over; serve.
16. Pass remaining orange sauce separately.

Yield: 4 servings

CANNELLONI

Meat Sauce
1/2 pound salt pork, diced
1/4 cup olive oil
1/4 cup butter
3/4 pound onions, peeled and diced
1 pound lean beef, cut into 1/2-inch cubes
1/2 pound lean pork shoulder, cut into 1/2-inch pieces
2 bay leaves, crumbled
5 cloves garlic, mashed
1 tablespoon fresh rosemary
1/2 teaspoon ground allspice
1 teaspoon freshly-ground black pepper
5 pounds ripe fresh tomatoes or 6 (1-pound) cans peeled plum tomatoes,
    chopped fine
1/4 pound carrots, scraped and minced
1/4 pound celery, minced
Salt
7 ounces tomato paste

Stuffing for Cannelloni
1 pound fresh spinach
Half of meat from sauce, ground
2 eggs, beaten
1/4 cup freshly grated Parmesan cheese
Pinch of freshly grated nutmeg
1/4 teaspoon freshly ground pepper
Salt

Bechamel Sauce
2 tablespoons butter
2-1/2 tablespoons all-purpose flour
1 cup boiling milk
1/2 teaspoon salt
Pinch of freshly grated nutmeg
1/4 cup heavy cream

15 crepes

For Meat Sauce
1. Combine salt pork, olive oil, and butter in a large saucepan; heat.
2. Add onions and saute to medium brown.
3. Add beef, pork, and bay leaves; stir.
4. Cook slowly, uncovered, for 30 minutes.
5. Chop garlic and rosemary together; add to the sauce with allspice
and pepper.
6. Stir well; continue to cook over low heat for 20 minutes; inhale
the aroma.
7. Cover; cook for 5 minutes.
8. Add tomatoes, carrots, celery, and 1/2 tablespoon salt.
9. Simmer slowly for 1-1/2 hours, stirring occasionally. Do not hurry
the cooking for a good sauce.
10. Remove sauce from the heat; allow to cool for 10 minutes. Strain
the sauce.

11. Put whatever remains in the strainer through a food mill and return it to the sauce.
12. Add the tomato paste; stir well; bring to a boil.
13. Check for salt, adding more if necessary.
14. Any sauce that is not for immediate use can be frozen for a future occasion.

Yield: 3-1/2 quarts

For Stuffing
1. Cook the spinach in very little salted boiling water for 10 minutes.
2. Drain thoroughly; chop fine; drain again so that it is quite dry.
3. Add the ground meat, beaten eggs, cheese, nutmeg, and pepper.
4. Taste and add salt if necessary. Mix well.

For Bechamel Sauce
1. Stir butter and flour in a saucepan over low heat for 2 minutes.
2. Remove from heat; add boiling milk and seasonings.
3. Boil, stirring for 1 minute.
4. Lower the heat; slowly add cream, stirring constantly until thick. Remove from heat.

To Assemble
1. Spread out the crepes.
2. Place some stuffing evenly across the center of each crepe, making a mound about 3/4-inch thick.
3. Fold crepe twice over the filling.
4. When all crepes are filled, arrange them in a buttered baking pan.
5. Spoon enough meat sauce over the crepes to cover them.
6. Sprinkle with 1/4 cup grated Parmesan cheese.
7. Stir 1/2 cup of the meat sauce into the warm Bechamel Sauce; mix well.
8. Spoon this over everything.
9. Place the baking pan in preheated 350F oven for about 12 minutes.
10. For each serving, allow 2 of the filled crepes.

Yield: 6 or 7 servings

PORC EN CROUTE

Pastry
1-1/4 cups flour
1/4 pound cold butter, cut into pieces
1/8 teaspoon salt
2 tablespoons cold water

Meat
3 pound boneless pork tenderloin
1/2 cup Dijon mustard
1 teaspoon crumbled dried tarragon
1 egg, lightly beaten

For Pastry
1. Place the flour in a bowl and add pieces of butter, blending with a pastry blender until mixture has the texture of oatmeal.
2. Add salt and water; mix lightly with your hands until dough can be gathered into a ball.
3. Wrap in waxed paper and chill for at least 1 hour or overnight.

For Meat
1. In a large skillet or Dutch oven, brown roast evenly on all sides over moderate heat.
2. Set aside to cool.
3. Preheat oven to 350F.
4. On a floured board, roll out pastry in a rectangle large enough to encase roast.
5. Spread mustard on pastry; sprinkle with tarragon.
6. Place roast in center; seal ends of pastry around roast, tucking them under.
7. Place seam side down in a shallow baking pan.
8. Brush pastry with beaten egg; bake for 1 hour or until pastry is golden.

Yield: 6 servings

PORK CHOPS A L'ORANGE

4 loin or rib pork chops, 1-1/2-inches thick
1/4 teaspoon black pepper
1/2 teaspoon paprika
2 teaspoons Season-All
3/4 cup orange juice
1 tablespoon sugar
1/4 teaspoon curry powder
10 whole cloves
1/2 teaspoon orange peel
Flour to thicken

1. Rub pork chops with mixture of pepper, paprika, and Season-All.
2. Brown chops on both sides in heavy skillet, no fat added.
3. Combine orange juice, sugar, curry powder, cloves, and orange peel; pour over chops.
4. Cover; reduce heat; simmer 1 hour or until tender.
5. Remove chops to warm platter.
6. Thicken remaining liquid with flour.
7. Spoon sauce over chops or serve in a small bowl.

Yield: 4 servings

ROAST PORK WITH THYME

1 (4-pound) pork loin

3 tablespoons olive oil
2 tablespoons lemon juice
1 teaspoon thyme
1 clove garlic
Salt and freshly ground pepper to taste

1. Combine olive oil, lemon juice, thyme, garlic, salt, and pepper.
2. Rub the mixture into the pork loin.
3. Roast about 35 to 45 minutes per pound in a 350F oven.

Yield: 6 servings

CROWN ROAST OF PORK

Note: Probably the most difficult part of this recipe is
finding a butcher to tie the racks of ribs into the crown. When they
do it, make certain that they "French" the chops and that it will
be possible for you to cut between the chops when it is time to
serve the roast.

This really is a very elegant and easy way to prepare a roast.
I made it for my first Christmas dinner for my in-laws; it also was
the main meat for the first Christmas luncheon we had in the Cafe.
Always makes an impression and is always delicious.

1 crown roast of pork made from 12-14 ribs
1/4 cup olive oil
2 cloves garlic, crushed
1 tablespoon thyme or rosemary
2 cups orange juice
1 box wild rice mix

1. Preheat oven to 450F.
2. Combine olive oil, garlic and either thyme or rosemary. Rub this
solution over the roast, making sure that you coat the exposed meat
surfaces.
3. Wrap ends of bones with foil to prevent their charring while the
roast cooks.
4. Place the roast in a roasting pan. Place in the hot oven; immediately reduce the temperature to 350F. Roast for forty minutes per
pound. As the roast is cooking, baste with the orange juice about every
half hour.
5. While the roast cooks, prepare the wild rice mix according to the
directions on the box. You may wish to add some sauteed mushrooms or
some plumped raisins to the mix.
6. About one-half hour before the roast is done, fill the center cavity
with the prepared rice; baste once more; finish roasting. As you are
basting, you may wish to scoop up some of the drippings from the pan.
7. When the roast is finished, remove to a platter using two large
spatulas. Any rice that falls out should be scooped back on top. Wrap
the ends of the bones with the French skirts. (If you cannot find these
in a store, they can easily be made. Cut sheets of white paper into 5
inch strips. Fold each strip in half lengthwise. Make cuts along the
fold about 1/4 inch apart to about 1 inch from edges. When you are finished cutting, reverse the fold which will open up the frills and make
them nice and soft.) Wrap each skirt around the bone and tape to secure.
8. Serve immediately.

PORK CASSEROLE WITH CASHEWS AND STIR-FRIED VEGETABLES

Pork
1 ounce dried Chinese mushrooms (about 12)
3 pounds lean pork, cut into 1/2x1/2x1-1/2-inch strips
1 (2-inch) length of fresh gingerroot, peeled and cut into 1/8-inch
   julienne strips

Marinade
1-1/2 cups (one 12-ounce can) apricot nectar
1/2 cup soy sauce
2 tablespoons dry sherry
2 teaspoons oyster sauce
1-1/2 tablespoons honey

Vegetable Topping
3 tablespoons peanut oil
1/2 cup coarsely chopped, unsalted cashews
3/4 pound fresh snow peas, cut into 1/8-inch julienne strips (about
   3 cups)
8 scallions, cut into quaters lengthwise and then into 2-inch lengths
1 (8-ounce) can water chestnuts, drained, rinsed, and cut into 1/8-inch
   julienne strips
1/2 cup (one 4-ounce can) bamboo shoots, drained, rinsed, and cut into
   1/8-inch julienne strips
1/2 teaspoon oriental sesame oil

For Pork
1. Place the mushrooms in a medium mixing bowl and pour 1 cup hot
water over them; let them sit for 15 minutes.
2. Drain and discard the juice or reserve it for another use.
3. In a shallow, 4-quart casserole, combine the pork with the mushrooms and ginger.

For Marinade
1. In a medium-sized mixing bowl, combine all the marinade ingredients
with 1/2 cup of water.
2. Pour the marinade over the meat and mushrooms, tossing them well.
3. Marinate 1 hour.
4. Preheat the oven to 350F.
5. Cover the casserole tightly; bake for 2 to 2-1/2 hours, or until
the meat is tender and easily pierced with a fork.
6. Remove from the oven and set aside.

For Vegetable Topping
1. In a wok or large, heavy skillet, warm the peanut oil over moderate
heat.
2. Add the cashews; stir-fry for about 30 seconds.
3. Stir in the snow peas, scallions, water chestnuts, and bamboo
shoots; stir-fry until the vegetables are heated through but still
crisp - 2 to 3 minutes.
4. Stir in the sesame oil for flavoring.
5. Transfer the pork and mushrooms to a platter; arrange the stir-
fried vegetables in a crescent shape over half the dish.

Yield: 6 to 8 servings

SWEET AND SOUR PORK (GOO LO YUKE)

Note: To do ahead, cook through making the sauce. Just before serving, add pork, vegetables, and fruit according to directions.

1 pound pork butt cut into 1-inch chunks

Meat Marinade
1 tablespoon sherry
1 tablespoon water
2 tablespoons Kikkoman Soy Sauce (this brand is best for this recipe)
4 teaspoons flour
4 teaspoons cornstarch

1 green pepper, cut into 1/2-inch chunks
1 onion, cut into wedges
12 maraschino cherries
1 cup canned lichee
1 cup pineapple chunks

Sauce Mixture
1/2 cup brown sugar
1/2 cup vinegar
1 teaspoon salt
4 tablespoons catsup
3/4 cup pineapple juice
4 teaspoons cornstarch

1. Marinate pork in meat marinade for 1/2 hour.
2. Drain cherries, lichee nuts, and pineapple chunks (save pineapple juice).
3. Prepare sauce mixture by combining all ingredients.
4. Deep-fry pork cubes in wok for about 3-4 minutes until golden brown. Drain.
5. Pour all the oil back into the bottle to save.
6. Add sauce mixture into wok; stir until thickened.
7. Add green pepper and onions; cook for 2 minutes.
8. Add pork cubes; stir until heated through.
9. Add fruits; stir until they're coated with the sauce.

Yield: 6 servings

BARBECUED PORK

2 whole pork tenderloins
1/4 cup soy sauce
2 tablespoons dry red wine
1 tablespoon brown sugar
1 tablespoon honey
2 teaspoons red food coloring, if desired
1/2 teaspoon ground cinnamon
1 clove garlic, crushed
1 green onion, cut in half
Green onion curls (optional)

1. Remove and discard fat from meat.
2. Combine soy sauce, wine, sugar, honey, food coloring, cinnamon, garlic, and onion in large bowl.
3. Add pork, turning tenderloins to coat completely.
4. Cover; let stand at room temperature 1 hour or refrigerate over-night, turning occasionally.
5. Drain pork, reserving marinade.
6. Place pork on wire rack over a baking pan.
7. Bake in preheated 350F oven until done - about 45 minutes.
8. Turn and baste frequently during baking.
9. Remove pork from oven.
10. Cool. Cut into diagonal slices.
11. Garnish with green onion curls.

Yield: 6 servings

COUNTRY HAM SALAD

Note: Our family had a mini-reunion in Williamsburg one year.
On Sunday, we had brunch at the Williamsburg Inn. On the side
of the fruit platter were these wonderful tea sandwiches. We knew
they had country ham in them, but what else, and how did they do it?
This is my adaptation and interpretation; I think it's wonderful and
versatile - hope you will, too!

8 ounces sliced country ham
1/4-1/2 cup Dijon mustard

1. Trim ham of all fat.
2. Grind ham in food processor.
3. Slowly add enough Dijon mustard to bind; you do not want it to be too wet. Taste as you add the mustard.

Variation:
You can also use this as an hor d'ouevre. Spread about 1 tablespoon on
a crepe and roll the crepe up. Cut the roll into 3 or 4 pieces and
insert a toothpick into each piece to secure. Just before serving,
heat in a 350F oven for 10 minutes.

Yield: 4-6 servings

PIZZA

Note: It really is fun to make your own pizzas, and inexpensive, too. It's something the whole family can get involved in. Of course, you can use this sauce and topping with a "prepared" crust such as English muffins, split hard rolls, or pita bread.

1 package or 1 tablespoon active dry yeast
1 teaspoon sugar
3/4 cup plus 2 tablespoons warm water
3 cups sifted flour (either all unbleached or 1/2 unbleached and 1/2
   whole wheat flour could be used)
1-1/2 teaspoons salt
1 tablespoon vegetable oil
2 tablespoons cornmeal

1 (8-ounce) can good-quality tomato or spaghetti sauce
1 teaspoon basil
1/2 teaspoon cumin
1 clove garlic crushed
1/2 teaspoon fennel seed
12 ounces mozzarella cheese, shredded
1 onion sliced
1/2 pound cooked Italian Sausage, ground beef, pepperoni, or any
   combination. Green pepper, mushrooms, and onions also make a good
   pizza.
Freshly ground black pepper to taste

1. Dissolve yeast in the warm water; add the sugar. Allow to sit until mixture becomes foamy. This is called proofing the yeast. If the yeast mixture does not foam, something is wrong with the yeast, and there is no point in going on with the dough. If you are in a hurry, you can add a minute amount of ginger to the yeast mixture. Ginger irritates the yeast and will get it started faster.
2. Combine the flour and the salt; stir them into the yeast mixture.
3. Add the oil; continue kneading until the dough is smooth and elastic.
4. Turn dough into an oiled bowl; allow to rise while you are preparing the toppings. It can rise up to one hour.
5. Simmer the tomato sauce and the seasonings. You may wish to add some oregano and/or some sugar to the sauce.
6. Sprinkle either a cookie sheet or a pizza pan with the cornmeal. Stretch the dough evenly to the edges of the sheet, making a small rim around the edge.
7. Spread the sauce over the crust with the back of a spoon.
8. Sprinkle the shredded mozzarella cheese over the sauce.
9. Top with your choice of topping. Don't be skimpy, but don't overload it so much that the crust cannot hold it. If you like a lot of toppings, make a thicker crust.
10. Bake in a pre-heated 450F oven for 10-20 minutes.

Yield: 4 servings

Seafood

188

QUICKIE CRAB BAKE

Note: This recipe won a contest. The woman who submitted it said that it was a great one to throw together when company surprises you. She was right; it's wonderful, and tastes much more complicated than it is!

6 ounces macaroni, shell shaped
8 ounces cream cheese, softened
1 cup dairy sour cream
1 cup cottage cheese
1/2 cup green onions and tops, finely chopped
1/2 cup parsley, finely chopped
2 (6-ounce) cans crabmeat, flaked
1-1/2 cups sharp cheddar cheese, shredded

1. Cook macaroni in boiling water for five minutes.
2. Rinse in cold water and drain. Keep moist.
3. Combine cream cheese, cottage cheese, sour cream, green onion, and parsley.
4. Arrange 1/2 of the macaroni in bottom of greased, two-quart casserole.
5. Spoon half of cream cheese mixture over macaroni.
6. Top with one can of crabmeat.
7. Repeat three layers, ending with second can of crab.
8. Spread cheddar cheese over all.
9. Top with sliced tomatoes.
10. Bake at 350F for 30 minutes or until bubbly on top.

Yield: 6 servings

LAND-LOCKED SEAFOOD CASSEROLE

1-1/2 cups chopped celery
1 chopped green pepper
1 chopped medium white onion
1/4 cup butter
1/4 cup chopped pimientos
2 (10-1/2-ounce) cans condensed cream of mushroom soup
1 cup shrimp
1 cup flaked crabmeat
1 (6-ounce) package long grain and wild rice, prepared as directed

1. Saute celery, pepper, and onion in butter.
2. Add all other ingredients.
3. Place mixture in buttered 9x13 baking dish.
4. Bake at 350F for 1 hour.

Yield: 8 servings

KING CRAB FETTUCINE

1/2 cup (1 stick) butter
1 garlic clove, minced
8 ounces fresh or frozen Alaskan king crabmeat, drained and separated
   into chunks
3/4 cup whipping cream
1/2 cup grated Parmesan cheese
1/2 teaspoon coarsely ground pepper
Salt
12 ounces fettuccine, cooked and drained
1 tablespoon freshly chopped parsley

1. Melt butter in heavy skillet over medium heat.
2. Add garlic; saute until golden.
3. Stir in crabmeat, cream, Parmesan, pepper, and salt; stir until
well blended.
4. Pour crab sauce over fettuccine in large serving bowl; toss well.
5. Sprinkle with fresh parsley; serve immediately.

Yield: 4 to 6 servings

GARIDES TOURKOLIMANO (GREEK SHRIMP)

3 pounds raw, large shrimp, peeled and de-veined
1/2 cup lemon juice
1/2 cup butter, whipped
1 garlic clove, minced
1 cup chopped green onion tops
3 large tomatoes, peeled and cut into wedges
1 teaspoon oregano
Salt and pepper
1 pound feta cheese, crumbled
3/4 cup cream sherry

1. Sprinkle shrimp with lemon juice; set aside.
2. Melt butter in large skillet.
3. Saute garlic, green onion tops, and tomato wedges.
4. Add shrimp; season with oregano, salt, and pepper to taste.
5. Check shrimp frequently and saute until pink.
6. Add feta cheese and cream sherry.
7. Bring to boil and cook 3-4 minutes.
8. Remove shrimp carefully to casserole.
9. Spoon cheese/sherry mixture over shrimp.

Yield: 4 to 6 servings

SHRIMP AND CRABMEAT AU GRATIN

3 pounds shrimp, peeled and de-veined
2 (9-ounce) packages frozen artichoke hearts
1/2 cup butter or margarine
1 pound fresh mushrooms, sliced
2 cloves garlic, crushed
4 tablespoons shallots, finely chopped (or onion)
1/2 cup flour
1/2 teaspoon pepper
2 tablespoons snapped, fresh dill weed (optional)
1-1/2 cups milk
2 (9-ounce) packages sharp cheddar cheese, shredded
1-1/2 cups dry white wine
4 (7-1/2-ounce) cans king crabmeat (or use frozen)
Seasoned corn flake crumbs
1/2 cup butter or margarine

1. Cook shrimp in salted boiling water to cover for 3 minutes or just until shrimp are pink. Drain.
2. Cook artichoke hearts as package directs. Drain.
3. Saute mushrooms in 4 tablespoons butter in skillet for 5 minutes.
4. Saute garlic and shallots in 4 tablespoons butter in saucepan for 5 minutes. Remove from heat.
5. Stir in flour, pepper, dill, then stir in milk.
6. Bring to boil, stirring constantly until thickened.
7. Remove from heat; add half the cheese; stir until melted.
8. Stir in wine.
9. Drain crabmeat and flake.
10. In a 2- to 2-1/2 quart casserole, combine sauce, mushrooms, shrimp, crab, artichokes, and remainder of the cheese. Mix lightly.
11. Sprinkle with crumbs; dot with butter.
12. Bake at 375F for 30 minutes or until bubbly and crumbs are browned.

Yield: 12 servings

SHRIMP MARINARA

3 cloves garlic, crushed
2 tablespoons olive oil
8 anchovy fillets
1-1/2 cups onion, chopped
1 green pepper, chopped
1 tablespoon basil
1 teaspoon oregano
1/8 teaspoon pepper
3 pounds tomatoes, peeled and chopped
2 pounds shrimp, shelled
1 pound mushrooms, sliced
Salt
1 pound spaghetti
1/4 cup Parmesan cheese, grated

1. Saute garlic in olive oil until lightly browned; drain and cool the oil (discarding garlic).
2. Dissolve the anchovies in the oil on low heat.
3. Add the onions; saute until soft.
4. Add the green pepper, basil, oregano, and pepper.
5. Saute two minutes more; add the tomatoes.
6. Simmer for about one hour.
7. Separately saute shrimp and mushrooms in olive oil and garlic.
8. Cook until the shrimp are done - about four to six minutes.
9. Salt to taste.
10. Serve over spaghetti with sauce.
11. Sprinkle with Parmesan cheese.

Yield: 4 to 6 servings

SUPER SHRIMP

1 bottle low-calorie Italian salad dressing
1/4 pound butter
Juice of 1 lemon
2 tablespoons crushed black pepper
4 pounds headless shrimp, in shells

1. Melt butter in heavy pot; add all other ingredients.
2. Cook in 450F oven up to 40 minutes - depending on size of shrimp - stirring every 10 minutes.
3. Test for doneness after 20 minutes and frequently thereafter.
4. Pour sauce into small bowls at each plate; serve shrimp on large platter in middle of table.

Yield: 8 servings

SHRIMP ARTICHOKE MOUTARDE

12 uncooked artichoke hearts, sliced 1/4-inch thick
2-1/2 cups water
6 tablespoons (3/4 stick) unsalted butter
3 cups whipping cream
2 tablespoons Dijon mustard
2 tablespoons fresh tarragon, chopped
30 large, uncooked shrimp, peeled, de-veined, and halved
Salt and freshly ground white pepper

1. Cook artichoke hearts with water and butter in heavy large skillet over medium heat until artichokes are tender and water evaporates - about 8 minutes.
2. Add cream, mustard, and tarragon; cook until reduced by 1/3.
3. Add shrimp; cook until opaque - about 3 minutes.
4. Season with salt and pepper.
5. Spoon into shallow bowls and serve.

Yield: 6 servings

MEDITERRANEAN STIR-FRY

1 tablespoon olive oil
4 large garlic cloves, finely diced
2 red bell peppers, seeded and cut julienne
1 large onion, thinly sliced
3 cups broccoli (about 1 pound), cut into bite-sized pieces and steamed
    until crisp-tender
2 tablespoons roasted, unsalted pine nuts
1 tablespoon raisins
8 ounces cooked, medium shrimp, shelled and de-veined
Salt and freshly ground pepper

1. Heat oil in wok or large skillet over medium heat.
2. Add garlic; cook, stirring constantly, until golden - about 1 minute (be careful not to burn).
3. Remove garlic using slotted spoon and set aside.
4. Increase heat to high.
5. When oil is very hot, add pepper and onion; stir-fry until slightly softened - about 2 minutes.
6. Mix in broccoli, nuts, and raisins; stir-fry until broccoli is heated through - about 1 minute.
7. Return garlic to wok with shrimp; stir-fry just until heated through.
8. Season with salt and pepper.
9. Serve immediately.

Yield: 2 servings

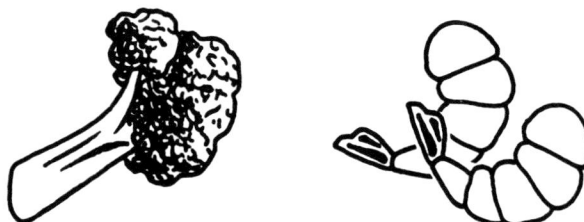

VIVE LA SPICY SHRIMP

16 large, headless shrimp, in shell

1/4 cup green onions, chopped
3 tablespoons olive oil
2 tablespoons French's Vive la Dijon Mustard
2 tablespoons lemon juice
2 teaspoons lemon peel, grated
1 teaspoon garlic, minced
1/4 teaspoon French's red pepper, crushed

2 tablespoons butter or margarine
1 cup dry white wine
1 tablespoon fresh parsley, chopped

1. Butterfly shrimp in shell and de-vein.
2. Combine next set of ingredients (green onions through red pepper);
add shrimp; toss to blend.
3. Marinate 2 hours in refrigerator.
4. Melt butter; remove shrimp from marinade; saute in butter 1
minute on each side.
5. Remove shrimp; keep warm.
6. Add wine; reduce heat for 3 minutes, stirring frequently.
7. Add marinade; cook 3 minutes more or until sauce thickens
slightly.
8. Add parsley; return shrimp to skillet; toss to coat and heat
through.

Yield: 2 servings

COQUILLES ST. JACQUES

Note: Coquilles may be served in a chafing dish or poured into a large casserole or individual ramekins or shells, topped with buttered breadcrumbs, and baked at 350F for about 15 minutes, just to brown the crumbs.

2 pounds fresh or frozen scallops
1 (10-ounce) can chicken bouillon, undiluted
3 pounds raw shrimp in the shell, boiled and cleaned
5 tablespoons butter or margarine
1 cup chopped green onions
2 (3-ounce) cans mushrooms, drained (reserve liquid)
4 tablespoons all-purpose flour
1/4 cup dry white wine
1 cup light cream
1/2 teaspoon seasoned salt
Generous dash white pepper
1/4 teaspoon paprika

1. Wash and drain scallops (if frozen, thaw).
2. Simmer in bouillon for 10 minutes. Drain, reserving cooking liquid.
3. Cut large scallops in half; set aside with cooked shrimp.
4. Heat butter in saucepan; add onions and mushrooms; saute for 3 minutes; remove and set aside.
5. Stir flour into the pan; stir until smooth.
6. Gradually add reserved cooking liquid, cream, mushroom liquid, and wine.
7. Cook slowly until thickened, stirring constantly.
8. Add seasonings; return onion and mushrooms, then add scallops and shrimp.
9. Let cook just a minute, then keep warm over hot water until ready to serve.

Yield: 10 servings

SEAFOOD AND VEGETABLES EN CASSEROLE

1 package (1 pound) fresh or frozen fish fillets (halibut, haddock,
    or cod)
1 small yellow onion
1/4 pound fresh mushrooms
2 tablespoons butter or margarine
2 tablespoons flour
1/2 cup milk
1/4 teaspoon salt
Dash pepper
1/2 cup dry white wine
1 (10-ounce) package frozen, mixed vegetables
2 cups hot, seasoned, freshly mashed potatoes
2 tablespoons butter or margarine, melted
2 tablespoons grated Parmesan cheese

1. If using frozen fish fillets, remove frozen block of fish from
package; let stand at room temperature for 5 minutes.
2. Using a large, sharp knife on a cutting board, cut block of fish
into 1-inch cubes.
3. Add frozen fish to sauce as directed below.
4. If using fresh fish fillets, cut pieces into 2-inch squares; set
aside.
5. Using a sharp knife, peel and chop onion; set aside.
6. Cut mushroom caps and stems into 1/4-inch-thick slices.
7. Have all ingredients gathered together to finish creamed fish mixture.
8. In a large skillet, heat 2 tablespoons butter over moderately high
heat.
9. When butter is hot and bubbly, add onion and mushrooms; cook 5
minutes, stirring constantly.
10. Stir in flour and cook 1 minute.
11. Remove from heat and gradually stir in milk.
12. Season sauce with salt and pepper; bring to a boil over moderate heat, stirring constantly until sauce thickens.
13. Reduce heat; stir in wine.
14. Add frozen or fresh fish and vegetables.
15. Simmer, covered, for 10 minutes, stirring occasionally until fish
is cooked.
16. Spoon mashed potatoes around each shell, or put potatoes in a large
pastry bag fitted with a number 5 star tube and pipe potatoes decoratively around edge of shells.
17. Spoon creamed fish mixture into four to eight individual baking
shells or a 4-cup casserole.
18. Drizzle melted butter over top and sprinkle with Parmesan cheese.
(Freshly-grated Parmesan will have the best flavor.)
19. Place 4 inches from heat; broil until fish mixture is hot and
bubbly and potatoes are browned.

Yield: 4 servings

FLOUNDER DIVAN

Cheese Sauce
1/4 cup butter or margarine
1 cup finely chopped onion
1/4 cup unsifted all-purpose flour
1/2 teaspoon salt
Dash pepper
Dash nutmeg
2 cups milk
1 egg yolk
1/2 cup grated Swiss cheese

2 (10-ounce) packages frozen whole broccoli spears
2 (1-pound) packages frozen flounder fillets, thawed
2 tablespoons lemon juice, preferably freshly squeezed
Salt
Pepper
2 tablespoons grated Swiss cheese

For Cheese Sauce
1. In a medium-sized saucepan, melt butter over moderately high heat; add onion; saute until soft but not browned.
2. Add flour and cook 1 minute longer, stirring constantly; remove from heat; stir in salt, pepper, and nutmeg.
3. Gradually add milk, stirring thoroughly after each addition until mixture is smooth and no lumps remain.
4. Return to heat; cook, stirring constantly, until mixture thickens.
5. Reduce heat; simmer 3 minutes longer while stirring constantly.
6. In a small bowl, beat egg yolk with a fork; stir in about 1/2 of the hot cream sauce; mix well.
7. Return egg yolk mixture, along with 1/2 cup cheese, to rest of sauce in saucepan, while stirring constantly.
8. Cook over low heat, stirring until thickened and cheese has melted. Do not boil.

For Divan
1. Preheat oven to 375F.
2. Butter a shallow, 2-quart baking dish and set aside.
3. Cook frozen broccoli in lightly salted water as package directs, separating spears as they thaw.
4. When almost tender, remove from heat and drain thoroughly; set aside.
5. Separate thawed fish fillets; place on paper towels to drain.
6. Cut each fillet into 4 pieces.
7. Brush each with lemon juice; sprinkle with salt and pepper.
8. Arrange broccoli over the bottom of the prepared dish.
9. Top with fish; pour on sauce.
10. Sprinkle with remaining grated Swiss cheese; bake 20 to 25 minutes or until fish flakes easily.
11. Run casserole under the broiler, about 6 inches from heat source, for a few seconds until cheese is browned.

Yield: 8 servings

MONKFISH TAILS EN PIPERADE

2 large green bell peppers
2 large red bell peppers (if you have none, use tomatoes or pimientos as
   noted in recipe)
1 large yellow onion
2 tablespoons or so olive oil
2 or 3 cloves garlic, pureed
1 teaspoon or so mixed herbs, like Italian or Provencal seasoning
1/4 teaspoon or so salt
Freshly ground pepper
3-1/2 pounds trimmed monkfish fillets
Salt, pepper, and flour
2 tablespoons or so olive oil
About 1 cup each dry white wine or French vermouth, and fish or chicken
   broth

1. Wash, halve, stem, and seed the peppers; cut into very fine long
thin slices. (If you have no red peppers, you may use peeled, seeded
tomatoes, cut into slices and added when the green peppers go over fish;
or use slices of canned red pimiento.)
2. Peel the onion; halve through the root; cut into thin, lengthwise
slices.
3. Film a large frying pan with the oil; add the sliced vegetables;
cook over moderate heat for 4 to 5 minutes while you add the garlic,
herbs, and seasonings. Vegetables should be partially cooked; they will
finish with the fish. (May be done in advance to this point; let cook
uncovered, then transfer to a bowl, cover, and refrigerate.)
4. Cut the fish into serving chunks.
5. Just before sauteing the fish, season all sides with a sprinkling
of salt and pepper; dredge lightly in flour; shake off excess.
6. In a second frying pan (or in the same one, if you have done the
vegetables ahead), pour in enough oil to film it; set over moderately
high heat.
7. When very hot, but not smoking, add the fish in one layer.
8. Saute for 2 minutes; then turn and saute for 2 minutes on the other
side--not to brown, merely to stiffen slightly.
9. Spread the cooked vegetables over the fish. (May be done several
hours in advance to this point; let cook uncovered, then cover and refrigerate.)
10. Pour in the wine and broth--enough to come halfway up the fish.
11. Cover; simmer about 10 minutes. Fish is done when it has turned
from springy to gently soft--it needs a little more cooking than other
fish, but must not overcook and fall apart.
12. Arrange fish and vegetables on a hot platter and cover. (Fish can
wait, unsauced, 15 minutes or so on its platter; cover and set over a
pan of hot water.)
13. Rapidly boil down the juices in frying pan until almost syrupy;
spoon them over the fish; serve. (Boil down the juices separately;
drain juices from waiting fish and add to sauce; spoon sauce
over fish just before serving.)
Yield: 6 servings

Variation:

To make a richer sauce, when you have boiled down the fish's cooking juices until almost syrupy, dribble the juices into a small mixing bowl containing 1/2 cup heavy cream blended with an egg yolk. Return sauce to the pan; stir over low heat just until thickened lightly but well below the simmer. Pour over fish and serve.

Vegetarian Entrees

RUSSIAN PIE

Pastry
1-1/4 cups flour
1 teaspoon sugar
1 teaspoon salt
4 ounces softened cream cheese
3 tablespoons butter

Filling
1 small head cabbage (about 3 cups shredded)
1/2 pound mushrooms
1 yellow onion
Basil, to taste
Marjoram, to taste
Tarragon, to taste
Salt and freshly ground pepper, to taste
3 tablespoons butter
4 ounces softened cream cheese
4 to 5 hard-cooked eggs
Dill weed

For Pastry
1. Make a pastry by sifting together the dry ingredients, cutting in the butter, and working it together with the cream cheese.
2. Roll out 2/3 of the pastry; line a 9-inch pie dish.
3. Roll out the remaining pastry; make a circle large enough to cover the dish.
4. Put away to chill.

For Filling
1. Coarsely shred a small head of cabbage.
2. Wash and slice the mushrooms.
3. Peel and chop the onion.
4. In a large skillet, melt about 2 tablespoons butter.
5. Add the onion and cabbage; saute for several minutes, stirring constantly.
6. Add at least 1/8 teaspoon each of marjoram, tarragon, and basil (all crushed), and some salt and freshly ground pepper.
7. Stirring often, allow the mixture to cook until the cabbage is wilted and the onions are soft.
8. Remove from the pan; set aside.
9. Add another tablespoon of butter to the pan; saute the mushrooms lightly for about 5 to 6 minutes, stirring constantly.
10. Spread the softened cream cheese in the bottom of the pie shell.
11. Slice the eggs; arrange the slices in a layer over the cheese.
12. Sprinkle them with a little chopped dill; cover them with the cabbage.
13. Make a final layer of the sauteed mushrooms; cover with the circle of pastry.
14. Press the pastry together tightly at the edges; flute them.
15. With a sharp knife, cut a few short slashes through the top crust.
16. Bake in a 400F oven for 15 minutes, then turn the temperature down to 350F and continue baking for another 20 to 25 minutes, or until the crust is light brown.

Yield: 4 to 6 servings

CHEESE SOUFFLE ROLL

Souffle
7 eggs, separated
Butter or regular margarine
6 tablespoons sifted all-purpose flour
Dash cayenne
3/4 teaspoon salt
1-1/4 cups milk
Grated Parmesan cheese
1/2 cup coarsely grated, sharp cheddar cheese
1/4 teaspoon cream of tartar

Spinach filling
2 (10-ounce) packages frozen chopped spinach
2 tablespoons butter or margarine
1/4 cup finely chopped onion
1/4 teaspoon salt
1/4 cup grated sharp cheddar cheese
1/2 cup dairy sour cream
1/4 pound cheddar cheese, sliced

For Souffle
1. Place whites and yolks in separate bowls.
2. Let whites warm to room temperature - about 1 hour.
3. Grease bottom of 15x10-1/2x1-inch jelly roll pan; line bottom with waxed paper; grease with butter.
4. Heat oven to 350F.
5. Melt 1/3 cup butter in saucepan. Remove from heat.
6. With wire whisk, stir in flour, cayenne, and 1/2 teaspoon salt until smooth.
7. Gradually stir in milk.
8. Bring to boil, stirring.
9. Reduce heat; simmer, stirring, until thick and leaves bottom of pan.
10. Beat in 1/2 cup Parmesan and 1/2 cup cheddar.
11. With whisk, beat yolks; beat in cheese mixture.
12. With mixer at high speed, beat whites with 1/4 teaspoon salt and cream of tartar until stiff peaks form when beater is slowly raised.
13. With under-and-over motion, fold one-third whites into the cheese mixture.
14. Carefully fold in remaining whites to combine.
15. Turn into pan.
16. Bake 15 minutes, or until surface is puffed and firm when pressed with fingertip.

For Filling
1. Cook spinach as package label directs.
2. Turn into sieve; press to remove the water.
3. In hot butter in medium-sized skillet, saute onion until golden.
4. Add spinach, salt, 1/4 cup cheddar, and the sour cream; mix well.

To Assemble
1. With metal spatula, loosen edges of souffle.
2. Invert on waxed paper sprinkled lightly with Parmesan.
3. Peel off waxed paper.

4. Spread surface evenly with filling.
5. From long side, roll up; place, seam side down, on greased cookie sheet.
6. Arrange cheese slices over top.
7. Broil, about 4 inches from heat, just until cheese melts.
8. Use large spatula to remove to serving dish or board.

Yield: 8 servings

CHEESE CLOUD

12 slices day-old white bread
1/2 pound cheddar cheese, sliced
4 eggs
2-1/2 cups milk
1/2 teaspoon prepared mustard
1 tablespoon onion, grated
1/4 teaspoon salt
Dash of cayenne pepper
1 teaspoon seasoned salt

1. Trim crusts from bread; arrange 6 slices in bottom of a 12x8x2-inch greased baking dish.
2. Cover with cheese slices, then with remaining bread slices.
3. Beat eggs; add milk, mustard, onion, and seasonings.
4. Pour over casserole; let stand at room temperature for 1 hour. May be prepared a day before and refrigerated overnight.
5. Bake at 350F for 1 hour.
6. Serve immediately.

Yield: 6 servings

PIZZA RUSTICA

Basic short crust pastry for double-crust pie
5 eggs
1 pound ricotta cheese
2 tablespoons chopped onion
1 cup grated Parmesan cheese
Chopped parsley, about 1 tablespoon
Salt and freshly ground black pepper
2 tablespoons olive oil
2 cloves garlic
10 ounces tomato puree
4 ounces tomato paste
1/4 teaspoon dried marjoram
1/2 teaspoon dried oregano
2/3 cup sliced ripe olives
1/2 pound thinly sliced mozzarella cheese
1 very large bell pepper

1. Prepare the short crust pastry as directed. It is especially good (for this pie) if you use only lemon juice and marsala instead of water to moisten it.
2. Line a 10-inch pie dish; roll out a top crust.
3. Beat the eggs; stir in the ricotta cheese, onion, parsley, and Parmesan cheese; season liberally with salt and pepper. Set aside.
4. Heat the olive oil in a small saucepan.
5. Crush the cloves of garlic into it; add the herbs.
6. When the garlic is clear and begins to turn gold, stir in the tomato puree, tomato paste, olives; once again, season well with salt and black pepper.
7. Slice the mozzarella thinly.
8. Seed the green pepper; slice it into matchsticks.
9. Spread half (or a little more) of the ricotta mixture in the prepared pie shell.
10. Arrange over it half the mozzarella slices.
11. Cover with half the tomato sauce; spread half the green pepper over it.
12. Repeat all the layers; cover with the top crust.
13. Pinch the edges securely together and flute.
14. With a very sharp knife, make 3 long, parallel slashes through the top crust.
15. Bake the pie in a preheated 425F oven for about 35 to 40 minutes or until it is well browned.
16. Let stand for 1/2 hour before serving.

Yield: 6 to 8 generous servings

CRESPELLE FIORENTINA (CREPES FLORENTINE), SPINACH CRISPELLE

Note: This may be completely assembled a day before serving. The sauce freezes well.

2 tablespoons butter
2 tablespoons minced shallots or white part of green onion
1 cup diced, fresh mushrooms
1 cup cottage or cream cheese, room temperature
1 egg
3 cups Bechamel Sauce (recipe follows)
1-1/2 cups drained, chopped spinach, fresh or frozen
20 (8-inch) crepes
1/4 cup grated Parmesan cheese
1 tablespoon butter

1. Melt butter in 10-inch skillet.
2. Add shallots; saute until transparent.
3. Stir in mushrooms; saute several minutes to remove raw taste.
4. Mix in cottage cheese, egg, and several tablespoons of Bechamel Sauce to make a thick paste. Set aside.
5. Mix 1/4 cup sauce with spinach.
6. Center a crepe in bottom of lightly oiled baking dish.
7. Spread with spinach mixture; cover with another crepe; spread with layer of mushroom/cheese mixture.
8. Repeat this process with remaining crepes, alternating fillings, finishing with last crepe.
9. Pour remaining sauce over crepes; sprinkle with grated Parmesan.
10. Dot with butter.
11. Refrigerate until 30 to 40 minutes before serving.
12. Preheat oven to 375F.
13. Place dish in upper third of oven; bake about 25 to 30 minutes until bubbling hot, with cheese lightly browned.

Yield: 4 to 6 servings

Bechamel Sauce
1/4 cup (1/2 stick) butter
1/4 cup all-purpose flour
2 cups milk, room temperature
2 tablespoons freshly grated Parmesan cheese

1. Melt butter in a 2-quart saucepan.
2. When butter foams, add flour; mix well.
3. Cook over moderate heat until lightly browned, stirring frequently.
4. Remove from heat; slowly add milk, mixing with whisk until smooth.
5. Stirring constantly, return to heat and allow to simmer 5 minutes.
6. Remove from heat and add Parmesan.

Yield: 2 cups

INDIVIDUAL FROZEN CHEESE SOUFFLES

2 tablespoons butter or margarine
1/4 cup flour
1/2 teaspoon salt
1/4 teaspoon pepper
1/4 teaspoon dry mustard
1 cup milk
1-1/2 cups cheddar cheese, shredded
6 eggs, separated

1. Melt butter over low heat.
2. Blend in flour, salt, pepper, and mustard. Cook 1 minute.
3. Gradually add milk; cook until mixture thickens.
4. Add cheese; continue cooking until cheese melts.
5. Beat egg yolks.
6. Add a little of the cheese sauce to the yolks; add the yolk mixture to the remaining cheese sauce.
7. Beat egg whites until stiff but not dry.
8. Fold whites into cheese mixture.
9. Pour into six 1-cup, buttered souffle dishes.
10. Cover with plastic wrap and freeze.
11. Bake at 350F for 40 minutes.
12. Serve immediately.

Yield: 6 servings

BASIL LASAGNE

1/2 pound lasagne noodles
1/2 cup Pesto (recipe follows)
1 cup ricotta cheese
1 egg
1/2 cup grated Parmesan cheese
1/2 pound mozzarella cheese, shredded

1. Put the lasagne noodles into a large pot of boiling water.
2. Meanwhile, using a wooden spoon or the food processor, beat the pesto, ricotta, egg, and Parmesan cheese until they are well blended.
3. Butter a shallow baking dish.
4. Drain the lasagne when just done; place a layer of it in the baking dish.
5. Cover it with the ricotta/pesto mixture and then with a second layer of lasagne.
6. Spread all the mozzarella over this and sprinkle with more Parmesan cheese.
7. Bake in a 350F oven for 25 minutes.

Yield: 3 to 4 servings

Pesto
4 cups basil leaves
3 cloves garlic
1/2 cup pignoli (pine nuts)
1/2 cup Italian parsley
1 teaspoon salt
1/2 to 1 cup oil
1/2 cup pecorino or Parmesan cheese

1. Put the basil, garlic, pignoli, parsley, and salt into the food processor or blender with 1/2 cup oil.
2. Process, adding enough additional oil to make a smooth paste.
3. Add the cheese and process a few seconds longer.

Yield: 2 cups

Variations:
Freezer pesto: To make pesto for the freezer, process the basil, garlic, parsley, salt, and oil. Freeze it in 1-cup portions.
To use, defrost the sauce and put it back into the processor with the nuts and cheese. To use it as a seasoning, you can eliminate the nuts and cheese and simply chip off teaspoonfuls from the frozen mass.

Pesto with walnuts: Instead of pignoli, use 1/2 cups walnuts and omit the cheese.

Pesto with parsley: Instead of basil, use 3 cups of Italian parsley.

CALZONE

Dough
1-1/2 teaspoons dry yeast
1 tablespoon honey
1 cup wrist-temperature water
1-1/2 teaspoons salt
2-1/2 to 3 cups flour (mixed whole wheat and white, or just white)

Filling
1 pound ricotta cheese
2 cloves garlic, crushed
1/2 cup onion, minced
1 pound fresh spinach
2 cups grated mozzarella cheese
Salt
Pepper
1/2 cup freshly grated Parmesan cheese
Dash of nutmeg
2 tablespoons butter

For Dough
1. Soften together the yeast, honey, and water.
2. Add the salt and the flour.
3. Knead 10-15 minutes.
4. Cover; set in a warm place to rise until double in bulk - about
1 hour.
5. Punch down.
6. Divide into six sections; roll out in rounds 1/4-inch thick.
7. Fill with 1/2-3/4 cup filling, placing on one half of the circle,
leaving a 1/2-inch rim.
8. Moisten the rim with water; fold the empty side over; crimp the
edge with your favorite fork.
9. Prick it here and there.
10. Bake on an oiled tray in a preheated 450F oven for 15-20 minutes,
or until crisp and lightly browned.
11. Brush each pastry with a little butter as it emerges from the oven.

For Filling
1. Wash, stem, and finely chop the spinach.
2. Steam it quickly on medium high heat, adding no additional water.
3. When wilted and deep green, it is done and should be removed to a
mixing bowl with slotted spoon.
4. Saute onion and garlic in butter until translucent and soft.
5. Combine all ingredients; mix well; salt and pepper to taste.

Yield: 6 servings

SPINACH-RICOTTA PIE

Crust
1 cup flour (A combination of white and whole wheat is nice.)
1/3 cup cold butter
3 tablespoons cold buttermilk

Filling
1 pound ricotta cheese
3 beaten eggs
1/2 pound chopped spinach
1 small onion, diced
1/2 teaspoon salt
1/2 teaspoon basil
Butter
3 tablespoons flour
1/2 cup grated sharp cheese
Dash nutmeg

1 cup dairy sour cream
Paprika

For Crust
1. Cut together flour and butter, using a pastry cutter or a food processor fitted with a steel blade.
3. When the mixture is uniformly blended, add enough buttermilk so that mixture holds together enough to form a ball.
4. Chill the dough at least one hour.
5. Roll it out; place in a 9-inch pie plate.

For Filling
1. Saute spinach and onion in butter with salt and basil.
2. Combine all filling ingredients and mix well.
3. Spread into unbaked pie shell.
4. Top with 1 cup sour cream; spread to edges of crust; sprinkle with a generous application of paprika.
5. Bake at 375F for 40 to 45 minutes.
6. Serve piping hot.

Yield: 6 servings

SPANAKOPITA

1-1/2 cups onions, chopped
3 cloves garlic, crushed
2 tablespoons olive oil
3 tablespoons flour
3 (10-ounce) packages frozen chopped spinach, thawed and drained
4 ounces feta cheese, crumbled
1/2 cup Swiss cheese, grated
1 cup milk, heated
1 teaspoon tamari
1/4 teaspoon pepper
3 eggs beaten
1 pound filo dough
1/2 pound butter, melted
2 teaspoons sesame seeds

1. Saute onions and garlic in olive oil until onions are soft.
2. Sprinkle with flour; make a roux.
3. Add spinach; stir until spinach is hot.
4. Add cheese and the heated milk.
5. Stir until thickened.
6. Add tamari and pepper.
7. Let cool five minutes.
8. Stir a little of the hot mixture into the eggs; add the warmed eggs back to the spinach mixture.
9. Reserve three of the sheets of filo dough.
10. Divide the remaining dough into two equal stacks.
11. On an oiled 10x15-inch baking sheet, lay out a sheet of filo.
12. Butter with a pastry brush; lay out the next sheet; butter, and so on until all of the first stack is used up. If sheets are slightly larger then the pan, just fold over the edges. If they are smaller, lay them out in a staggered fashion so they cover the pan completely.
13. Spread 1/2 of the spinach mixture directly on top of the last sheet.
14. Layer the three reserved filo sheets, buttering each one.
15. Spread the rest of the filling; layer the remaining stack of filo dough, again buttering between the sheets.
16. Butter the top sheet and sprinkle with sesame seeds.
17. Bake at 350F for 45 minutes or until it rises up slightly and browns.

Yield: 4 to 6 servings

SPINACH QUICHE

1 unbaked 9-inch pie shell
1 tablespoon butter
1 cup minced onion
1 (10-ounce) package frozen spinach, thawed
1 (15-ounce) package Ricotta cheese
2 eggs
1/8 teaspoon pepper
1/8 teaspoon nutmeg
1/4 cup Parmesan cheese

1. Prick pie shell with fork; bake 15 minutes at 400F.
2. Melt butter in medium saucepan; add onion and cook until tender.
3. Squeeze spinach in hands to remove all moisture.
4. Add spinach to onion; toss over heat until all liquid has evaporated.
5. Mix remaining ingredients in bowl.
6. Add spinach mixture; mix until it looks like green and white marble.
7. Pour into shell.
8. Bake at 350F for 40 to 45 minutes.
9. Cool 10 minutes before serving.

Yield: 5 or 6 servings

OLD-TIME WELSH RABBIT

3 tablespoons butter or margarine
1/2 cup flour
1/2 teaspoon salt
1/8 teaspoon dry mustard
Dash cayenne pepper
3/4 teaspoon Worcestershire sauce
3 cups milk
1/2 pound (2 cups) sharp cheddar cheese, grated
Crisp crackers or toast

1. Melt butter in double boiler.
2. Stir in flour, salt, mustard, cayenne, Worcestershire, then milk; cook, stirring, until thickened and smooth.
3. Add cheese; cook, stirring occasionally, until melted.
4. Serve over crisp crackers or toast.

Yield: 6 servings

MANICOTTI

3 cups sifted all-purpose flour
4 eggs
4-1/2 tablespoons cold water
Pinch of salt
1 tablespoon olive oil

Stuffing
3/4 cup ricotta or cottage cheese
3/4 pound mozzarella cheese, diced
3 eggs, lightly beaten
2 tablespoons butter
2 tablespoons grated Parmesan cheese
1/2 teaspoon salt
Pinch of black pepper

Meat Sauce
1/2 pound salt pork, diced
1/4 cup olive oil
1/4 cup butter
3/4 pound onions, peeled and diced
1 pound lean beef, cut into 1/2-inch cubes
1/2 pound lean pork shoulder, cut into 1/2-inch cubes
2 bay leaves, crumbled
5 cloves garlic, mashed
1 tablespoon fresh rosemary
1/2 teaspoon ground allspice
1 teaspoon freshly ground black pepper
5 pounds ripe fresh tomatoes or 6 (1-pound) cans peeled plum tomtoes,
    finely chopped
1/4 pound carrots, scraped and minced
1/4 pound celery, minced
Salt
7 ounces tomato paste

For Manicotti
1. Place flour on a pastry board; make a well in the center.
2. Break the eggs into the well; add water, a little at a time, and
the salt.
3. Knead for about 10 minutes.
4. Let stand, covered, for about 1 hour.
5. Cut dough into 4 pieces; roll as thin as you can.
6. Cut into rectangles 4-inches wide and 6-inches long.
7. Place between pieces of wax paper. You should have about 12 pieces.
8. Cook half at a time in 4 quarts salted, boiling water with the olive
oil added.
9. Cook for 5 minutes.
10. Drain and place between 2 towels.

For Stuffing
Combine all ingredients and mix well.

For Meat Sauce

1. Combine salt pork, olive oil, and butter in a large saucepan; heat.
2. Add onions; saute to medium brown.
3. Add beef, pork, and bay leaves; stir.
4. Cook slowly, uncovered, for 30 minutes.
5. Chop garlic and rosemary together; add to sauce with allspice and pepper.
6. Stir well; continue to cook over low heat for 20 minutes; inhale the aroma.
7. Cover; cook for 5 minutes.
8. Add tomatoes, carrots, celery, and 1/2 tablespoon salt.
9. Simmer slowly for 1-1/2 hours, stirring occasionally. Do not hurry the cooking for a good sauce.
10. Remove sauce from the heat and allow to cool for 10 minutes.
11. Strain the sauce and put whatever remains in the strainer through a food mill. Return it to the sauce.
12. Add the tomato paste; stir well; bring to a boil.
13. Check for salt; add more if necessary. Any sauce that is not used can be frozen.

Yield: 3-1/2 cups

To Assemble
1. Divide stuffing into 12 parts.
2. Place a mound of stuffing on each dough rectangle about 1/3-inch from the edge; mound should be about 1/2-inch thick and 1/2-inch wide.
3. Fold dough over twice.
4. Spread a thin layer of the meat sauce on the bottom of a baking pan.
5. Arrange manicotti about 1/4-inch apart in the pan; spoon the rest of the sauce over the top.
6. Sprinkle a teaspoon of Parmesan cheese over each of the manicotti.
7. Bake in a preheated, 300F oven for 15 to 20 minutes.

Yield: 6 or 7 servings

BAKED PASTA SHELLS MARINARA

Pasta Shells
6 quarts water
1 tablespoon vegetable oil
1 tablespoon salt
24 jumbo pasta shells

Cheese Filling
2 medium carrots
1 large yellow onion
1 clove garlic
1 stalk celery
1 tablespoon butter or margarine
8 hard-cooked eggs, peeled and chopped
1 cup cottage cheese
1 raw egg
2 tablespoons Italian-flavored dry bread crumbs
2 tablespoons chopped parsley
1/2 teaspoon dried oregano leaves
Dash pepper

Marinara Sauce
1 tablespoon vegetable oil
1 cup slice onion
1 clove garlic, cracked
1 (16-ounce) can whole peeled tomatoes, undrained
1 (8-ounce) can tomato sauce
1/2 teaspoon salt
1/2 teaspoon dried oregano leaves
1/2 teaspoon dried basil leaves

1/4 cup freshly grated Parmesan cheese

For Pasta Shells
1. In an 8- to 10-quart saucepan, bring water, oil, and salt to a rolling boil.
2. Add pasta shells all at once; stir with a wooden spoon or fork to separate.
3. Cook, stirring occasionally, as package directs, until pasta is tender.
4. Drain.

For Cheese Filling
1. Peel carrots, onion, and garlic; cut carrots, onion, and celery into large chunks.
2. Using a food processor or large sharp knife, chop all vegetables until fine. You should have about 2-1/2 cups of the mixed vegetables.
3. In a large skillet, heat butter over high heat.
4. Add vegetables all at once; saute, stirring constantly, until tender and golden brown.
5. Cool slightly; mix with chopped eggs, cottage cheese, raw egg, bread crumbs, parsley, oregano, and pepper.

For Marinara Sauce
1. Heat oil in a medium-sized saucepan.
2. Add sliced onion; saute until golden brown.
3. Add garlic, undrained tomatoes, tomato sauce, salt, oregano, and basil.
4. Bring mixture to a boil; reduce heat; simmer 20 minutes.

To Fill Pasta Shells
1. Using a small spoon, fill drained pasta shells with cheese mixture.
2. Arrange shells in a lightly greased, shallow baking dish or casserole about 12 inches in diameter.
3. Top with Marinara Sauce; sprinkle with Parmesan cheese.
4. Baked pasta shells can be prepared ahead of time.
5. Arrange in baking dish as directed; cover with aluminum foil or plastic wrap.
6. Chill until ready to bake.
7. Preheat oven to 350F.
8. Bake 25 to 35 minutes or until hot and bubbly.

Yield: 8 servings

TOMATO CHEESE STRATA

1 cup butter, melted
2 teaspoons dry mustard
1 teaspoon garlic powder
Italian bread, cubed in 1-inch pieces
2 quarts prepared spaghetti sauce with mushrooms
1/2 cup green onions, chopped
1 teaspoon Italian seasonings
3 pounds Swiss cheese, shredded
3/4 cup butter
1 cup flour
1-1/2 quart milk
12 eggs, beaten

1. Combine butter, mustard, and garlic powder; drizzle over bread cubes. Set aside.
2. Add onions and Italian seasoning to spaghetti sauce.
3. Butter two 9x13x3-inch casseroles and layer as follows: 1/3 bread cubes, 2 cups spaghetti sauce mixture, and 1 quart shredded cheese.
4. Repeat layer two more times in each casserole.
5. Pour remaining sauce on top. Set aside.
6. Melt butter in a saucepan.
7. Add flour; blend to make a roux.
8. Remove from heat; gradually add milk, stirring constantly until smooth.
9. Return to medium heat for 1 minute, stirring constantly.
10. Remove from heat; add a small amount to the eggs.
11. Add egg mixture to the white sauce; cook over medium heat for 1 minute, stirring constantly.
12. Pour sauce over the bread in the pan.
13. Cover; refrigerate several hours or overnight.
14. Remove; let sit, covered, for 1 hour.
15. Bake at 350F for 35 minutes.
16. Remove; top with additional cheese.
17. Bake 15 minutes or until inserted knife comes out clean.
18. Let stand 5 minutes before serving.

Yield: 24 servings

ALMOND-RICOTTA PIE

Crust
1 cup graham cracker crumbs
1/4 cup sugar
1/4 cup toasted, ground almonds
6 tablespoons butter, melted

Filling
2-1/2 cups ricotta cheese
1 tablespoon almond extract
3/4 cup sugar
1-1/4 cups toasted, ground almonds
1/2 cup semisweet chocolate chips, chilled and then ground in food
   processor or blender
3/4 cup heavy cream, whipped until it forms stiff peaks

Topping
1/3 cup toasted slivered almonds

For Crust
1. Combine all ingredients.
2. Press firmly and evenly into the bottom and sides of a 9-inch pan.
3. Bake 10 minutes in a 350F oven. Let cool completely.

For Filling
1. Combine all ingredients.
2. Pour over crust.
3. Sprinkle on topping.
4. Refrigerate.

Yield: 8 servings

Vegetables

SWEET AND SOUR VEGETABLES

2 tablespoons oil
1 slice ginger, minced
1 medium green pepper
1 medium red pepper
1 large onion, cut into 1/2- to 3/4-inch pieces
1 carrot sliced
1 tomato, peeled, seeded, and cubed
1/2 cup pineapple chunks

Sauce
1/2 cup chicken broth
2 tablespoons cornstarch
1 tablespoon soy sauce
1/2 cup brown sugar
1/2 cup vinegar
1 teaspoon salt

1. Combine chicken broth and cornstarch in saucepan.
2. Add soy sauce, brown sugar, vinegar, and salt.
3. Cook until thick.
4. Heat oil in wok.
5. Stir-fry ginger to release flavor.
6. Add vegetables; stir-fry 1 minute.
7. Add pineapple and sauce.
8. Heat through.

Yield: 4 servings

PINEAPPLE SURPRISE

3/4 cup sugar
1 stick butter
4 eggs
5 slices bread, cubed
1 can crushed pineapple, drained

1. Combine all ingredients and place in a casserole.
2. Bake at 350F for 45 minutes to 1 hour.
3. Serve hot.

Yield: 4 servings

SESAME BROCCOLI

1 pound fresh broccoli, cut in spears, or 1 (10-ounce) package frozen
    broccoli spears
2 tablespoons vinegar
1 tablespoon soy sauce
1/4 teaspoon sesame oil
1 teaspoon sugar
1 tablespoons sesame seeds, toasted

1. Bias-slice broccoli stems in 1/2-inch thick pieces (leave florets whole).
2. Cook stems, covered in 1-inch of boiling salted water, for 5 minutes.
3. Add broccoli florets.
4. Cook 5 to 10 minutes longer or until crisp-tender. (If using frozen broccoli, prepare according to package directions, cutting the cooking time in half.)
5. Drain; cover; chill broccoli.
6. In screw-top jar, combine vinegar, soy sauce, sesame oil, and sugar; cover; shake to mix well.
7. Just before serving, drizzle vinegar mixture over broccoli; toss gently.
8. Arrange on cold plate.
9. Sprinkle with toasted sesame seeds.

Yield: 4 servings

SWISS CHEESE AND CORN CASSEROLE

2 packages frozen, 1 (2-pound) can, or 3 cups fresh corn
6 ounces evaporated milk
1 egg, beaten
2 tablespoons onion, finely chopped
1/2 teaspoon salt
Dash pepper
1/2 cup soft bread crumbs
1 tablespoon butter, melted
4 ounces Swiss cheese, grated

1. Cook corn in 1 cup salted water for 3 minutes. Drain.
2. Combine corn, milk, egg, onion, salt, pepper, and all but 1/4 cup cheese.
3. Turn into 10x6-inch baking dish.
4. Toss bread crumbs with butter; sprinkle on top of casserole.
5. Sprinkle cheese on top.
6. Bake at 350F for 30 minutes.

Yield: 6 servings

PENNY'S FRIED TOMATOES

Note: My parents belonged to a Gourmet Group when we lived outside of Philadelphia. These were served with a Pennsylvania Dutch meal and really are wonderful. Using the heavy cream makes the gravy more like a cheese sauce. You can use milk or half-and-half, but they will not be as yummy!

It's best to use tomatoes past the green stage but not fully ripened.

My father and brother are not real tomato fans like my mother and myself. In the summer, when Dad would work late and John was not home, my mother and I would treat ourselves to these wonderful things. We would eat ourselves silly.

6-8 orange-colored tomatoes (not fully ripened but not green)
6-8 strips bacon
1-1/2 cups heavy cream
1 cup flour
1/2 cup dark brown sugar

1. Mix flour and brown sugar together in a shallow bowl.
2. Fry bacon in skillet. Remove bacon but do not drain skillet.
3. Cut top and bottom off of partially ripened tomatoes.
4. Cut tomatoes into 3/4-inch slices.
5. Coat both sides of tomatoes with flour and brown sugar by turning them lightly over in the bowl.
6. Fry tomatoes on both sides in the skillet.
7. When lightly browned, remove to an oven-proof platter; keep warm in a low oven.
8. When all tomatoes are fried, crumble bacon on top of tomatoes.
9. Usually one of the tomatoes has fallen apart in the pan. Leave it in the pan as it will enrich the gravy.
10. Using a cooking fork, stir up all residue in the bottom of the pan.
11. Slowly add cream to make a white gravy.
12. Continue cooking until gravy has thickened nicely.
13. Pour gravy over tomatoes; serve immediately.

Yield: 6 to 8 servings

HOLIDAY CASSEROLE

2 bunches fresh or 3 boxes frozen broccoli
1 large head or 2 boxes frozen cauliflower
1/4 pound butter
10 tablespoons flour
1 quart milk
1 teaspoon dry mustard
2 teaspoons salt
1 teaspoon dried minced onion
1/2 teaspoon white pepper
1 cup sharp cheddar cheese
8 ounces salami, diced

1. Cook broccoli and cauliflower until just done.
2. Heat the butter.
3. Stir in the flour; add half the milk, stirring until smooth.
4. Add the remaining milk, the mustard, salt, onion, pepper, and cheese.
5. Continue to stir until smooth and slightly thickened.
6. Cover; turn down the heat.
7. Simmer for 15 minutes.
8. Pour some of the sauce into a shallow, round casserole.
9. Put the broccoli in a ring around the edge of the casserole.
10. Use the cauliflower to fill in the center; in the very center, put the salami.
11. Pour the rest of the sauce over all.
12. Cool before covering, wrapping, and freezing.
13. Before serving, heat for 45 minutes at 300F.

Yield: 8 to 12 servings

SQUASH CASSEROLE

2 pounds cooked squash
1 stalk diced celery
2 tablespoons chopped pimiento
1 can cream of chicken soup
1 cup dairy sour cream
1 carrot, grated
1 onion, diced
1 stick margarine, melted
1 small package Pepperidge Farm Stuffing

1. Combine all ingredients.
2. Bake in an 8x8x2-inch pan in a 325F oven for 30 minutes.

Yield: 4 to 6 servings

RATATOUILLE WITH GRATED CHEESE

3 cloves garlic, finely chopped
2 onions, cut in thin slices
1/3 cup olive oil
1 green pepper, cut in thin rounds
2 medium eggplants, diced
6 to 8 very ripe tomatoes, peeled, seeded, and diced, or 1 (20-ounce)
    can Italian plum tomatoes
1 teaspoon dry basil, or 1/4 cup fresh basil, chopped
1-1/2 teaspoon salt
1 pound mushrooms, sliced
Grated Parmesan cheese

1. Saute garlic and onions in oil until soft.
2. Add pepper and eggplant; cook for 5 minutes over medium heat,
tossing well and shaking pan.
3. Add tomato and seasonings; simmer 30 minutes, covered for half
that time.
4. Add mushrooms; correct seasoning; continue cooking till mushrooms are just cooked through.
5. Serve sprinkled with grated cheese.

Yield: 6 servings

STUFFED TOMATOES

6 medium tomatoes
1/4 cup chopped green pepper
1/4 cup Parmesan cheese
1/3 cup croutons
1 teaspoon salt
Parsley or chopped bacon

1. Remove stem ends and pulp from each tomato, leaving 1/2-inch wall.
2. Chop pulp to measure 1/3 cup.
3. Stir together tomato pulp and remaining ingredients, except parsley
or bacon.
4. Fill tomato with mixture.
5. Place filled tomato in ungreased baking dish.
6. Bake 20 to 25 minutes at 350F until tomatoes are heated.
7. Garnish with parsley or bacon.

Yield: 6 servings

FRENCH RICE

1 (10-1/2-ounce) can onion soup, undiluted
1/2 cup butter or margarine, melted
1 (4-1/2-ounce) jar sliced mushrooms, undrained
1 (8-ounce) can sliced water chestnuts, undrained
1 cup uncooked regular rice

1. Combine soup and butter; stir well.
2. Drain mushrooms and water chestnuts, reserving liquid.
3. Add enough water to reserved liquid to make 1-1/3 cups.
4. Add mushrooms, water chestnuts, liquid, and rice to soup mixture; stir well.
5. Pour into a lightly greased, 10x6x2-inch baking dish.
6. Cover and bake at 350F for 1 hour.

Yield: 6 servings

NO DATE SEVEN FLAVOR RICE (GNAW MAI FAAN)

Note: To do ahead, prepare in advance and reheat, loosely covered with foil, in 350F oven for 1/2 hour.

3 dried mushrooms, soaked for 2 hours
4 strips bacon
1 set chicken giblets (liver, heart, and gizzard optional)
2 stalks green onion
1 1/2 cups long grain rice, washed
1/2 cup celery, diced
1/2 cup onion, diced
1/2 teaspoon salt
1-2 tablespoons light soy sauce
1 teaspoon sesame oil
2-1/4 cups water

1. Stem mushrooms and finely dice the caps.
2. Cut bacon into small strips.
3. Dice liver, heart, gizzard, and green onion.
4. Cook rice in 2-1/4 cups water according to boiled rice directions.
5. While rice is cooking, heat wok and stir-fry bacon with the giblets until done - about 3-4 minutes. Set aside.
6. There should be some bacon fat left. If not, add 1 tablespoon oil and stir-fry celery, onion, and mushrooms for 2 minutes.
7. Add meat mixture.
8. When rice is done, add it while still hot to the mixture in wok.
9. Add salt, soy sauce, sesame oil, and green onion.
10. Mix well and serve.

Yield: 4 to 5 servings

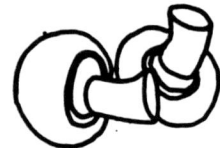

FRIED RICE

Note: Can be made ahead and reheated in warm oven.

2 to 3 cups cooked rice
8 pieces bacon, diced
1/2 cup celery, diced
1/2 cup green pepper, diced
1/2 cup mushrooms, sliced
1/2 cup cashews
1/2 cup diced onion and/or scallions
2 to 3 tablespoons soy sauce
1 teaspoon sesame oil

1. Cook bacon until almost crisp. Remove from pan.
2. In bacon fat, saute celery, green pepper, mushrooms, cashews, and onion for 1 to 2 minutes.
3. Return bacon and rice to pan; stir.
4. Add soy sauce and sesame oil.
5. Stir well.
6. Serve warm.

Yield: 6 servings

RICE WITH ALMONDS

1 tablespoon unsalted butter
3/4 cup long-grain rice
1-1/2 cups chicken stock or canned broth
Salt
1/4 cup toasted slivered almonds

1. Heat the butter in a heavy, 1-quart saucepan over medium heat until melted.
2. Stir in the rice until coated.
3. Add the chicken stock; salt to taste.
4. Adjust the heat to simmering; simmer, covered, until the liquid is absorbed and the rice is tender - about 17 minutes.
5. Remove the rice from the heat; let stand 5 minutes.
6. Stir in the almonds with a fork; transfer the rice to a serving platter.
7. Serve hot.

Yield: 4 servings

TEA LEAF EGGS

8 to 10 eggs
3 tablespoons soy sauce
5 teaspoons aniseed
2 inches cinnamon stick
1 tablespoon black tea leaves
1 teaspoon sugar
1 teaspoon salt
2 cups cold water

1.   In saucepan, cover eggs with cold water to a depth of at least 1 inch above eggs.
2.   Rapidly bring to boiling; cover pan tightly.
3.   Reduce heat; simmer 15 minutes.
4.   Rinse quickly in cold water until eggs are cool enough to handle; drain.
5.   Tap eggs gently all over until shells are a network of fine cracks (do not remove shells).
6.   Return eggs to saucepan.
7.   Add soy sauce, aniseed, stick cinnamon, black tea, sugar, salt, and 2 cups cold water.
8.   Bring to boiling; reduce heat.
9.   Simmer, covered, 2 hours (add boiling water to keep eggs covered, if needed).
10.   Drain; chill.
11.   To serve, roll eggs between palms of hands to loosen shell.
12.   Peel, starting from large end of egg.

Yield: 8 to 10 servings

DIRTY RICE

2 pounds ground beef
2 pounds ground sausage
1 pound ground gizzards and hearts
1 cup onion
1 cup green onion
2 tablespoons garlic
1/2 cup bell pepper
1 teaspoon black pepper
3 tablespoons Worcestershire sauce
1/2 pound margarine
3 teaspoons salt
4 bay leaves
4 cups rice

1. Mix all ingredients together, except rice; cook them down for 4 hours.
2. Add 2 cans of mushroom soup; simmer for 30 minutes.
3. Add rice; steam for 30 minutes to 1 hour.
4. Remove bay leaves; serve.

Yield: 10 servings

PENNIES' FRIES

Note: It's really fun to make your own French fries, and with the help of a food processor, it can be really easy, too! They're so much better than the store-bought variety.

8 new potatoes
1 tablespoon white vinegar
Lawry's seasoned salt
Vegetable oil

1. Scrub potatoes well, but do not peel.
2. Using the thinnest blade on the processor, slice the potatoes.
3. Combine the white vinegar with enough water to cover the potatoes. Allow the potatoes to sit in this solution for about 5 minutes. (This will prevent discoloration.) Remove potatoes and allow to drain well. If there is much moisture left on the potatoes, the oil will foam when the potatoes are added.
4. Heat oil to 375F. Drop the sliced potatoes into the oil in small batches. It is much better to cook many small batches than several large batches. Fry until the potatoes are golden brown. As soon as they come out of the oil, salt with the seasoned salt. May be served warm or at room temperature.

POTATO AND LEEK PUREE

3 or 4 leeks, about 3/4 pound, trimmed
5 Maine or Idaho potaotes, about 1-1/4 pounds
2 tablespoons butter
1/2 cup milk
Salt, if desired, and freshly ground pepper to taste
1/8 teaspoon freshly grated nutmeg

1. Remove root ends of leeks.
2. Split leeks lengthwise almost through to root end.
3. Rinse thoroughly between leaves.
4. Cut into finest possible dices. There should be 4 cups.
5. Peel potatoes; cut into quarters. There should be 4 cups.
6. Add cold water, enough to cover; bring to boil.
7. Cook 15 to 20 minutes until tender.
8. Drain potatoes; put through food mill or ricer and into saucepan.
9. Heat 1 tablespoon of butter in heavy saucepan; add leeks.
10. Cook, stirring occasionally, until wilted.
11. Cover; cook 10 minutes.
12. Heat milk.
13. Add leeks to potatoes.
14. Add heated milk, stirring with wooden spoon.
15. Add remaining tablespoon butter, salt, pepper, and nutmeg.
16. Heat, stirring about 15 seconds, and it is ready for the table.

Yield: 4 servings

GRILLED POTATOES

4 large baking potatoes (about 2 pounds)
1 tablespoon plus 1 teaspoon reduced-calorie margarine
1 tablespoons plus 1 teaspoon Parmesan cheese
1 teaspoon chopped chives
1/4 to 1/2 teaspoon pepper
1/8 teaspoon garlic powder
1 medium onion, thinly sliced

1. Scrub potatoes and peel.
2. Cut potatoes in half crosswise.
3. Cut slices crosswise into potatoes, 3/4-inch apart, leaving bottom edge intact; set aside.
4. Combine next 5 ingredients; mix well.
5. Divide mixture evenly and place into slit potatoes.
6. Place onion slices into slits of potato halves.
7. Wrap each potato in aluminum foil. Place potato bundles in baking pan.
8. Bake at 400F for 45 to 55 minutes or until done.

Yield: 8 servings

HAM AND CHEESE STUFFED POTATOES

4 large baking potatoes
1 teaspoon shortening
6 tablespoons margarine or butter
2 tablespoons grated onion
1/4 teaspoon pepper
2 eggs
6 ounces (1-1/2 cups) shredded cheddar or American cheese
6 ounces (1 cup) diced ham
Paprika, if desired

1. Heat oven to 375F.
2. Rub each potato with shortening; prick several places with a fork.
3. Bake for about 1 hour or until done.
4. Cut potatoes in half lengthwise; scoop out inside, leaving a thin shell.
5. In large bowl, beat potatoes 1 minute.
6. Add margarine, onion, pepper, and eggs; continue beating until mixture is smooth and fluffy.
7. Fold in 1 cup cheese (reserve remaining cheese for topping) and ham.
8. Fill potato shells with mixture; top with reserved 1/2 cup cheese.
9. Sprinkle with paprika.
10. Bake at 375F for 15 minutes or until potatoes are heated through and cheese is melted.

Yield: 4 servings

SWEET POTATO CASSEROLE

3 cups mashed sweet potatoes
1/3 cup milk
1 stick butter
1/4 cup sherry
2 eggs
1 cup white sugar

Topping
Brown sugar
Flour
Butter
Pecans

1. Preheat oven to 350F.
2. Mix together potatoes, milk, butter, sherry, eggs, and sugar.
3. Pour into casserole.
4. Combine flour and brown sugar.
5. Sprinkle over potato mixture.
6. Dot top of casserole with butter.
7. Sprinkle top with pecans.
8. Bake for 30 minutes.

Yield: 4 to 6 servings

MARINADE FOR SHISH KABOBS

Note: Generally, I use quartered onions, green peppers, and tomatoes, and end with a large, fresh button mushroom on each skewer.

5-1/2 pounds sirlion, cut in cubes
1/2 cup olive or salad oil
1/4 cup soy sauce
1/2 cup Taylor N.Y. State claret or burgundy
2 tablespoons candied ginger, finely chopped (optional)
2 cloves garlic, grated
2 tablespoons tomato sauce or catsup
1 tablespoon curry powder
1/2 teaspoon black pepper

1. Mix all ingredients thoroughly; add no salt, since soy sauce provides ample. Marinate meat in refrigerator 12 to 36 hours, depending on how pungent you like it. Turn cubes several times for even flavor.
2. When ready to grill, drain meat; arrange on skewers alternately with vegetables or fruit.
3. Grill for 10-15 minutes or until meat reaches desired doneness.

Yield: 12 servings

PESTO ALLA GENOVESE

Note: You can use walnuts instead of pine nuts, about 1/2 cup spinach or chard and more basil for the same amount of oil and butter. You can also use half Parmesan and half Romano (Parmesan alone yields a milder pesto).

This keeps in refrigerator with a skim of oil, or freezes well.

1/2 cup pignoli
1/4 cup chopped fresh basil
2 tablespoons chopped, raw spinach
2 teaspoons finely minced garlic
1/2 rounded cup freshly grated cheese
6 tablespoons butter, softened
1/2 cup olive oil
1/4 teaspoon salt
1/8 teaspoon freshly ground pepper

Combine all ingredients and puree in blender or food processor.

Yield: 3 cups

BARBECUE SAUCE

Note: This recipe was given to me by the pastry chef of a local restaurant famous for its ribs. While he would share the rib recipe, I never could get any of his dessert recipes from him! You can make this as hot as you like, depending on the amount of pepper you add.

Use this on chicken, pork, or beef ribs, or anything else you can think of.

1 cup oil
1-1/2 cups brown sugar
5 tablespoons mustard
3 teaspoons salt
5 teaspoons Worcestershire sauce
5 cups ketchup
1/2 cup vinegar
Red pepper to taste

Combine all ingredients.

Yield: 2 quarts

SECRET MUSTARD SAUCE

1 cup milk
2 egg yolks
1 tablespoon flour
1 tablespoon dry mustard
3/4 cup sugar
1/2 cup vinegar

1. Beat egg yolks and milk.
2. Combine and add ingredients; cook over hot water until thickened.
3. Gradually stir in the vinegar; heat thoroughly.

Yield: 1-1/2 cups

SWEET AND SOUR SAUCE

1/2 cup sugar
1/2 cup vinegar
2 tablespoons soy sauce
2 tablespoons sherry
3 tablespoons tomato sauce or catsup
2 tablespoons cornstarch, dissolved in 1/2 cup pineapple juice

1. Combine the sugar, vinegar, soy sauce, sherry, and tomato sauce in a heavy saucepan; bring to a boil.
2. Add the cornstarch mixture, stirring constantly until the sauce thickens.

Yield: 2 cups

JOY'S BEEF MARINADE

Note: This marinade will make even the poorest cut of meat tasty and tender. If you like, you can sprinkle your meat with MSG and/or Accent. I never do, however, and it is always tender.

2 cloves garlic, minced
2 tablespoons oil
6 tablespoons wine vinegar
2 tablespoons catsup
1 tablespoon soy sauce
1 tablespoon Worcestershire sauce
1 teaspoon prepared mustard

1. Combine marinade ingredients.
2. Marinate roast for 48 hours.

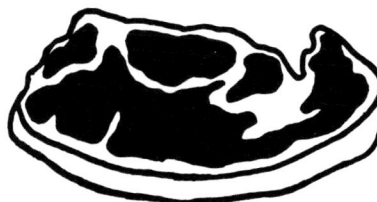

Desserts

PRALINES AND CREAM CAKE

Cake
1 cup pecan halves
1 package Pillsbury Plus Yellow Cake Mix
3/4 cup water
1/3 cup Praline liqueur or water
1/3 cup oil
1 teaspoon vanilla
3 eggs
1 (3-ounce) package Philadelphia Brand cream cheese, softened

Frosting
1 (3-ounce) package Philadelphia Brand cream cheese, softened
2 tablespoons liquid brown sugar*
1 tablespoon Praline liqueur or water
Reserved toasted pecan halves

1. Heat oven to 350F.
2. In shallow pan, toast pecan halves 8 to 10 minutes or until crisp, stirring occasionally.
3. Reserve 15 halves for garnish. Finely chop remaining pecans.
4. Grease and flour 10-inch tube pan or 12-cup fluted tube pan.
5. In a large bowl, combine cake mix, water, liqueur, oil, vanilla, eggs, and cream cheese.
6. Combine at low speed until moistened; beat 2 minutes at highest speed.
7. Fold in chopped pecans; pour into prepared pan.
8. Bake for 40 to 50 minutes or until toothpick inserted in center comes out clean.
9. Cool 15 minutes. Remove from pan and turn upright on a serving plate. Cool completely.
10. In small bowl, beat all frosting ingredients except reserved pecan halves until smooth.
11. Spoon over cake.
12. Garnish with reserved pacan halves.
13. Store in refrigerator.

*To substitute for liquid brown sugar, use 1 tablespoon brown sugar and 1 tablespoon water.

Yield: 16 servings

KAHLUA PARTY CRUNCH CAKE

Cake
1-1/4 cups sifted cake flour
1-1/2 cups sugar
1/2 cup egg yolks (6 large)
2 tablespoons Kahlua
2 tablespoons water
1 tablespoon lemon juice
1 cup egg whites (8 large)
1 teaspoon cream of tartar
1 teaspoon salt

Kahlua Cream
2 cups whipping cream
2 tablespoons Kahlua
1 tablespoon sugar

Kahlua Crunch
1-1/2 cups sugar
2 tablespoons water
1/4 cup Kahlua
1/4 cup white corn syrup
3 tablespoons baking soda

For Cake
1. Sift flour with 3/4 cup sugar into small bowl of mixer.
2. Make a well in the center; add egg yolks, Kahlua, water, and lemon juice.
3. Beat until smooth.
4. Beat egg whites in large mixing bowl with cream of tartar and salt to very fine foam.
5. Gradually add remaining 3/4 cup sugar, 2 tablespoons at a time, and beat until firm meringue.
6. Pour batter slowly over meringue, folding until blended. Do not stir.
7. Pour into 10x4-inch tube pan; bake at 350F for 50 minutes or until top springs back when lightly touched.
8. Turn pan upside down, placing tube over neck of a bottle. Let stand until cool.

For Kahlua Cream
1. Beat whipping cream, Kahlua, and sugar until stiff.

For Kahlua Crunch
1. Put sugar, water, Kahlua, and corn syrup into narrow, deep, heavy pan.
2. Stir, then bring to a boil and cook to 310F (hard crack stage).
3. Remove from heat and add soda (free from lumps). Mixture will foam rapidly when soda is added. Stir briskly just until mixture thickens. Do not break down foam with excessive stirring.
4. Turn out into ungreased 9-inch square pan; do not stir. Let stand until cold.
5. Knock out of pan; crush with rolling pin to coarse crumbs.

To Assemble
1. Remove cake from pan; cut into 4 even layers.
2. Re-assemble layers with about 1/2 of the Kahlua cream between layers.
3. Spread remainder over sides and top.
4. Cover cake generously with crushed Kahlua crunch, pressing gently with hands.
5. Mark cutting lines on top and down sides of cake with knife.
6. Refrigerate until served.

Yield: 16 servings

COCONUT-FROSTED PINEAPPLE CAKE

2 cups sifted all-purpose flour
2-1/2 cups sugar
2 teaspoons baking soda
1 (20-ounce) can crushed pineapple, in syrup
2 eggs
1/2 cup vegetable oil
1/2 cup (1 stick) butter or margarine
1 (5.33-ounce) can evaporated milk
1 cup shredded coconut
1 cup chopped walnuts
1/2 teaspoon vanilla

1. Preheat oven to 350F.
2. Lightly grease 9x13-inch pan.
3. Combine flour, 1-1/4 cups sugar, and baking soda in large mixing bowl.
4. Add undrained pineapple, eggs, and oil; mix thoroughly.
5. Turn batter into prepared pan.
6. Bake until tester inserted in center comes out clean - about 30 minutes.
7. Bring to boil over medium-high heat; continue boiling, without stirring, for 3 to 4 minutes. Cool slightly.
8. Stir in coconut, walnuts, and vanilla.
9. Spread frosting evenly over hot cake.
10. Let cool on rack.
11. Serve warm or at room temperature.

Yield: 10 to 12 servings

ANGEL FOOD CAKE WITH ORANGE-ALMOND CREAM

Note: The cake may be baked a day ahead; but once the filling is made and the cake assembled, it should be eaten within 1 to 2 hours.

Cake
1-1/4 cups cake flour, sifted
1/2 cup plus 1-1/3 cups sugar
12 egg whites
1 teaspoon vanilla extract
1-1/4 teaspoon cream of tartar
1/4 teaspoon salt

Orange-Almond Cream
2 sticks (1/2 pound) unsalted butter, softened
3/4 cup confectioner's sugar
1/4 cup orange liqueur, such as Grand Marnier, Cointreau, or Triple Sec
2 teaspoons grated orange zest (from 1 large orange)
1-1/3 cups finely ground blanched almonds (about 5 ounces)
2 cups heavy cream

For Cake
1. Preheat the oven to 325F.
2. In a large bowl, sift together the flour and 1/2 cup sugar.
3. In a large bowl, beat the egg whites with an electric mixer on high speed until foamy.
4. Add the vanilla, cream of tartar, and salt. Continue beating until soft peaks form.
5. Beating on high speed, gradually add the 1-1/3 cups of sugar.
6. Beat until glossy and forms stiff peaks.
7. Taste; the consistency should be smooth, not grainy. If some sugar is still undissolved, beat until smooth.
8. Fold in 1/3 of the flour-sugar mixture until blended.
9. Repeat two more times, stirring occasionally to thoroughly incorporate the flour.
10. Spoon the batter into an ungreased 10-inch tube pan.
11. Bake for 50 minutes, until a cake tester inserted near the center comes out clean.
12. Cool the cake upside-down in the pan before unmolding.

For Orange-Almond Cream
1. In a medium bowl, beat the butter with the sugar until pale and fluffy - about 3 minutes.
2. Slowly add the orange liqueur, 1 tablespoon at a time, beating after each addition until smooth.
3. Add the orange zest and almonds; beat until evenly distributed.
4. In a medium bowl, beat the cream until the beaters leave light traces when drawn across the top of the cream.
5. Stir 1/4 of the whipped cream into the butter mixture to lighten it.
6. Fold in the remaining cream in three more additions.
7. Place in the refrigerator for 10 minutes to firm slightly before filling and frosting the cake.

To Assemble

1. Cut the cake horizontally in half with a serrated knife to make 2 even layers.
2. Spread the bottom layer with about 1/3 of the Orange-Almond Cream.
3. Place the second cake layer on top; cover the top and sides with the remaining cream.
4. Place the cake, uncovered, in the refrigerator until ready to serve.

Yield: 10 servings

ANGEL MERINGUE TORTE WITH RASPBERRIES

6 egg whites
1/2 teaspoon cream of tartar
1/4 teaspoon salt
1-1/2 cups sugar
1/2 teaspoon vanilla
1/2 teaspoon almond extract
1 cup chilled whipping cream
Raspberry topping

1. Heat oven to 450F.
2. Butter bottom only of a 9-inch springform pan or 10x4-inch tube pan.
3. Beat egg whties, cream of tartar, and salt in large mixing bowl on medium speed until foamy.
4. Beat in sugar, 2 tablespoons at a time. Continue beating until stiff and glossy.
5. Beat in flavorings.
6. Spread evenly in pan.
7. Place in oven; immediately turn off oven. Leave pan in oven at least 8 hours.
8. After removing from oven, run knife around torte to loosen and invert on serving plate.
9. In chilled bowl, beat whipping cream until stiff.
10. Frost torte with whipped cream.
11. Refrigerate several hours.
12. Serve with raspberry topping.

Yield: 12 servings

POUND CAKE

Cake

8 egg whites (1 cup)
3 cups all-purpose flour, sifted
1 teaspoon baking powder
Salt
2 cups granulated sugar
8 egg yolks
2 cups butter or margarine (4 sticks)
1 tablespoon grated orange peel
2 tablespoons grated lemon peel
2 tablespoons lemon juice

Glaze

1 tablespoon butter
1 package (1 pound) confectioner's sugar
1 teaspoon grated lemon peel
1/3 cup lemon juice

1. Separate eggs, turning yolks into one large bowl and whites into another. Let egg whites warm to room temperature - about 1 hour.
2. Preheat oven to 350F.
3. Lightly grease and flour bottom and sides of a 10-inch tube pan.
4. Sift and measure 3 cups of flour.
5. Sift again with baking powder and 1/4 teaspoon salt. Set aside.
6. With mixer at high speed, beat egg whites with 1/4 teaspoon salt until foamy throughout.
7. Beat in 1 cup sugar, 1/4 cup at a time, beating well after each addition. Beat until soft peaks form.
8. Grate orange and lemon peels on a fine grater. Measure.
9. In a large bowl, at high speed, with same beater (don't wash), beat butter with remaining cup of sugar 5 minutes until light and fluffy.
10. Beat in yolks until light and fluffy.
11. At high speed, beat in peels, lemon juice, and 1 tablespoon water until smooth.
12. Divide flour mixture into thirds. At low speed, blend in 1/3 at a time just until combined - about 1 minute.
13. At low speed, fold in egg whites, half at a time, just until blended, scraping bowl and guiding batter into the beater. (Be sure not to overmix.)
14. Turn batter into prepared pan.
15. Bake in middle of oven 60 minutes, or until cake tester inserted in center comes out clean.
16. Cool on rack 15 minutes. Turn out of pan and cool.
17. To make glaze, blend butter, sugar, lemon juice, and peel until smooth.
18. Drizzle over cake.

Yield: 12 servings

COFFEE CHIFFON CAKE

7 eggs, separated
1 teaspoon cream of tartar
1/2 teaspoon salt
1 cup sugar
3 teaspoons instant coffee
1/3 cup water
1 cup all-purpose or unbleached flour*
2 ounces (2 squares) semisweet chocolate, grated
2 teaspoons vanilla

Frosting
2 cups whipping cream
1/3 cup powdered sugar
2 ounces (2 squares) semisweet chocolate, grated
1-1/2 teaspoons instant coffee
1 teaspoon vanilla

1. Heat oven to 325F. In large bowl, beat egg whites, cream of tartar, and salt until mixture forms soft peaks. Gradually add 1/2 cup of the sugar, beating until stiff peaks form.
2. In small bowl, beat egg yolks until thick and lemon colored. Gradually add remaining 1/2 cup sugar, beating until thick.
3. Dissolve 3 teaspoons instant coffee in 1/3 cup water. Lightly spoon flour into measuring cup; level off. Blend coffee mixture, flour, 2 ounces grated chocolate and 2 teaspoons vanilla into egg yolk mixture. Beat 1 minute at low speed or just until blended.
4. Fold egg yolk mixture into egg whites. Pour into ungreased 10-inch tube pan. Bake at 325F for 50 to 60 minutes or until top springs back when touched lightly in center. Invert cake on funnel or bottle; cool completely. Remove from pan.
5. In large bowl, beat cream until slightly thickened. Reserving 3 teaspoons grated chocolate for top, add remaining grated chocolate, powdered sugar, 1-1/2 teaspoons instant coffee, and 1 teaspoon vanilla to cream; beat until firm peaks form (do not overbeat).
6. Slice cake into 2 layers. Fill and frost top and sides; sprinkle reserved 3 teaspoons grated chocolate over top. Store in refrigerator.

*Self-rising flour is not recommended.

Yield: 20 servings

STRAWBERRY CREAM CAKE

6 egg whites
1-3/4 cups sifted (sift before measuring) all-purpose flour
1/2 teaspoon salt
1-1/2 cups granulated sugar
6 egg yolks
1/4 cup fresh lemon juice
1 tablespoon grated lemon peel
2 pints strawberries, washed and hulled
2 cups heavy cream, chilled
1/2 cup confectioner's sugar
1/2 teaspoon vanilla extract
1/4 cup currant jelly, melted

1. In large electric mixer bowl, let egg whites warm to room temperature - 1 hour.
2. Sift flour with salt.
3. With mixer at high speed, beat egg whites until foamy.
4. Beat in 3/4 cup of the granulated sugar, 2 tablespoons at a time, beating after each addition.
5. Beat until soft peaks form when beater is slowly raised.
6. Preheat oven to 350F.
7. In small mixer bowl, at high speed; with the same beater, beat yolks until very thick and lemon colored.
8. Gradually beat in remaining granulated sugar; beat 2 minutes.
9. At low speed, gradually beat in flour mixture.
10. Add lemon juice, 2 tablespoons water, and the lemon peel, beating just to combine - 1 minute.
11. Using a wire whisk, with a under-and-over motion, gently fold egg-yolk mixture into egg whites just to blend.
12. Pour batter into an ungreased 10x4-inch tube pan; bake 40 minutes, or until top springs back when gently pressed with fingertip.
13. Invert pan over neck of bottle; let cake cool completely - 1 hour.
14. With spatula, carefully loosen cake from pan; remove cake.
15. Divide cake into thirds with toothpicks. With these as guides, split cake into three layers, using a long-bladed serrated knife.
16. Place bottom layer, cut side up, on plate.
17. Slice 1 pint berries.
18. In medium bowl, beat cream with confectioner's sugar and vanilla.
19. Spread bottom layer with 3/4 cup cream and half of sliced berries.
20. Repeat with second layer.
21. Top with last layer, cut side down.
22. Frost top and side with rest of whipped cream.
23. Toss 1 pint berries with jelly.
24. Arrange on the cake.
25. Refrigerate 1 hour.

Yield: 12 servings

BLUEBERRY LEMON POUND CAKE

2 sticks (1 cup) unsalted butter, softened
2 cups granulated sugar
6 large egg yolks
4 teaspoons grated lemon rind
2 tablespoons fresh lemon juice
3 cups cake flour
1 teaspoon baking soda
1/4 teaspoon salt
1 cup plain yogurt
6 large egg whites, room temperature
Pinch cream of tartar
1-1/2 cups blueberries, picked over and tossed with 1 tablespoon flour
1 tablespoon confectioner's sugar

1. In a large bowl cream the butter, then add 1-1/2 cups of granulated sugar, a little at a time, beating constantly.
2. Beat the mixture until it is light and fluffy.
3. Beat in the egg yolks, 1 at a time, beating well after each addition.
4. Add the lemon rind and the lemon juice.
5. Stir in the flour mixture alternately with the yogurt.
6. In a bowl with an electric mixer, beat the egg whites with the cream of tartar and a pinch of salt until they hold soft peaks.
7. Beat in gradually the remaining 1/2 cup granulated sugar; beat the meringue until it holds stiff peaks.
8. Stir one fourth of the meringue gently but thoroughly into the batter.
9. Fold in remaining meringue.
10. Fold in the blueberries.
11. Spoon the batter into a buttered and floured 4-quart tube pan, 4-inches deep, and smooth the top.
12. Bake the cake in a preheated moderately hot oven (375F) for 1 hour or until a cake tester inserted halfway between the center and the edge comes out clean.
13. Let the cake cool in the pan on a rack for 10 minutes; invert it onto the rack, and let it cool completely.
14. Sift the confectioner's sugar over the cake; transfer the cake to a platter, or serve the cake sliced, toasted lightly, and buttered.

Yield: 16 servings

NORWEGIAN STRAWBERRY CREAM CAKE

Cake
Butter
Flour
1/2 cup all-purpose flour
1/3 cup cornstarch or potato flour
1 teaspoon baking powder
6 eggs, separated, room temperature
Pinch of cream of tartar
1 cup sugar

Vanilla Custard
1/4 cup sugar
1 tablespoon cornstarch
1-1/2 cups half-and-half
3 egg yolks, room temperature
2 tablespoons (1/4 stick) unsalted butter, room temperature
1 tablespoon vanilla

1 quart fresh strawberries
1/2 cup strawberry jam, sieved

1-1/2 cups whipping cream, well chilled
2 tablespoons powdered sugar
1 teapsoon vanilla

For Cake
1. Preheat oven to 350F.
2. Butter two 9-inch round cake pans and dust with flour.
3. Combine 1/2 cup flour, cornstarch, and baking powder.
4. Beat yolks in small bowl until frothy.
5. Beat whites with cream of tartar in large bowl with electric mixer until soft peaks form.
6. Add sugar 1 tablespoon at a time, beating until stiff and shiny.
7. Fold yolks and dry ingredients alternately into whites.
8. Divide batter between prepared pans.
9. Bake until center of layers springs back when touched, about 30 minutes.
10. Cool in pans. (Can be prepared 1 day ahead, removed from pans, and wrapped tightly.)

For Custard
1. Combine 1/4 cup sugar and cornstarch in small saucepan.
2. Slowly mix in half-and-half, then yolks and butter.
3. Cook over medium-low heat until mixture thickens, stirring constantly - about 10 minutes.
4. Place plastic wrap on surface and cool to room temperature.
5. Stir in 1 tablespoon vanilla.

To Assemble
1. Reserve several berries for garnish; slice remainder.
2. Cut each cake layer in half horizontally.
3. Place 1 layer on cake plate, cut side up.
4. Spread with half of custard.

5. Add next layer, cut side down.
6. Spread with jam.
7. Arrange sliced berries over jam, spreading to edges.
8. Cover with third layer, cut side up.
9. Spread with remaining custard.
10. Top with last layer, cut side down. (Can be prepared 4 hours ahead to this point and refrigerated.)
11. Up to an hour before serving, whip cream to soft peaks.
12. Stir in powdered sugar and 1 teaspoon vanilla.
13. Mound whipped cream atop cake.
14. Garnish with reserved strawberries.

Yield: 16 servings

STRAWBERRY CAKE

Note: You may wish to use a cream cheese frosting on this cake and garnish it with whole strawberries.

Cake
1 small box strawberry gelatin
1 package white cake mix
4 eggs
3/4 cup salad oil
3 tablespoons flour
1 (10-ounce) package frozen strawberries

Strawberry Icing
3/4 stick margarine, softened
2 cups powdered sugar
1 (10-ounce) package frozen strawberries

1. Combine all cake ingredients, including gelatin; beat with mixer for 5 minutes.
3. Bake in greased tube pan in 325F oven for 55 minutes.
4. For icing, combine margarine, powdered sugar, and remaining strawberries and beat well.
5. Pour over cooled cake.

Yield: 16 servings

STRAWBERRY SURPRISE CAKE

Note: This recipe must be made ahead of time.

1 (10-inch diameter) angel food cake
1 recipe Strawberry Mousse (see recipe)
2 cups whipping cream
1/4 cup Grand Marnier
Whole strawberries (garnish)

1. Using a serrated knife, cut a 1-inch layer from top of cake; set aside.
2. Starting 1 inch from outer edge, remove inside of cake, reserving pieces.
3. Place hallowed cake on serving plate.
4. Use some of reserved pieces and fill in bottom layer about 1-inch thick.
5. Spoon mousse into center until even with top of cake.
6. Replace layer and use reserved pieces to fill tube and make top level.
7. Whip cream with Grand Marnier.
8. Place about 1/2 cup cream in pastry bag fitted with star tip.
9. Spread cake completely with remaining cream.
10. Pipe top with rosettes, placing strawberry in center of each.
11. Refrigerate overnight.

Strawberry Mousse
2 pints fresh strawberries, pureed (about 2 cups puree)
1 cup sugar
1 envelope unflavored gelatin
1/4 cup lemon juice
2 eggs whites

1-1/2 cups whipping cream
Whole strawberries
2 tablespoons chopped pistachio nuts

1. Combine puree and sugar in medium bowl.
2. Soften gelatin in lemon juice; dissolve over hot water.
3. Stir into puree.
4. Beat egg whites until foamy; add to puree.
5. Place mixture in freezer.
6. When partially frozen, about 45 to 60 minutes, beat in food processor or blender until pale pink. Transfer to bowl.
7. Whip 1 cup cream and fold into berry mixture.
8. Place in serving dishes or glass bowl.
9. Refrigerate until firm - at least 2 hours.
10. Decorate with whipped cream rosettes, made from remaining 1/2 cup cream.
11. Top with whole strawberries and dust with pistachio nuts.

Yield: 10 to 12 servings

ITALIAN CREAM CAKE

Note: This recipe originally came from Ann Goodnight. It is one of the Cafe's favorites. Since it such a high cake, it makes a very pretty presentation.

Cake
1 stick butter
1/2 cup shortening
2 cups sugar
5 egg yolks
2 cups plain flour, sifted
1 teaspoon soda
1 teaspoon vanilla
1 cup buttermilk
1 cup coconut
1 cup chopped pecans or walnuts
5 egg whites, beaten until stiff

Cream Cheese Icing
1 stick butter, softened
8 ounces cream cheese, softened
1 pound confectioner's sugar
1 teaspoon vanilla
1 cup chopped peacans or walnuts

For Cake
1. Cream together butter, shortening, sugar, and egg yolks.
2. Stir in flour, soda, buttermilk, and vanilla.
3. Mix in coconut and nuts.
4. Fold in egg whites.
5. Pour into 3 greased and floured cake pans.
6. Bake at 350F for 25 to 30 minutes.
7. Frost with Cream Cheese Icing.

For Cream Cheese Icing
1. Beat together all ingredients until creamy and of spreading consistency.
2. Spread on cake layers.

Yield: 16 servings

NORWEGIAN ORANGE CREAM CAKE

Cake
1 package Pillsbury Plus Yellow Cake Mix
1 cup dairy sour cream
3/4 cup orange juice
3 eggs

Fillings
1-1/2 cups milk
3 (3/4-ounce) packages instant vanilla pudding and pie filling mix
1/2 cup raspberry preserves
1/2 cup apricot preserves

Frosting
1-1/2 cups whipping cream, whipped

For Cake
1. Heat oven to 350F.
2. Grease and flour two 8- or 9-inch round cake pans.
3. In a large bowl, combine all cake ingredients at low speed until moistened.
4. Beat 2 minutes at highest speed.
5. Pour batter evenly into prepared pans.
6. Bake at 350F for 25 to 30 minutes; remove from pans. Cool completely.

For Filling
1. In small bowl, combine milk and pudding mix.
2. Beat 2 minutes at low speed until well blended; refrigerate until set - about 5 minutes.

To Assemble
1. Slice cooled cake into 4 layers.
2. Place 1 layer on serving plate; spread with raspberry preserves.
3. Top with second layer; spread with vanilla filling.
4. Place third layer on filling; spread with apricot preserves.
5. Top with remaining layer.
6. Frost cake with whipped cream.
7. If desired, pipe rim of rosettes of whipped cream around top edge of cake; decorate with small dots of raspberry and apricot preserves.
8. Store in refrigerator.

Yield: 16 servings

POPPY SEED CAKE

Cake
3/4 cup poppy seeds
3/4 cup milk
3/4 cup margarine
1-1/2 cups sugar
2 cups flour
2 teaspoons baking powder
3 egg whites

Filling
3 egg yolks
3/4 cup brown sugar
1/2 cup milk
1 tablespoon butter
2 tablespoons cornstarch

Icing
1 pound confectioner's sugar
1 cup shortening
1 egg white
3 tabelspoons water

For Cake
1. Grease and flour 2 cake pans; preheat oven to 350F.
2. Soak poppy seeds in milk for 20 minutes.
3. Cream butter and sugar until light and fluffy.
4. Add poppy seeds and milk.
5. Sift together flour and baking powder; slowly add to batter.
6. Beat egg whites until stiff peaks form.
7. Fold egg whites into batter.
8. Pour batter into pans; bake for 30 minutes.
9. Cool for 10 minutes; remove from pans. Cool completely.

For Filling
1. Combine all ingredients.
2. Place in double boiler; cook slowly, stirring constantly until thickened.

For Icing
1. Blend together shortening and sugar.
2. Add egg white and water; beat until fluffy.

To Assemble
1. Put filling between layers.
2. Frost top and sides of cake with icing.

Yield: 16 servings

SPICED PECAN CAKE WITH PECAN FROSTING

Note: This is a cross between the Italian Cream Cake
and a very good spice cake. The glazed pecans on top are really
wonderful. Don't let the directions scare you off; it's not that bad.

Cake
2 cups coarsely chopped pecans
1/4 cup firmly packed, light brown sugar
2 tablespoons cinnamon
1 teaspoon freshly grated nutmeg
1 cup (2 sticks) unsalted butter, room temperature
2 tablespoons plus 2 teaspoons vanilla
2 cups sugar
3 cups sifted all-purpose flour
2 tablespoons baking powder
1 cup plus 2 tablespoons milk
3 egg whites, room temperature

Glaze
1 cup water
1/2 cup sugar
1 teaspoon vanilla

Frosting
1-1/2 cups sugar
3/4 cup water
8 egg yolks, room temperature
1-1/2 cups (3 sticks) margarine, cut into pieces, room temperature
2-1/2 cups powdered sugar
4-1/2 teaspoons vanilla
2-1/2 cups coarsely chopped pecans, toasted
Whipping cream (if necessary)
Pecan halves

For Cake
1. Position rack in upper third of oven and preheat to 425F.
2. To candy pecans, place in large, ungreased metal pan. Roast 10
minutes, stirring every 2 minutes.
3. Combine brown sugar, cinnamon, and nutmeg in medium bowl.
4. Mix in 1/4 cup butter.
5. Stir in hot pecans to coat thoroughly.
6. Return mixture to pan and roast 10 minutes, stirring every 2
minutes.
7. Mix in 2 tablespoons vanilla; roast 5 minutes, stirring frequently.
8. Cool candied pecans to room temperature.
9. Preheat oven to 350F.
10. Grease and flour three 8-inch round cake pans.
11. Cream remaining 3/4 cup butter with 1-1/2 cups sugar in large bowl
of electric mixer at high speed until very light and fluffy - about 6
minutes.
12. Sift flour and baking powder into another bowl.
13. Combine milk and remaining 2 teaspoons vanilla.
14. Add dry ingredients and milk mixture alternately to butter, beating

at high speed until well blended and scraping down sides of bowl occasionally.
15. Gently stir in candied pecans.
16. Beat whites until frothy.
17. Add remaining 1/2 cup sugar 1 tablespoon at a time, beating at high speed until mixture is stiff but not dry - about 2 minutes.
18. Gently fold whites into batter in 3 additions.
19. Divide batter among prepared pans, forming slight depression in center of each.
20. Bake until toothpick inserted near center comes out clean - about 40 minutes.
21. Cool 10 minutes. Invert layers onto wire racks and cool to room temperature.

For Glaze
1. Heat water and sugar in heavy small saucepan over low heat until sugar dissolves, swirling pan occasionally.
2. Increase heat; bring mixture to boil.
3. Remove from heat; stir in vanilla.
4. Immediately brush glaze over top of each layer.

For Frosting
1. Heat sugar and water in heavy 1-quart saucepan over low heat, swirling pan occasionally, until sugar dissolves.
2. Increase heat and boil, without stirring, until mixture registers 230F (thread stage) on candy thermometer, swirling pan occasionally - about 15 minutes.
3. Blend yolks in large bowl of electric mixer at high speed for 5 seconds.
4. Reduce speed to low; add hot syrup in thin stream, then beat at high speed until cool - about 10 minutes. (Do not scrape down sides of bowl).
5. Gradually add margarine, beating at medium speed until smooth - about 5 minutes.
6. Reduce speed to low; blend in powdered sugar and vanilla.
7. Add chopped pecans; beat at high speed until mixture is very thick. Thin the frosting with cream if necessary.
8. Stack layers on serving platter, spreading 1 cup frosting between each, refrigerating frosting as necessary to firm.
9. Smooth remaining frosting on sides and top of cake.
10. Arrange pecan halves around top edge.
11. Serve at room temperature.

Yield: 16 servings

RASPBERRY CONTINENTAL

Note: This one's a diet buster; no one can resist it. What a combination!

Cake
1/2 cup butter
1 cup sugar
1/2 teaspoon salt
1/3 cup milk
1 egg
1 teaspoon vanilla
1/4 cup toasted, blanched almonds, chopped
1-1/4 cups unbleached flour

Raspberry Filling
1/4 cup sugar
2 tablespoons cornstarch
1 (10-ounce) package frozen raspberries

Butter Filling
1/2 cup butter or margarine
1-1/2 cups powdered sugar
1 egg

Topping
3/4 cup whipping cream
3 tablespoons sugar
Chopped walnuts, if desired

For Cake
1. Heat oven to 350F.
2. Grease an 8-inch square pan.
3. In a large bowl, cream butter and sugar until light and fluffy.
4. Add salt, milk, egg and vanilla; mix well.
5. Lightly spoon flour into measuring cup; level off.
6. Stir flour and almonds into creamed mixture.
7. Pour into prepared pan.
8. Bake at 350F for 30-35 minutes or until toothpick inserted in center comes out clean.
9. Remove from pan; cool.

For Raspberry Filling
1. In medium saucepan, combine sugar, cornstarch, and all frozen raspberries.
2. Cook over medium heat until thickened, stirring constantly.
3. Cool completely.

For Butter Filling
1. In medium bowl, cream butter; gradually add powdered sugar. Cream well.
2. Add egg; beat until light and fluffy. Set aside.

For Topping
1. In small bowl, beat whipping cream until firm peaks form. Do not overbeat.
2. Stir in sugar.

To Assemble
1. Slice cooled cake horizontally into two layers; remove top layer.
2. Spread butter filling and then raspberry filling over bottom layer.
3. Replace top layer; top with whipped cream.
4. Sprinkle with walnuts.
5. Refrigerate until served.

Yield: 6 to 8 servings

RASPBERRY CAKE

9 tablespoons unsalted butter
1-1/2 cups sugar
4 egg yolks
3/4 cup ground almonds
2-1/4 cups flour
4 cups fresh raspberries
4 egg whites

1. Heat oven to 375F.
2. Cream butter and 1/2 cup of the sugar in large bowl until light and fluffy.
3. Stir in egg yolks, almonds, and flour until smooth. Do not overmix.
4. Roll dough out to a 10-inch circle; use to line a 9-inch, straight-sided tart pan with a removable base.
5. Ease dough into pan, pressing gently to line bottom and sides and use a scissors or knife to cut away excess dough.
6. Bake 30 minutes, or until cooled through completely but not browned.
7. Cool on wire rack.
8. Meanwhile, mix raspberries with 1/2 cup of the remaining sugar.
9. Beat egg whites until soft peaks form.
10. Beat in remaining 1/2 cup sugar until stiff but not dry.
11. Using a slotted spoon, spread raspberries and sugar over the baked crust, leaving a narrow rim around the edge free of fruit.
12. Pile on the meringue, right up to the edge of the cake.
13. Return cake to the oven for 15 to 20 minutes--not by precise timing, but by the color of the meringue. It should be golden.
14. Serve warm or cold.

Yield: 8 servings

THREE-LAYER LEMON CAKE

Cake Layers
4-1/2 cups flour
3/4 teaspoon baking soda
3/4 teaspoon salt
1-1/2 cups butter
4-1/2 cups sugar
8 eggs
1-1/2 cups buttermilk
5 tablespoons lemon juice
Grated rind of three lemons

White Lemon Icing
4 egg whites
3 cups sugar
6 tablespoons cold water
1/2 teaspoon cream of tartar
1 tablespoon light honey
2 teaspoons vanilla
4 tablespoons lemon juice
1 teaspoon grated lemon rind
Ground almonds (optional)

For Cake
1. Sift flour, baking soda, and salt.
2. Cream butter.
3. Add sugar and beat thoroughly.
4. Add eggs one at a time, beating after each one.
5. Beat two minutes more.
6. To this mixture, add dry ingredients alternately with the buttermilk in three additions, beating until smooth after each one.
7. Stir in the lemon juice and rind.
8. Turn into 3 greased and floured pans.
9. Bake at 350F for 30 minutes, or until done when tested.
10. Cool completely.

For Icing
1. In top of a double boiler, beat the egg whites, sugar, water, cream of tartar, and honey until thoroughly blended.
2. Place over boiling water.
3. Beat constantly for seven minutes.
4. Add the lemon juice and rind.
5. Ice the cake and, if desired, sprinkle the top with ground almonds.

Yield: 16 servings

CARROT CAKE

Note: This is our favorite Carrot Cake recipe. Not only is it delicious, it is also very easy.

Cake
2 cups sugar
1-1/2 cups oil
4 eggs, unbeaten
2 cups flour
2 teaspoons baking powder
1 teaspoon salt
1 teaspoon baking soda
2 teaspoons cinnamon
2 cups raw carrots, shredded
1 cup chopped nuts

Glaze
1 pound confectioner's sugar
2 teaspoons vanilla
1 (8-ounce) package cream cheese
1/2 stick margarine

For Cake
1. Cream oil and sugar until fluffy. Don't underbeat.
2. Add eggs and beat well.
3. Sift flour, baking powder, soda, salt, and cinnamon.
4. Add to creamed mixture.
5. Fold in carrots and nuts.
6. Pour into a greased fluted pan, or a 9x13-inch pan.
7. Bake 1 hour at 300F.

For Glaze
1. Cream butter and cream cheese.
2. Add sugar and vanilla.
3. Beat until smooth.
4. Glaze cooled cake with cream cheese frosting.

Yield: 16 servings

CASHEW PINEAPPLE CAKE

Cake
2-1/2 cups all-purpose or unbleached flour
3 teaspoons baking powder
1/2 teaspoon salt
3/4 cup margarine or butter, softened
1-1/4 cups sugar
3 eggs
1 teaspoon vanilla
3/4 cup milk
1 (8-ounce) can crushed pineapple

Frosting
3/4 cup margarine or butter
2 cups powdered sugar
1 egg
1/2 cup coarsely chopped cashews

For Cake
1. Heat oven to 350F.
2. Grease and flour two 8- or 9-inch round cake pans.
3. Lightly spoon flour into measuring cup; level off.
4. In medium bowl, combine flour, baking powder, and salt.
5. In large bowl, cream margarine and sugar until light and fluffy.
6. Add eggs and vanilla; beat well.
7. Alternately add dry ingredients and milk to creamed mixture, mixing well after each addition.
8. Drain pineapple, reserving 1/4 cup pineapple for frosting.
9. Stir in remaining pineapple.
10. Spread evenly in prepared pan.
11. Bake at 350F for 25 to 35 minutes or until toothpick inserted in center comes out clean.
12. Cool 10 minutes; remove from pans.
13. Cool completely.

For Frosting
1. In medium bowl, cream margarine; gradually add powdered sugar, beating well.
2. Add egg; beat until light and fluffy.
3. Stir in reserved 1/4 cup pineapple.
4. Place 1 layer on serving plate; spread with half the frosting.
5. Repeat with other layer. Do not frost sides.
6. Sprinkle top of cake with cashews.
7. Store in refrigerator.

Yield: 12 servings

DIXIE SPICE CAKE WITH CARAMEL FROSTING

Cake
2-1/4 cups all-purpose or unbleached flour
1-1/4 cups firmly packed brown sugar
1/2 cup sugar
1 teaspoon soda
1/2 teaspoon salt
1/2 teaspoon nutmeg
1/2 teaspoon allspice
1 cup buttermilk
2/3 cup shortening
1 teaspoon vanilla
3 eggs
1 cup chopped black walnuts or pecans

Frosting
1/2 cup margarine or butter
1 cup firmly packed brown sugar
1/4 cup milk
3 cups powdered sugar
1/2 teaspoon vanilla

For Cake
1. Heat oven to 350F.
2. Generously grease and flour bottom only of 13x9-inch pan.
3. Lightly spoon flour into measuring cup; level off.
4. In large bowl, blend flour and remaining ingredients, except nuts, at low speed until moistened.
5. Beat 3 minutes at medium speed.
6. Stir in nuts.
7. Pour into prepared pan.
8. Bake at 350F for 40 to 45 minutes or until center springs back when lightly touched. Cool completely.

For Frosting
1. In medium saucepan, melt margarine; add brown sugar.
2. Cook over low heat 2 minutes, stirring constantly.
3. Add milk; continue cooking until mixture comes to a rolling boil.
4. Remove from heat.
5. Gradually add powdered sugar.
6. Add vanilla; mix well. If necessary, thin with a few drops milk.
7. Spread over cooled cake.

Yield: 12 servings

CHUNKY APPLE WALNUT CAKE

Cake
1-1/2 cups vegetable oil
2 cups sugar
3 eggs
2 cups unbleached all-purpose flour, sifted
1/8 teaspoon ground cloves
1-1/4 teaspoons ground cinnamon
1/4 teaspoon ground mace
1 teaspoon baking soda
3/4 teaspoon salt
1 cup whole wheat flour, sifted
1-1/4 cups shelled walnuts, coarsely chopped
3-1/4 cups coarse chunks of peeled and cored Rome Beauty apples
3 tablespoons Calvados or applejack

Apple Cider Glaze
4 tablespoons sweet butter
2 tablespoons brown sugar
6 tablespoons granulated sugar
3 tablespoons Calvados or applejack
4 tablespoons sweet cider
2 tablespoons fresh orange juice
2 tablespoons heavy cream

For Cake
1. Preheat oven to 325F.
2. In large bowl, beat vegetable oil and sugar until thick and opaque.
3. Add eggs, one at a time, beating well after each addition.
4. Sift together all-purpose flour, cloves, cinnamon, mace, baking soda, and salt; stir in whole-wheat flour.
5. Add to oil and egg mixture; mix until well blended.
6. Add walnuts, apple chunks, and Calvados all at once; stir batter until pieces are evenly distributed.
7. Pour batter into a greased, 10-inch round cake pan.
8. Bake for 1 hour and 15 minutes, or until a cake tester inserted in the center comes out clean.
9. Let cake rest for 10 minutes, then unmold and pour glaze over warm cake, or cut cake and pour glaze over slices.

For Apple Cider Glaze
1. Melt butter in a small saucepan; stir in both sugars.
2. Add remaining ingredients; stir; bring to a boil.
3. Reduce heat slightly; cook for 4 minutes.
4. Remove from heat; cool slightly.
5. Pour while still warm over warm cake.

Yield: 10 to 12 servings

AMARETTO CAKE

Cake
1 cup chopped almonds
1 (18-1/2-ounce) package yellow cake mix*
1 (3-3/4-ounce) package Jell-O Vanilla Instant Pudding and Pie Filling
4 eggs
1/2 cup cold water
1/2 cup oil
1/2 cup Amaretto

*If using yellow cake mix with pudding already in the mix, omit instant pudding, use 3 eggs instead of 4, and 1/3 cup oil instead of 1/2.

Glaze
1/4 pound butter
1/4 cup water
1 cup granulated sugar
1/2 cup Amaretto

For Cake
1. Preheat oven to 325F.
2. Grease and flour 10-inch tube or 12-cup bundt pan.
3. Sprinkle nuts over bottom of pan.
4. Mix all cake ingredients together.
5. Pour batter over nuts.
6. Bake 1 hour. Cool.
7. Invert on serving plate.
8. Prick top.
9. Spoon and brush glaze evenly over top and sides.
10. Allow cake to absorb glaze.
11. Repeat till glaze is used up.

For Glaze
1. Melt butter in saucepan.
2. Stir in water and sugar.
3. Boil 5 minutes, stirring constantly.
4. Remove from heat.
5. Stir in Amaretto.
6. Decorate cake with border of whipped cream.

Yield: 16 servings

FRUIT FANTASIA (A THREE-LAYER CAKE)

Banana Nut Layer
1-1/4 cups sifted flour
5/6 cup sugar
5/8 teaspoon baking powder
5/8 teaspoon soda
1/2 teaspoon salt
1/3 cup margarine
1/6 cup buttermilk
5/8 cup mashed ripe bananas
1 or 2 eggs
1/6 cup buttermilk
1/3 cups chopped nuts

Cherry Cake Layer
1 cup plus 1 tablespoon flour
2/3 cup sugar
1-1/2 teaspoons baking powder
1/2 teaspoon salt
1/4 cup margarine
1/8 cup maraschino cherry juice
10 maraschino cherries, cut into eighths
1/4 cup milk
3 egg whites, unbeaten
1/4 cup chopped nuts

Apple Cake Layer
1-1/2 cups sifted flour
1 cup sugar
1-1/2 teaspoons cinnamon
1/2 teaspoon salt
1/2 teaspoon baking soda
1-1/2 cups diced apples
1/2 cup chopped nuts
1/2 cup oil
2 eggs, beaten

Pudding Filling
2 packages instant vanilla pudding

Frosting
1 cup butter
1 pound powdered sugar
1 egg white
1 teaspoon vanilla extract
Milk

For Banana Nut Layer
1. Grease and flour a 9-inch layer pan.
2. Sift all dry ingredients together.
3. Cream margarine; add mashed bananas and first 1/6 cup of buttermilk.
4. Add flour mixture alternately with buttermilk.
5. Beat 2 minutes or stir by hand, if preferred.
6. Fold in nuts.
7. Pour batter into pan.

For Cherry Layer
1. Grease and flour a 9-inch layer pan.
2. Sift all dry ingredients together.
3. Cream margarine; add cherry juice, cherries, and milk.
4. Stir in flour.
5. Beat 2 minutes or until well blended with spoon or whisk.
6. Add egg white and nuts; beat 2 more minutes.
7. Pour batter into prepared pan.

For Apple Layer
1. Grease and flour a 9-inch layer pan.
2. Mix dry ingredients together; mix in eggs and oil; add to dry ingredients.
3. Blend well.
4. Add apples and nuts.
5. Pour into prepared pan. (If this layer appears taller than the rest, use some of the batter to make cupcakes.)

For Pudding Filling
1. Prepare according to package directions.

For Frosting
1. Cream butter and sugar until light and fluffy.
2. Add egg and extract.
3. Add enough milk to bring frosting to spreading consistency.

To Assemble
1. Bake cake layers at 350F for 20 to 30 minutes. Cool completely.
2. Decide order of layers.
3. Spread filling between layers; refrigerate until set.
4. Frost top and sides of cake with frosting.

Yield: 16 servings

CREOLE CHOCOLATE CAKE

Note: This is always very popular when we serve it.

2 cups unsifted all-purpose flour
1 teaspoon baking soda
1/2 cup butter or regular margarine
1/2 cup salad oil
3 squares unsweetened chocolate
2 cups sugar
2 eggs, beaten
1/2 cup sour milk
1 teaspoon vanilla extract

Filling
1 (5.3-ounce) can evaporated milk
3/4 cup sugar
1/4 cup chopped seedless raisins
1/2 cup chopped dates
1 teaspoon vanilla extract
1/2 cup chopped walnuts or pecans
1/2 cup chilled heavy cream

Frosting
1 (6-ounce) package semisweet chocolate pieces
1/2 cup dairy sour cream
Dash salt

1. Preheat oven to 350F.
2. Sift flour with soda into large bowl.
3. Grease well and flour two 8x8x2-inch square cake pans.
4. In small saucepan, combine butter, oil, and chocolate; stir over low heat to melt the chocolate. Add 1 cup water; cool 15 minutes.
5. To flour mixture, add 2 cups sugar, the eggs, sour milk, and 1 teaspoon vanilla; mix with wooden spoon. Stir in cooled chocolate to combine.
6. Quickly turn into prepared pans; bake 30 to 35 minutes, until surface springs back when pressed with finger. Cool in pans 5 minutes.
7. Carefully loosen sides with spatula. Turn out on racks; cool.
8. Make filling in small saucepan by combining milk, sugar, and 1/4 cup water. Cook over medium heat, stirring to dissolve sugar.
9. Add raisins and dates. Stir with wooden spoon.
10. Cook, stirring, until mixture is thickened - about 5 minutes.
11. Add vanilla and nuts. Cool completely.
12. In small bowl, beat cream with rotary beater just until stiff.
13. Spread raisin mixture on top of first layer, top this with cream.
14. For frosting, melt chocolate pieces in top of double boiler over hot water. Remove top of double boiler from hot water.
15. Stir in sour cream and salt. With wooden spoon, beat until smooth.
16. Cool 5 minutes, until frosting is of spreading consistency.
17. With spatula, frost top of cake, swirling decoratively; use rest of frosting to cover sides.
18. Refrigerate 1 hour before serving.
19. With sharp thin knife, mark top of cake into four quarters; cut each quarter into four slices.

Yield: 16 servings

CHOCOLATE CHIP CAKE

Note: In Ardmore, Pennsylvania, a bakery named the Viking
Bakery makes a wedding cake that is the perfect reason to get re-
married, so you can have another cake! Even if your marriage is a happy
one or if you have no desire to marry, this cake is as close to the
Viking's as I could come.

Use a good grade of chocolate for the chips. I use bittersweet
chocolate and chop it up for my chips. Stir the chips into the
dry ingredients so that they will not sink to the bottom. If you forget
to do that, just toss them with some flour before putting them in the
cake.

I use the frosting from the Poppy Seed Cake or the Buttercream Frosting
from Raspberry Continental. Top the cake with shaved white chocolate.
The Viking Bakery covers its wedding cakes with white chocolate curls.

1 white cake mix, prepared according to package directions
8 ounces chocolate chips (at least) coated with about 2 tablespoon flour
Buttercream Frosting recipe (see Raspberry Continental recipe)
Shaved white chocolate, about 8 ounces

1. Prepare cake mix.
2. Coat chips with flour and fold into cake mix. If you are using pre-
packaged chocolate chips, you may wish to zap them once or twice in your
food processor.
3. Pour batter into three 8- or 9-inch cake pans.
4. Bake according to package directions.
5. Cool cake; frost with Buttercream Frosting.
6. Heavily sprinkle top and sides of cake with white chocolate chips.

Yield: 12 servings

BROWNIE SUNDAE CAKE

Note: We added Heath Bits on top.

1 (15-ounce) package fudge brownie mix
Ice cream
Chocolate sauce

1. Prepare brownie mix according to directions on package.
2. Spread in greased, 9x1-1/2-inch round layer pan.
3. Bake 30 to 35 minutes.
4. Cool.
5. Cut into wedges; serve with ice cream and chocolate sauce.

Yield: 8 to 10 servings

PEANUT BUTTER COOKIE CAKE

1/2 roll Pillsbury Slice 'n Bake Refrigerated Peanut Butter Cookies
1 (6-ounce) package (1 cup) semisweet chocolate chips
1 package Pillsbury Plus Yellow Cake Mix
1 cup water
1/2 cup chunky peanut butter
3 eggs

1. Heat oven to 350F.
2. Slice cookie dough into 1/8-inch slices.
3. Press on bottom and sides (about 1-inch from top) of 12-cup fluted tube pan, making sure there are no holes.
4. In small saucepan, combine chocolate chips and margarine over low heat, stirring constantly, until chocolate melts.
5. Spoon mixture onto cookie dough, spreading lightly up sides.
6. In large bowl, blend remaining ingredients at low speed until moistened.
7. Beat 2 minutes at highest speed.
8. Pour into prepared pan.
9. Bake at 350F for 45 to 55 minutes or until toothpick inserted in center comes out clean.
10. Cool upright in pan 10 minutes; invert onto wire rack. Cool completely.
11. Cover cake (cookie crust softens upon standing).
12. If desired, sprinkle with powdered sugar.

Yield: 12 servings

FRENCH CHOCOLATE CAKE WITH CHOCOLATE GLAZE

Note: This cake freezes successfully if wrapped and sealed securely. Bring to room temperature before serving and glaze will become shiny.

Cake
1 cup or one (5-1/2-ounce) bag or can of almonds, skins on
4 squares (4 ounces) semisweet chocolate or 3/4 cup chocolate pieces
1/2 cup (1 stick) butter at room temperature, cut up
2/3 cup sugar
3 eggs
Grated rind of 1 large orange
1/4 cup very fine dry breadcrumbs

Chocolate Glaze
2 squares (2 ounces) unsweetened chocolate
2 squares (2 ounces) semisweet chocolate or 1/4 cup chocolate pieces
1/4 cup (1/2 stick) butter, softened and cut up
2 teaspoons honey
Toasted slivered almonds

For Cake
1. Butter sides of an 8-inch round cake pan. Line bottom with kitchen parchment. Set aside.
2. Grind almonds as fine as possible in electric food processor or electric blender. Set aside.
3. Preheat oven to 375F.
4. Melt chocolate in top of a double boiler over hot, not boiling, water.
5. Work butter with an electric beater until very soft and light.
6. Graduallly work in sugar, beating constantly.
7. Once all sugar has been added, add eggs, one at a time, beating hard after each addition. At this point, batter may look curdled, but don't be alarmed.
8. Stir in melted chocolate, ground nuts, orange rind, and breadcrumbs thoroughly.
9. Pour into prepared pan and bake for 25 minutes.
10. Take from oven and cool for 30 minutes on a cake rack.
11. Turn out onto rack. If cake does not drop out easily, give it a good bang with your hands.
12. Lift off and discard parchment. Cool. Center of cake will not seem thoroughly cooked, hence its soft texture and delicious flavor.

For Chocolate Glaze
1. Combine two chocolates, butter, and honey in top of double boiler.
2. Melt over hot water.
3. Remove from heat; beat until cold but still pourable (until it begins to thicken).
4. Place cake on a rack over a piece of waxed paper; pour glaze over all. Smooth sides, if necessary, with a metal spatula.
5. Garland rim of cake with plenty of toasted slivered almonds, placing them close together.

Yield: 6 to 8 servings

SAUCEPAN CHOCOLATE CAKE WITH BUTTERCREAM FROSTING

Cake
2 cups all-purpose flour
2 cups sugar
1 teaspoon soda
1 cup margarine or butter
1 cup water
1/4 cup cocoa
1/2 cup buttermilk
2 eggs
1 teaspoon vanilla

Buttercream Frosting
2/3 cup butter, softened
4 cups powdered sugar
1 teaspoon vanilla
2 to 4 tablespoons half-and-half cream or milk

For Cake
1. Heat oven to 375F. Grease and flour 13x9-inch pan.
2. In medium bowl, combine flour, soda, and sugar; set aside.
3. In large saucepan, combine butter, water and cocoa; heat until blended; remove from heat.
4. Add flour mixture, buttermilk, eggs, and vanilla to saucepan.
5. Using electric hand mixer, beat 2 minutes at medium speed.
6. Pour batter into prepared pan.
7. Bake at 375F for 20 to 30 minutes or until toothpick inserted in center comes out clean. Cool.

For Buttercream Frosting
1. In large bowl, cream butter until light and fluffy.
2. Gradually add powdered sugar, beating well after each addition.
3. Add vanilla and half-and-half; beat until light and of spreading consistency. Frost cake.
4. If desired, sprinkle with chopped nuts; chopped, well drained marashino cherries; coarsely crushed peppermint stick candy; or grated orange peel.

Yield: 12 servings

CHOCOLATE BUTTERMALLOW CAKE

Note: What a way to go!!

1 (18.5-ounce) package devil's food cake mix with pudding

1 cup packed brown sugar
3 tablespoons flour
3/4 cup half-and-half
2 tablespoons margarine or butter
1 teaspoon vanilla
1/2 cup chopped nuts
Marshmallow Frosting (see recipe below)
1/2 ounce melted unsweetened chocolate

Marshmallow Frosting
2 egg whites (1/4 cup)
1-1/2 cups sugar
1/4 teaspoon cream of tartar
1 tablespoon light corn syrup
1/3 cup water
1-1/2 cups miniature marshmallows

For Cake
1. Heat oven to 350F. Grease and flour a 13x9-inch pan.
2. Bake cake mix as directed on package. Cool cake in pan.
3. Stir together sugar and flour in small saucepan.
4. Stir in half-and-half gradually. Cook over medium heat, stirring constantly, until mixture thickens and boils. Boil and stir 1 minute.
5. Remove from heat; blend in margarine and vanilla. Cool.
6. Spread filling over top of cake. Sprinkle nuts over filling.
7. Frost top with marshmallow frosting.
8. Using teaspoon, drizzle melted chocolate in lengthwise lines on frosting; immediately draw a spatula or table knife across lines to form a pattern.

For Marshmallow Frosting
1. Combine egg whites, sugar, cream of tartar, corn syrup, and water in top of double boiler. Blend 1 minute on low speed with electric mixer.
2. Place over boiling water; beat 7 minutes on high speed until stiff peaks form. Remove from heat.
3. Add marshmallows; beat until spreading consistency.

Yield: 16 servings

OLD FASHIONED CHOCOLATE FUDGE CAKE

Note: This one is always a favorite. My husband's uncle owns a chocolate factory and this was the cake I chose to make for his birth-. day. All the family loved it and when they saw the recipe, they were so pleased that it was so easy.

Cake
2 cups flour
2 cups sugar
1-1/2 teaspoons baking soda
1/4 teaspoon salt
1/2 cup cocoa
1 cup oil
1 cup buttermilk
2 eggs, beaten
3 teaspoons vanilla
3/4 cup hot water

Icing
4 tablespoons cocoa
6 tablespoons milk
1 stick butter
1 box (1 pound) powdered sugar
1 tablespoon vanilla
1 cup chopped pecans (optional)

For Cake
1. Sift together flour, sugar, soda, salt, and cocoa.
2. Add oil, buttermilk, eggs, vanilla, and hot water; mix well.
3. Bake in greased, 9x13-inch pan at 350F for 30 to 40 minutes.

For Icing
1. Make a paste of the cocoa and milk in a saucepan.
2. Add butter; bring to a boil, stirring constantly.
3. Remove from heat; add powdered sugar and vanilla.
4. Beat well; add pecans.
5. Pour over hot cake while still in baking pan.

Yield: 16 servings

MISSISSIPPI MUD

Note: This is so rich and gooey. Your sweet tooth will be so glad!

2 sticks margarine
2 cups sugar
1/3 cup cocoa
4 eggs
1 teaspoon vanilla
1-1/2 cups flour
1 cup chopped pecans
Dash salt
1 (8-ounce) jar marshmallow cream
1 stick melted margarine
1/2 cup evaporated milk
1 teaspoon vanilla
1 box powdered sugar
1/2 cup cocoa
Chopped pecans (optional)

1. Cream margarine, sugar, and cocoa; add eggs and vanilla; mix.
2. Add flour, nuts, and salt; beat two minutes.
3. Bake in a greased 9x13-inch pan at 350F for 35 minutes.
4. Spread marshmallow cream on hot cake; cool.
5. Melt one stick of margarine; add milk and vanilla.
6. Stir in powdered sugar and cocoa until smooth.
7. Spread on top of marshmallow cream.
8. Sprinkle with more chopped pecans, if desired.

Yield: 16 servings

CHOCOLATE ICE CREAM CAKE

Note: Don't be confused as my baker once was: the ice cream goes into the cake; it's not a layer when you construct the cake! The ice cream adds a incredible moistness to the cake.

Cake
1 package Pillsbury Plus Devil's Food Cake Mix
1 pint (2 cups) chocolate ice cream, slightly softened
3/4 cup water
3 eggs

Frosting
6 tablespoons all-purpose flour
1 cup milk
1 cup margarine or butter, softened
1 cup sugar
4 ounces (4 squares) unsweetened chocolate, melted and cooled
2 teaspoons vanilla

For Cake
1. Heat oven to 350F. Grease and flour two 9-inch round cake pans.
2. In large bowl, beat all cake ingredients at medium speed for 4 minutes. Pour into prepared pans.
3. Bake at 350F for 35 to 45 minutes or until toothpick inserted in center comes out clean.
4. Cool cake in pans 10 minutes; invert onto cooling racks to cool completely.
5. Split each layer in half horizontally, forming four layers.

For Frosting
1. In small sauce pan, combine flour and milk. Cook over low heat, stirring constantly, until mixture is smooth and thick; cool completely.
2. In large bowl, beat margarine until light and fluffy.
3. Gradually add sugar, beating until well blended.
4. Add cooled milk mixture, chocolate and vanilla; beat until light and fluffy.

Yield: 12 servings

CHOCOLATE PASTRY TORTE

Note: This is a wonderful, different dessert. Please try it the next time you have a dinner party; your guests will be really impressed and pleased.

1 (16-ounce) can chocolate syrup (1-1/2 cups)
2 teaspoons powdered instant coffee
1 teaspoon cinnamon
1 (11-ounce) package pie crust mix or sticks
2 teaspoons vanilla
2 cups chilled whipping cream (do not substitute dessert topping mix for the whipping cream)

1. Heat oven to 425F.
2. Blend syrup, coffee, and cinnamon.
3. Add 1/2 cup syrup mixture to pie crust mix; mix thoroughly.
4. Divide into 6 equal parts.
5. Roll each part into a 7-inch circle on a well floured, cloth-covered board. Trim edges to make even.
6. Place circles on ungreased baking sheets (two on each sheet).
7. Prick with fork.
8. Bake until almost firm - 6 to 8 minutes.
9. Cool pastry circles slightly; loosen while warm with 2 wide spatulas. Cool on wire racks.
10. In chilled bowl, beat remaining syrup mixture, the vanilla, and whipping cream until mixture forms soft peaks.
11. Stack pastry circles, spreading chocolate cream between layers and over top.
12. Refrigerate at least 8 hours.

Yield: 9 to 12 servings

MAHOGANY CHIFFON CAKE

Cake
3/4 cup boiling water
1/2 cup cocoa
1-3/4 cups cake flour or 1-1/2 cups all-purpose flour
1-3/4 cups sugar
1-1/2 teaspoons baking soda
1 teaspoon salt
1/2 cup salad oil
7 egg yolks
2 teaspoons vanilla
1 cup egg whites (7 or 8)
1/2 teaspoon cream of tartar
Chocolate glaze or cake toppings (recipes follow)

1. Blend boiling water and cocoa; set aside to cool.
2. Heat oven to 325F.
3. Stir together flour, sugar, soda, and salt.
4. Make a well and add in order: oil, egg yolks, cooled cocoa mixture, and vanilla. Beat until smooth.
5. Beat egg whites and cream of tartar in large mixer bowl until whites form very stiff peaks.
6. Gradually pour egg yolk mixture over beaten whites, gently folding just until blended.
7. Pour into ungreased 10x4-inch tube pan.
8. Bake until top of cake springs back when touched lightly, 65 to 70 minutes.
9. Invert pan on funnel; let hang until cake is completely cool.
10. Spread with glaze or serve with one of the toppings.
Yield: 12 servings

Chocolate Glaze
1/3 cup margarine or butter
2 ounces unsweetened chocolate
2 cups powdered sugar
1-1/2 teaspoons vanilla
2 to 4 tablespoons hot water

1. Melt butter and chocolate in saucepan over low heat.
2. Remove from heat.
3. Stir in sugar and vanilla.
4. Stir in water, 1 tablespoon at a time, until glaze is desired consistency.

Cocoa Fluff Topping
1 cup chilled whipping cream
1/2 cup powdered sugar
1/4 cup cocoa

In chilled bowl, beat whipping cream, powdered sugar, and cocoa. Also good on chocolate or angel food cake.

Yield: 2 cups

Creme de Cacao Topping

1 cup chilled whipping cream
1/4 cup Cream de Cacao

In chilled bowl, beat whipping cream. Fold in Cream de Cacao. Delicious on any cake.

Yield: 2 cups

Mint Fluff Topping

1 cup chilled whipping cream
3 tablespoons green Creme de Menthe

In chilled bowl, beat 1 cup chilled whipping cream. Fold in Creme de Menthe. Try on angel food cake, too.

Yield: 2 cups

Pink Peppermint Fluff Topping

1 cup chilled whipping cream
1/2 cup crushed peppermint stick candy

In chilled bowl, beat cream. Fold in peppermint stick candy. Also good on chocolate or angel food cake.

Yield: 2-1/2 cups

Chocolate Crunch Topping

1 cup whipping cream
3 (3/4-ounce) chilled chocolate-covered toffee candy bars

In chilled bowl, beat whipping cream. Crush candy bars and fold into whipped cream. Also good on gingerbread, chocolate, or angel food cake.

Yield: 3 cups

CHOCOLATE-CHOCOLATE-CHOCOLATE-CHOCOLATE-CHOCOLATE-CHIP FUDGE CAKE

Note: The name says it all. A chocoholic's delight!!

Cake
2/3 cup unsalted butter, room temperature
2 cups granulated sugar
3 eggs
2 cups sifted all-purpose flour
3/4 cup unsweetened cocoa powder, preferably Dutch processed
1-1/4 teaspoons baking soda
1/4 teaspoon baking powder
1/2 teaspoon salt
1-1/2 cups milk
1 teaspoon vanilla extract
1/4 cup chocolate-mint liqueur, such as Vandermint

Chocolate Fudge Filling
2/3 cup granulated sugar
1/2 cup heavy cream
2-1/2 ounces (2-1/2 squares) unsweetened baking chocolate
1 tablespoon light corn syrup
2 tablespoons unsalted butter

Chocolate Cream
2-1/2 cups heavy cream
3-1/2 tablespoons unsweetened cocoa powder, preferably Dutch processed
7 tablespoons confectioner's sugar

Assembly and Chocolate Syrup
3 tablespoons chocolate chips
2 tablespoons unsweetened cocoa powder, preferably Dutch processed
2 tablespoons light corn syrup
1 tablespoon granulated sugar

For Cake
1. Preheat the oven to 350F.
2. Line two 9-inch round cake pans with waxed paper; butter and flour the pans; tap out any excess flour.
3. In a mixer bowl, beat the butter until light and fluffy.
4. Gradually add the sugar; continue beating until smooth.
5. Beat in the eggs, one at a time, until well-blended.
6. Sift together the flour, cocoa, baking soda, baking powder, and salt.
7. Add to the egg mixture in thirds, alternating with the milk, mixing only until blended.
8. Blend in the vanilla and liqueur.
9. Divide the batter evenly between the two prepared pans.
10. Bake until the tops of the cakes are springy to the touch - 40 to 45 minutes.
11. Remove from the oven; set on racks to cool for 30 minutes.
12. Loosen the edges with a knife and unmold. Peel off the waxed paper.
13. Set the cakes on a rack; let cool completely.

For Chocolate Fudge Filling
1. Combine the sugar, cream, chocolate, and corn syrup in a small heavy saucepan.
2. Bring to a simmer over moderate heat, stirring frequently.
3. Reduce the heat to low; cook for 10 minutes, or until mixture thickens.
4. Remove from heat; dot the top with the butter; let cool to room temperature - about 15 minutes.
5. When cool, stir in the butter until the fudge filling is smooth and creamy.

For Chocolate Cream
1. Beat the cream and cocoa until soft peaks form.
2. Gradually add the confectioner's sugar and continue beating until stiff.

To Assemble
1. Cover one cake layer with all of the fudge filling.
2. Sprinkle evenly with the chocolate chips.
3. Spread 1/2 cup of the chocolate cream on top of the chips.
4. Cover with the second cake layer; cover the top and sides of the cake with half of the remaining chocolate cream.
5. Use the remainder in a pastry bag to decorate the cake as desired.
6. Refrigerate for up to 3 hours before serving time.

For Syrup
1. Combine the cocoa, corn syrup, sugar, and 2 tablespoons of water in a small saucepan.
2. Bring to a simmer over low heat; cook, stirring constantly, for 2 minutes.
3. Cover the syrup to prevent a skin from forming.
4. Just before serving, drizzle the syrup over the top of the cake in a lacy design.

Yield: 10 to 12 servings

CHOCOLATE NUTMEG CAKE

Note: See recipes for Cocoa Buttercream, Chocolate Icing, and European-style Marzipan in next recipe. This cake looks like a chocolate present with a Marzipan bow. The buttercream piping decorates the ribbon.

1 recipe European-style Marzipan (see note)
Powdered sugar
2 cups all-purpose flour
1-1/4 teaspoons baking soda
3/4 teaspoon fresh grated nutmeg
1/2 teaspoon salt
2/3 cup butter or margarine
1-3/4 cups granulated sugar
1 teaspoon vanilla
2 eggs
3 squares (3 ounces) unsweetened chocolate, melted and cooled
1-1/4 cups cold water
1 recipe Cocoa Buttercream (see note)
1 recipe Chocolate Icing (see note)

For Marzipan Ribbon
1. Prepare European-style Marzipan according to recipe directions, except mix in 1 additional tablespoon of water.
2. On surface dusted with powdered sugar, roll half of the marzipan to form a 16x8-inch rectangle. (Wrap and refrigerate the remaining marzipan for another use.)
3. Using a ruler, cut the marzipan lengthwise into 8 strips 1-inch wide and 16 inches long.
4. Wrap 2 strips in clear plastic wrap; refrigerate.
5. Cut the remaining strips into 1-inch lengths (should have 24 strips).
6. Shape each strip to form a loop; pinch ends of each strip together.
7. On a baking sheet, lay each loop on its side; let dry 3 to 4 hours.
8. Cover with plastic wrap and store overnight.

For Cake
1. Grease and lightly flour two 8x8x2-inch baking pans; set aside.
2. Stir together the flour, baking soda, nutmeg, and salt; set aside.
3. In a mixer bowl, beat butter or margarine with electric mixer 30 seconds.
4. Add granulated sugar and vanilla; beat till well combined.
5. Add eggs one at a time, beating on medium speed for 1 minute after each addition.
6. Stir in cooled chocolate.
7. Add the dry ingredients and cold water alternately to beaten mixture.
8. Turn batter into prepared pans.
9. Bake in a 350F oven for 25 to 30 minutes or until cakes test done.
10. Cool in pans 10 minutes on wire racks. Remove from pans and cool thoroughly.

To Assemble

1. Spread about 1 cup cocoa buttercream between cake layers.
2. Spread the chocolate icing on top and sides of cake.
3. Let the icing partially dry in refrigerator before adding the marzipan ribbon.
4. For ribbon, unwrap and place the reserved strips of marzipan, centered over top and down sides of cake, crossing in center.
5. Using pastry fitted with writing tip, pipe the buttercream along edges and two lines, side by side, down centers of ribbons.
6. Place a dollop of the cocoa buttercream where marzipan ribbon strips meet on top.
7. Arrange loops of marzipan ribbon, one at a time, in a dollop of buttercream, piping buttercream along the edges and two lines, side by side, down centers of loops as they are placed in buttercream.
8. Pipe small dots of buttercream on the chocolate icing.
9. Store cake in refrigerator until serving time.

Yield: 12 servings

COCOA BUTTERCREAM, CHOCOLATE ICING, EUROPEAN-STYLE MARZIPAN

Cocoa Buttercream
4 egg yolks
2/3 cup sugar
1/3 cup unsweetened cocoa powder
1/4 cup water
1 cup butter or margarine

1. In small mixer bowl, beat egg yolks at high speed for 5 minutes, until thick and lemon colored; set aside.
2. In a small saucepan, stir together sugar, cocoa, and water.
3. Bring mixture to a boil, stirring till dissolved.
4. Cook over medium heat, stirring constantly, till mixture reaches the soft ball stage (236F degrees).
5. Quickly pour hot mixture in a steady stream over beaten egg yolks, beating till mixture is thick and smooth; cool 15 minutes.
6. Beat in butter, one tablespoon at a time.

Yield: 2 cups

Chocolate Icing
1/2 cup sugar
4 teaspoons cornstarch
1/4 teaspoons salt
2/3 cup water
1 square (1 ounce) unsweetened chocolate, cut up

1. In a saucepan combine sugar, cornstarch, and salt.
2. Stir in water; add chocolate.
3. Cook and stir till chocolate is melted and mixture is thickened and bubbly. Cook and stir 2 minutes more. Remove from heat; stir in vanilla.
4. Cool for 5 minutes.

Yield: 3/4 cup

European-style Marzipan

1 cup (6 ounces) whole blanched almonds or 1-1/3 cups slivered almonds
1-1/3 cups sifted powdered sugar
2 tablespoons water
1/2 teaspoon almond extract
2-1/4 cups sifted powdered sugar
1 tablespoons slightly beaten egg white
Few drops desired food coloring (optional)

1. Place the whole blanched almonds or slivered almonds in a blender or food processor. Cover and blend or process until nuts are ground.
2. In a mixer bowl, beat together the ground almonds, the 1-1/3 cups powdered sugar, the water, and almond extract until mixture forms a ball. Beat in the remaining powdered sugar.
3. Stir in enough egg white to form a claylike mixture.
4. Tint with a few drops food coloring, if desired.
5. Mold the nut mixture by using mint molds lightly dusted with powdered sugar, or shape the nut mixture as desired.
6. Store the marzipan mixture in a covered container at room temperature.

Yield: 2 cups

VIENNESE CHOCOLATE TORTE

Torte
11 tablespoons unsalted butter, softened
6 tablespoons all-purpose flour
3 ounces semisweet chocolate
1/2 cup sugar
3 eggs, separated, at room temperature
6 tablespoons finely ground walnuts
1 cup canned, pitted, tart red cherries, drained

Glaze
6 ounces semisweet chocolate
1/4 cup strongly brewed coffee

For Torte
1. Preheat the oven to 350F.
2. Using 1 tablespoon of the butter and 2 tablespoons of the flour, lightly grease and flour a 9-inch springform pan; tap excess flour and set aside.
3. In a double boiler, melt the chocolate over boiling water; cool to room temperature.
4. Meanwhile, in a large bowl, beat the remaining 10 tablespoons butter until creamy.
5. Gradually beat in the sugar until the mixture is light and fluffy.
6. Beat in the melted chocolate and then the egg yolks one at a time.
7. In a separate bowl, combine the walnuts and the remaining flour.
8. Working in three additions, gently fold the egg whites into the chocolate mixture alternately with the walnut mixture.
9. Spoon the mixture into the prepared pan and shake it until evenly distributed.
10. Pat the cherries dry with paper towels; scatter them evenly over the top of the batter.
11. Bake for 50 to 55 minutes, or until a cake tester inserted in the center comes out clean.
12. Cool the torte thoroughly on a rack; remove the springform ring.

For Glaze
1. Place the chocolate and the coffee in the top portion of a double boiler set over boiling water.
2. Stir occasionally until the chocolate is melted.

To Assemble
1. Spread the glaze over the top and sides of the torte.
2. Chill until the glaze has set.
3. Cut into thin slices to serve.

Yield: 8 to 10 servings

QUEEN OF SHEBA CAKE

Cake
4 ounces semisweet chocolate
1 stick unsalted butter
3 egg yolks
2/3 cup sugar
1/2 teaspoon vanilla
1-1/3 cups ground almonds
1/3 cup flour, sifted
4 egg whites

Glaze
4 ounces semisweet chocolate
4 tablespoons unsalted butter

For Cake
1. Preheat oven to 350F.
2. In a small pan, melt chocolate over low heat. Cool to room temperature.
3. In a mixing bowl, cream butter and mix in melted, cooled chocolate.
4. Add egg yolks, one by one, and half of the sugar, beating well after each addition.
5. Mix in vanilla.
6. Fold in ground almonds and then flour.
7. In another bowl, whip egg whites just until they are stiff.
8. Add remaining half of the sugar; beat until egg whites are glossy - about 30 seconds more.
9. Stir 1/4 of the egg whites into chocolate mixture; then fold in the rest of them.
10. Pour mixture into an 8-inch buttered and floured cake pan.
11. Bake until cake shrinks slightly from sides of the pan and the top springs back when lightly pressed with a fingertip - about 30 minutes.
12. Cool cake in pan for a few minutes before turning it out onto a cake rack to cool completely. At this point, cake can be stored in an air-tight container for a week.

For Glaze
1. A few hours before servng, melt chocolate with butter over very low heat. Stir gently.
2. Put cake on a rack and spread warm glaze over its top and sides, working quickly to finish before glaze sets.

Yield: 8 to 10 servings

ORANGE FUDGE MARBLE LOAF CAKES

1 package Pillsbury Plus Fudge Marble Cake Mix
1 cup dairy sour cream
1/3 cup oil
3 eggs
2 tablespoons grated orange peel
1/2 cup currants or chopped raisins
2 tablespoons water
1/2 cup orange juice
2 tablespoons sugar

1. Heat oven to 350F.
2. Grease two 8x4-inch loaf pans; line with waxed paper and grease and flour again.
3. Trim waxed paper evenly with edges of pan.
4. In large bowl, blend cake mix (reserve marble pouch), sour cream, oil, and eggs at low speed until moistened; beat 2 minutes at highest speed.
5. Pour 1 cup batter into small bowl; set aside.
6. To remaining batter, add orange peel; blend well.
7. Divide evenly between 2 prepared pans.
8. To reserved batter, add marble pouch from cake mix package, currants, and water; blend well.
9, Pour evenly over batter in pans.
10. Marble with knife in a folding motion, turning the pan while folding.
11. Bake at 350F for 50 to 60 minutes or until toothpick inserted in center comes clean.
12. Cool for 5 minutes.
13. Combine orange juice and sugar; pour slowly and evenly over warm cakes. Cool completely.
14. Remove from pans; remove and discard waxed paper.
15. For best flavor, store cake, tightly wrapped, overnight in refrigerator.

Yield: 12 to 16 servings

COCOA-NUT LAYER CAKE

Cake
1/2 cup unsweetened cocoa
1/2 cup boiling water
1-3/4 cups unsifted all-purpose flour
1 teaspoon baking powder
1 teaspoon baking soda
1/8 teaspoon salt
1/2 cup butter or regular margarine, softened
2 cups granulated sugar
2 eggs
1 teaspoon vanilla extract
1-1/3 cups buttermilk
1/2 cup finely chopped pistachio nuts or walnuts
1 cup heavy cream

Chocolate Frosting
1/3 cup light cream
1/3 cup butter or regular margarine
2/3 cup unsweetened cocoa
2-2/3 cups sifted confectioner's sugar
1 teaspoon light corn syrup
1 teaspoon vanilla extract
1/4 cup coarsely chopped pistachio nuts or walnuts

For Cake
1. In small bowl, mix cocoa with boiling water. Cool completely.
2. Preheat oven to 350F.
3. Grease and flour three 8x8x1-1/2-inch layer-cake pans.
4. Sift flour, baking powder, soda, and salt.
5. In large bowl of electric mixer, combine the butter, sugar, eggs, and vanilla.
6. Beat at high speed until fluffy - about 5 minutes - occasionally scraping side of bowl and guiding mixture into beaters with rubber scraper.
7. At low speed, blend in flour mixture (in fourths), alternately with buttermilk, beginning and ending with flour mixture. Beat just until smooth.
8. Measure 1-2/3 cups batter into a small bowl. Stir in 1/2 cup chopped nuts; pour into one of the prepared pans.
10. Add cocoa mixture to remaining batter; mix until smooth; divide evenly between other prepared pans.
11. Bake 30 to 35 minutes, until cake tester inserted in center of cake comes out clean.
12. Cool 10 minutes on rack; remove from pans; cool completely.
13. Whip heavy cream until stiff; refrigerate.

For Frosting
1. In saucepan, heat cream until bubbles form; remove from heat.
2. Add the hot cream to butter, cocoa, 1-1/2 cups confectioner's sugar, corn syrup, and vanilla.
3. With portable mixer or wooden spoon, beat frosting until smooth.
4. Add remaining confectioner's sugar, beating until smooth and thick enough to spread.

To Assemble
1. Place one chocolate layer on cake plate, right side down; spread with half of the whipped cream.
2. Place the nut cake layer on next; spread with rest of whipped cream.
3. Top with remaining chocolate layer, right side up.
4. With spatula, spread frosting on the side and top.
5. Garnish top edge of cake with the coarsely chopped nuts.
6. Refrigerate until serving.

Yield: 12 servings

PIG PICKIN' CAKE

Cake
1 yellow cake mix
1 large can mandarin oranges and juice
4 eggs
1 cup vegetable oil

Icing
1 (3-inch size) can crushed pineapple
1 medium-sized container Cool Whip
1 small package vanilla instant pudding

For Cake
1. Combine cake mix, juice from mandarin oranges, eggs, and oil in a large bowl.
2. Blend on high speed for 3 minutes.
3. Stir in mandarin oranges.
4. Pour into two 9-inch cake pans and bake as directed on cake mix box.

For Icing
1. Combine pudding mix and juice from crushed pineapple.
2. Mix with a spoon until stiff.
3. Add Cool Whip and pineapple.
4. Spread icing between cooked cake layers and on top and sides of cake.

Yield: 16 servings

BLACK FOREST CHERRY CAKE

Note: This is the best Black Forest Cake I've ever had.

Cherry Filling
2 cans (16 ounces) pitted tart red cherries, drained, reserving
   2/3 cup juice
2/3 cup granulated sugar
1/4 cup cornstarch

Chocolate Buttercream
3 tablespoons butter
2 cups sifted powdered sugar
1 ounce unsweetened chocolate, melted and cooled
2 tablespoons light cream
1 teaspoon vanilla

Cake
2 egg whites
1-1/2 cups granulated sugar
1-3/4 cups sifted cake flour
3/4 teaspoon baking soda
1 teaspoon salt
1/3 cup cooking oil
1 cup milk
2 egg yolks
2 ounces unsweetened chocolate, melted and cooled
1 teaspoon unflavored gelatin
2 tablespoons cold water
3 cups whipping cream
1/2 cup Kirshwasser or cherry liqueur
3/4 cup toasted sliced almonds
1 ounce semisweet chocolate, shaved

For Cherry Filling
1. Combine all ingredients and cook until mixture is thick and bubbly.
Cool.
For Chocolate Buttercream
1. Mix all ingredients until of piping consistency--one or two teaspoons of cream may have to be added.

For Cake
1. Beat egg whites; gradually add 1/2 cup sugar; beat until stiff peaks
form.
2. Sift flour, rest of sugar, soda, and salt; add oil and 1/2 cup
milk; beat 1 minute; add rest of the milk and egg yolks.
3. Fold in egg whites.
4. Pour 1/3 batter into lightly greased and floured 9-inch round cake
pan.
5. Add chocolate to remaining batter; pour chocolate mixture into 2
lightly greased and floured 9-inch cake pans.
6. Bake all 3 layers in 350F oven for 20 to 25 minutes. Cool.

To Assemble

1. Soften gelatin in water; heat just until dissolved.
2. Whip cream, add gelatin; beat until soft peaks form.
3. Place one chocolate layer on serving plate; fill pastry bag with Chocolate Buttercream.
4. Pipe three rings of buttercream 1-inch apart; fill area in between with cherry filling; spread a thin layer of whipped cream on top.
5. Place yellow cake layer atop; drizzle Kirsch over very slowly.
6. Pipe a ring of whipped cream on outside of layer and fill center with cherry filling.
7. Place second chocolate layer atop.
8. Frost cake with remaining whipped cream.
9. Press almonds onto sides and sprinkle shaved chocolate on top.
10. Make rosettes with whipped cream and garnish with maraschino cherries. Chill.

Yield: 18 servings

CHOCOLATE BOURBON CAKE

Note: This very rich, mousse-like cake is perfect for a large crowd during the holidays. It freezes very well.

This recipe must be made ahead.

2 cups butter
1 cup sugar
1 cup powdered sugar
1 dozen eggs, separated
4 ounces unsweetened chocolate, melted
1 teaspoon vanilla extract
1 cup chopped pecans
1 dozen double ladyfingers
1 pound dry Italian macaroons (approximately 4 dozen), broken and soaked
  in 1 cup bourbon
1-1/2 cups heavy cream, whipped

1. Cream butter and sugars until light and fluffy.
2. Beat egg yolks until light; blend into butter mixture.
3. Beat in chocolate; add vanilla and pecans.
4. Beat egg whites until stiff but not dry; fold into chocolate mixture.
5. Line a 10-inch springform pan around sides and bottom with split ladyfingers.
6. Alternate layers of soaked macaroons and chocolate mixture over ladyfingers. You should have two layers of each.
7. Chill overnight.
8. Remove sides of springform pan and cover top with whipped cream. If it is frozen, add whipped cream after defrosting.

Yield: 16 to 18 servings

CHOCOLATE AND VANILLA BUTTER CAKE

Note: The first time we made this in the cafe, we had lots of requests to do it again. It is a wonderful birthday cake.

Chocolate Syrup
1/2 cup sifted unsweetened cocoa powder, preferably Dutch process
1/4 cup sugar
1/4 cup light corn syrup
1/2 cup water
Pinch of salt
1/2 teaspoon vanilla

Cake
3/4 cup Chocolate Syrup (see recipe above)
3-1/4 cups sifted, unbleached, all-purpose flour
2-1/8 teaspoons baking powder
1/2 teaspoon salt
1 cup milk
2-1/2 teaspoons vanilla
1 cup unsalted butter, room temperature
2 cups granulated sugar
4 jumbo eggs
1/4 teaspoon baking soda
Chocolate Glaze (see recipe below)

Chocolate Glaze
3 ounces unsweetened chocolate, coarsely chopped
6 tablespoons unsalted butter, cut into 6 pieces
1/2 cup sugar
Pinch of salt
1/4 cup milk
1 tablespoon cornstarch
1/4 cup light cream or half-and-half
1 teaspoon vanilla

For Chocolate Syrup
1. Combine cocoa, sugar, corn syrup, water, and salt in small heavy saucepan; stir over low heat until blended.
2. Still on low heat, heat mixture to boiling; cook, stirring constantly until mixture is smooth - about 2 minutes.
3. Remove from heat; stir in vanilla.
4. Cool to room temperature.

For Cake
1. Heat oven to 350F.
2. Butter and flour a 10-inch tube pan, plain or fluted, preferably a bundt pan.
3. Sift 3-1/4 cups flour, the baking powder, and salt onto sheet of waxed paper or into bowl.
4. Combine milk and vanilla in separate bowl.
5. Beat 1 cup butter in mixer bowl on moderately high speed until light and fluffy - about 3 minutes.

6.   Add granulated sugar in two additions, beating for 2 minutes after each addition.
7.   Add eggs, one at a time, beating thoroughly after each addition.
8.   After all the eggs have been added, beat mixture on high speed for 2 minutes, scraping down sides of bowl often with rubber spatula.
9.   On low speed, beat in flour mixture in three additions and milk mixture in two, beginning and ending with flour mixture.
10. Pour two thirds of batter into prepared pan.
11. Combine chocolate syrup mixture into remaining third of batter, blending well.
12. Pour chocolate batter evenly over top of vanilla batter; do not stir chocolate batter in.
13. Bake in lower third of oven until wooden pick inserted into cake is withdrawn clean and dry - about 55 minutes.
14. Cool cake in pan 10 minutes.
15. Turn out of pan onto wire rack to cool completely; if plain tube pan was used, invert cake onto second rack to cool right side up.
16. Make Chocolate Glaze.
17. Thirty minutes before serving, pour Chocolate Glaze evenly over cake.

For Chocolate Glaze
1.   Heat chocolate, butter, sugar, and salt in small heavy saucepan over low heat, stirring occasionally, until chocolate and butter are melted and sugar is dissolved.
2.   Meanwhile, stir milk into cornstarch in cup; blend well.
3.   Add milk/cornstarch mixture and light cream to chocolate mixture in saucepan.
4.   Heat over medium heat to boiling, stirring constantly.
5.   Remove from heat; stir in vanilla.
6.   Let glaze cool for 2 minutes, stirring occasionally.
7.   Transfer to measuring cup or other container with a lip before pouring over cooled cake.

Yield: 12 servings

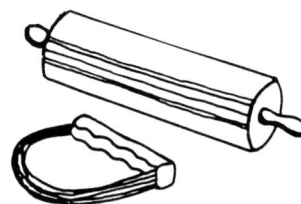

BLACK AND WHITE LAYER CAKE

White Sponge Sheet
5 eggs (large or extra-large), separated
1/3 cup granulated sugar
1 teaspoon vanilla extract
1/4 cup sifted all-purpose flour
Pinch of salt
Pinch of cream of tartar

Chocolate Sponge Sheet
6 ounces semisweet chocolate
1 teaspoon instant coffee (powdered or granular)
1/4 cup boiling water
4 large eggs, separated
1/3 cup granulated sugar
1 teaspoon vanilla extract
1/3 cup sifted all-purpose flour
Pinch of salt
Pinch of cream of tartar

Chocolate Buttercream
6 ounces semisweet chocolate
2 tablespoons heavy cream
8 ounces (2 sticks) plus 1 tablespoon unsalted butter
7 egg yolks
1 cup strained confectioner's sugar
Pinch of salt
1 teaspoon vanilla extract

For White Sponge Sheet
1. Adjust a rack to the middle of the oven.
2. Preheat the oven to 350F.
3. Line a 10-1/2x15-1/2x1-inch jelly roll pan with foil.
4. Butter the foil by placing a piece of butter in the pan and placing the pan in the oven to melt the butter.
5. Brush the butter all over the foil. Set aside.
6. Place the yolks in the small bowl of an electric mixer.
7. Add 3 tablespoons of the sugar and the vanilla and beat at high speed for a few minutes until pale (almost white) and thick.
8. On low speed add the sifted flour, scraping the bowl with a rubber spatula, and beating only until smooth.
9. Transfer the mixture to a larger mixing bowl. (It is easier to fold in a large bowl.)
10. Using a small bowl, beat the egg whites with the salt and cream of tartar until they hold a soft shape.
11. Gradually add the reserved sugar and beat until the whites hold a definite shape but are not dry.
12. Fold about a third of the whites into the yolks--don't be too thorough--and then fold the remaining whites into the yolks, folding carefully only until blended.
13. Transfer the mixture to the prepared pan. Spread it smooth.
14. Bake for 20 to 23 minutes until the top springs back when it is lightly pressed with a fingertip and the cake begins to pull away from the sides of the pan.

15. Place a long piece of wax paper over the baked cake.
16. Cover with a flat cookie sheet.
17. Holding them firmly together, invert the cake pan and the cookie sheet.
18. Remove the cake pan; carefully peel off the foil. Do not allow the cake to remain upside down any longer than necessary or the top will stick to the paper.
19. Quickly cover the cake with another cookie sheet; turn over again; remove wax paper; leave cake right side up to cool.

For Chocolate Sponge Sheet

1. Prepare the oven and the jelly roll pan as in the above directions for the White Sponge Sheet.
2. Break up or coarsely chop the chocolate; place it in the top of a small double boiler over hot water on moderate heat.
3. Dissolve the coffee in the water; add to the chocolate.
4. Stir occasionally until the chocolate is melted.
5. Remove the top of the double boiler; set it aside to cool slightly.
6. In the small bowl of an electric mixer, beat the yolks with 3 tablespoons of the sugar and the vanilla.
7. Beat for a few minutes until the mixture is thick and pale.
8. On low speed, add the tepid chocolate, scraping the bowl with a rubber spatula and beating only until mixed.
9. Mix in the flour.
10. Remove from the mixer; transfer to a larger bowl.
11. Using a small bowl, beat the egg whites with the salt and cream of tartar until they hold soft shape.
12. Gradually add the reserved sugar; continue to beat until the whites hold a definite shape but are not dry.
13. Fold about one-third of the remaining whites into the chocolate mixture--do not be too thorough--and then fold in the remaining whites, folding carefully only until blended; do not handle any more than necessary.
14. Turn the batter into the prepared jelly roll pan and spread it smooth.
15. Bake at 350F for 15 minutes or until it feels set and firm when lightly pressed with a fingertip.
16. Cover the cake with a long piece of wax paper; cover the paper with a flat cookie sheet; invert the pan and the sheet.
17. Remove the pan and gently peel off the foil; quickly cover with another cookie sheet and turn over again; remove the wax paper; leave the cake right side up to cool.

For Chocolate Buttercream

1. Break up or coarsely chop the chocolate; place it in the top of a small double boiler over hot water on low heat.
2. Add the heavy cream and 1 tablespoon of the butter.
3. Stir until smooth.
4. Meanwhile, in the small bowl of an electric mixer, beat the egg yolks at high speed for a few minutes until pale and thick.
5. On low speed, gradually add the warm chocolate mixture, scraping the bowl constantly with a rubber spatula.
6. Transfer the mixture to the top of the double boiler over hot water on low heat; cook for 5 minutes, scraping the bottom and sides con-

stantly with a rubber spatula. The mixture must never get really hot.
7. Transfer the chocolate mixture to a mixing bowl.
8. Place some ice water in a larger mixing bowl.
9. Place the bowl of chocolate into the bowl of ice water; stir gently
until the chocolate cools to tepid.
10. Meanwhile, in the large bowl of an electric mixer, beat the reserved
2 sticks of butter with the confectioner's sugar, salt, and vanilla
until soft and smooth.
11. Add the chocolate mixture; continue to beat for just a minute or
two until smooth, creamy, and gorgeous.

To Assemble

1. You will need a long, narrow, flat serving tray - a chocolate-roll
board (measuring about 5x18-inches) is perfect.
2. Use a ruler and toothpicks to mark the cakes, the long way, into
thirds (you will have three strips measuring 15-1/2x3-1/2-inches). It
is important that they are all the same width. Use a long, thin, sharp
knife to cut the cakes.
3. Carefully place a strip of white cake on the serving tray or board.
4. Spread a thin layer of buttercream over the cake; the buttercream
should completely cover the cake, but keep it thin or you will not have
enough.
5. Now place a chocolate layer on top. (The chocolate cake is fragile
and does not want to cooperate, cut the chocolate strip crosswise into
2 or 3 pieces, and transfer each piece separately, using a metal spatula.)
6. Spread more buttercream over the chocolate layer.
7. Continue to alternate white and chocoalte layers with buttercream
between them.
8. Do not ice the top and sides yet. Reserve the remaining buttercream
at room temperature.
9. Make room for the cake in the freezer or refrigerator.
10. Cover the top of the cake with a piece of plastic wrap.
11. To flatten cake slightly - and to level the top - place a tray or a
cookie sheet or another chocolate-roll board on top of cake.
12. Place in freezer for about half an hour or in the refrigerator for
a little longer.
13. Just before you are ready to finish icing the cake, beat the reserved buttercream well with the mixer.
14. Spread it to coat the top and sides completely.
15. Reserve about 1/2 cup or so of the buttercream to use as decoration.
16. Place the 1/2 cup buttercream in a pastry bag fitted with a small
star-shaped tip.
17. Form a row of small rosettes touching each other on each long edge
of the top. Wow - gorgeous!
18. Refrigerate the cake and serve it cold.

Yield: 10 to 12 servings

ᴛE MOUSSE CAKE

)aking chocolate, preferably Van Leer
:ter, cut into small pieces

;ugar

tened cocoa powder
oner's sugar

ᴈd chocolate
ɪtter, cut into small pieces

;25F.
and sides of 8-inch springform pan.
late and 1/2 cup butter in top of double boiler over
ɪeat, stirring frequently, until chocolate is melted.
eat; let cool.
5. Beat egg yolks and granulated sugar in large bowl until light and lemon colored.
6. Add cooled chocolate mixture, stirring to blend thoroughly.
7. Beat egg whites in medium bowl with clean beaters until stiff peaks form.
8. Stir half the egg whites into chocolate batter to lighten; fold in remaining whites.
9. Pour batter into prepared pan.
10. Bake until wooden pick inserted in center of cake is withdrawn clean - about 1 hour.
11. Remove to wire rack; let cool 15 to 20 minutes.
12. Remove sides of pan; invert cake onto serving plate to cool completely.
13. While cake is cooling, make Chocolate Icing.
14. Spread icing evenly over top and sides of cake, using thin, flexible metal spatula.
15. Sieve cocoa powder evenly over cake; sieve confectioner's sugar evenly over cocoa powder.

For Chocolate Icing
1. Combine chocolate and butter in top of double boiler over simmering water; heat, stirring frequently, until chocolate is melted.
2. Remove from heat; let cool.
3. Beat egg yolks and sugar in large bowl until light and lemon colored.
4. Add cooled chocolate mixture, stirring to blend thoroughly.
5. Beat egg whites in medium bowl with clean beaters until stiff peaks form.
6. Beat half the egg whites into chocolate mixture to lighten; fold in remaining whites.
7. Use immediately.

Yield: 10 servings

SUPER CHOCOLATE CAKE

Cake
Fine, dry bread crumbs
4 squares unsweetened chocolate
3/4 cup boiling water
3 cups all-purpose flour
2-1/2 teaspoons baking powder
1-1/2 teaspoons baking soda
1/2 teaspoon salt
1-1/4 cups butter or margarine, softened
1 tablespoon vanilla
1-1/2 cups granulated sugar
1 cup firmly packed, light brown sugar
5 eggs
1-1/2 cups dairy sour cream
Rich Chocolate Frosting (see recipe below)
Pecans or walnuts

Rich Chocolate Frosting
4 squares unsweetened chocolate
3 tablespoons butter or margarine
1 (8-ounce) carton dairy sour cream
1-1/2 teaspoons vanilla
1/4 teaspoon salt
1 pound confectioner's sugar

For Cake
1. Grease three 9-inch layer cake pans; sprinkle with fine, dry bread crumbs to coat lightly.
2. Combine chocolate and water in a small heavy saucepan.
3. Stir over low heat until chocolate melts and mixture is smooth; cool.
4. Sift flour, baking powder, baking soda, and salt onto wax paper.
5. Beat butter or margarine in a large bowl of electric mixer at high speed until soft.
6. Add vanilla, granulated sugar, and brown sugar; beat until fluffy.
7. Add eggs, one at a time, beating well after each addition.
8. Blend cooled chocolate into sour cream in a medium bowl until smooth.
9. Add all at once to egg mixture, beating just until well mixed.
10. Add sifted dry ingredients about 1/4 at a time, mixing by hand after each addition.
11. Divide batter evenly among prepared pans.
12. Bake in 375F oven for 35 minutes or until layers come away from sides of pans.
13. Cool in pans on wire racks 5 minutes; loosen cakes around edges of pans and turn out; cool on racks.
14. Put cake together and frost with Rich Chocolate Frosting.
15. Garnish with pecan or walnut halves.

For Rich Chocolate Frosting
1. Melt chocolate with butter or margarine in top of double boiler over simmering water.
2. Stir until smooth; cool at least 15 minutes.

3. Combine sour cream, vanilla, and salt in small bowl of electric mixer.
4. Gradually beat in confectioner's sugar at low speed; when smooth, increase speed; beat in cooled chocolate.
5. If mixture is not thick enough to spread and hold swirls, set bowl in a larger bowl or pan filled with ice and water.
6. Continue stirring and folding until mixture thickens and holds its shape.

Yield: 16 servings

KAHLUA CAKE

3/4 cup butter, softened
2 cups sugar
3/4 cup cocoa
4 eggs, separated
1 teaspoon baking soda
2 tablespoons cold water
1/2 cup cold coffee
1-1/2 cups Kahlua
1-3/4 cups cake flour
1 tablespoon vanilla extract
1/2 cup powdered sugar
Whipped cream to garnish
Strawberries to garnish

1. Cream butter and sugar well; add cocoa and one egg yolk at a time, beating well.
2. Dissolve soda in water; combine soda, coffee, and 1/2 cup Kahlua.
3. Add liquids to creamed mixture alternately with flour.
4. Stir in vanilla.
5. Fold in stiffly beaten egg whites.
6. Pour into a greased and floured 10-inch bundt pan.
7. Bake at 325F for 45 minutes or until done.
8. Remove cake from pan while warm; pierce cake with fork.
9. For glaze, combine remaining Kahlua and powdered sugar until smooth and pour over cake.
10. Cover and store in refrigerator.
11. Garnish with whipped cream and strawberries, if desired.

Yield: 16 servings

PERFECT APPLE PIE

Note: Good pie apples are tart, firm, and juicy, such as Northern Spy, Greening, and McIntosh.

In rolling pastry, it's best to use a pastry cloth. Rub flour well into cloth, and brush off excess, then roll out with covered rolling pin. This keeps pastry from sticking without picking up excess flour. Roll Roll pastry from center out, using light strokes and alternating directions to form an even circle.

1 (9-1/2- to 11-ounce) package pie crust mix
1 cup sugar
2 tablespoons flour
1 teaspoon cinnamon
1/8 teaspoon nutmeg
1/4 teaspoon salt
7 cups thinly sliced, pared, tart cooking apples (2-1/2 pounds)
2 tablespoons lemon juice
2 tablespoons butter or margarine
Ice cream or cheddar cheese

1. Make pastry as package label directs.
2. Handling gently, shape pastry into a ball.
3. Divide in half; form each half into a round; then flatten each with palm of hand.
4. On lightly floured pastry cloth, roll out half of pastry into a 12-inch circle, using a ball-bearing rolling pin.
5. Roll with light strokes from center to edge, lifting rolling pin as you reach edge.
6. Place a 9-inch, heat-resistant glass pie plate on pastry circle; it should measure 1 inch wider all around.
7. Fold rolled pastry in half; carefully transfer to pie plate, making sure fold is in center of pie plate.
8. Unfold pastry, and fit carefully into pie plate, pressing gently with fingers, so pastry fits snugly all around. Do not strech pastry.
9. Refrigerate until ready to use.
10 Preheat oven to 425F.
11 In small bowl, mix sugar, flour, cinnamon, nutmeg, and salt.
12 In large bowl, toss the apples with the lemon juice.
13 Add sugar mixture to sliced apples; toss lightly to combine.
14 Roll out remaining pastry into 12-inch circle.
15 Fold over in quarters; cut slits for steam vents.
16 Turn apple mixture into pastry-lined pie plate, mounding up high in center. This supports top crust.
17 Dot apples with butter cut in small pieces.
18 Using scissors, trim overhanging edge of pastry so it measures 1/2-inch from rim of pie plate.
19 Carefully place folded pastry so that point is at the center of filling, and gently unfold.
20 Using scissors, trim overhanging edge of pastry (for top crust), so it measures 1 inch from edge all around.
21. Moisten the edge of the bottom pastry with a little water.
22. Fold top pastry under edge of bottom pastry.
23. With fingers, press edges together to seal, so juices won't run

out.
24. Press upright to form a standing rim.
25. Crimp edge: place thumb on edge of pastry at an angle. Pinch dough between index finger and thumb. Repeat at same angle all around.
26. Bake 45 to 50 minutes, or until apples are fork-tender and crust is golden.
27. Serve warm with ice cream or cheddar cheese.

Yield: 8 servings

PECAN PIE

1 unbaked 9-inch pie crust
4 eggs
1 cup dark brown sugar
3/4 cup light corn syrup
1/2 teaspoon salt
1/4 cup melted sweet butter
1 teaspoon vanilla extract
2 cups shelled pecans, chopped
1/3 cup shelled pecan halves

1. Preheat oven to 400F.
2. Beat eggs well in a large bowl.
3. Add brown sugar, corn syrup, salt, melted butter, and vanilla to the eggs; mix thoroughly.
4. Sprinkle chopped pecans in pastry-lined pan.
5. Pour egg mixture over pecans.
6. Arrange pecan halves around edge of filling next to crust for decoration.
7. Set on the middle rack of the oven; bake for 25 to 30 minutes longer, or until set.
8. Remove from oven; let cool to room temperature before serving.

Yield: 8 servings

COLORADO HIGH PIE

Crumb Crust
1-1/4 cups graham cracker crumbs
1/4 cup granulated sugar
1/4 (scant) teaspoon nutmeg
1/2 stick unsalted butter, melted

Apple Filling
2 pounds firm and tart apples (3 to 4 large apples, such as Granny
   Smith)
2 tablespoons unsalted butter
3 tablespoons granulated sugar

Rum Chiffon Bavarian
1 envelope unflavored gelatin
1/4 cup cold tap water
3/4 cup milk
3 eggs (large or extra large), separated, plus 1 egg white
1/2 cup granulated sugar
1 teaspoon vanilla extract
1/4 cup dark rum
1 cup heavy cream
Pinch of salt

Whipped Cream Topping
1 cup heavy cream
1/2 teaspoon vanilla extract
2 tablespoons confectioner's or granulated sugar
Shaved semisweet chocolate (optional)

For Crumb Crust
1. Adjust a rack to the center of the oven and preheat the oven to
375F.
2. Mix together the crust ingredients.
3. Press the mixture into a 9-inch pie pan.
4. Bake in preheated oven for 10 minutes. Cool.

For Apple Filling
1. Peel, quarter, and core the apples.
2. Cut each piece in half the long way; then cut crossways into
slices 1/2- to 3/4-inch wide.
3. Melt the butter in a frying pan with a tight cover.
4. Add the apples and sugar; stir to mix; cover tightly; cook over
moderate heat for a few minutes until the apples have given off their
juice.
5. Uncover; stir over high heat until the apples are tender and all
of the liquid has evaporated. The mixture should be like a chunky
applesauce.
6. If the liquid evaporates before the apples are tender, cover the
pan again, reduce the heat a bit, and let the apples steam, then uncover
and stir over high heat again to dry a bit if necessary. Do not overcook.
7. Set aside the pan; let the apples cool. The apples can be used
soon or can be refrigerated until you are ready for them.

For Rum Chiffon Bavarian
1. Sprinkle the gelatin over the water in a small cup; let stand.
2. Heat the milk, uncovered, over moderate heat until scalded.
3. In the top of a double boiler, off the heat, stir the yolks just to mix.
4. When the milk has formed a slightly wrinkled skin on its surface, gradually add it to the yolks, stirring as you do.
5. Stir in 1/4 cup of the sugar.
6. Place the top of the double boiler over hot water; cook on moderately high heat, scraping sides and bottom continuously, until mixture thickens enough to coat a spoon (180F on a candy thermometer).
7. Add the softened gelatin; stir to dissolve.
8. Transfer the mixture to a medium-sized bowl and stir in the vanilla and rum.
9. Place the bowl of custard into a larger bowl of ice water.
10. Stir constantly until mixture has cooled but not thickened. Set aside.
11. In chilled bowl, whip the cream until it holds a definite shape but not really stiff; set aside.
12. In a small bowl, beat the 4 egg whites with the salt until they hold a soft shape.
13. Reduce the speed to moderate, gradually add 1/4 cup sugar, increase speed to high; continue to beat until the whites hold a definite shape, but not too stiff. Set aside.
14. Return the custard mixture to the ice water; stir constantly until it barely begins to thicken.
15. Gradually fold it (about 1/3 at a time) into the whipped cream; fold this mixture and the whites together. Do not handle any more than necessary; keep it light and airy.

To Assemble
1. Spread the apples in the crust.
2. Create some temporary room for the pie in the freezer.
3. Pour about half of the Bavarian over the apples.
4. Place the pie in the freezer for about 5 minutes, just until the Bavarian is slightly set.
5. Pour or spoon on about 1/4 or 1/3 of remaining Bavarian, or as much as it will hold without running over.
6. Replace in freezer.
7. Continue until all the Bavarian is safely mounded on the pie. Do not allow it to freeze; it will only take a few minutes in the freezer each time.

For Whipped Topping
1. A few hours before serving, place the cream, vanilla, and sugar in a chilled bowl and, with chilled beaters, whip only until the cream is stiff enough to hold a shape. Be careful not to whip any more than necessary.
2. Place the cream by spoonfuls over the top, starting at the edges.
3. Use the back of the spoon to shape the cream into swirls and peaks.
4. Sprinkle the middle of the top with optional bits of shaved chocolate.

Yield: 8 servings

DOUBLE CHOCOLATE SOUR CREAM CAKE

Cake
1 package Pillsbury Plus Devil's Food Cake Mix
1 cup dairy sour cream
1 cup water
1/3 cup oil
3 eggs
1 cup miniature semisweet chocolate chips

Frosting
3 cups powdered sugar
3 tablespoons cocoa
3 tablespoons margarine or butter, softened
5 to 6 tablespoons orange juice
1/4 teaspoon orange extract
Mandarin oranges (optional)

For Cake
1. Heat oven to 350F.
2. Grease and flour two 8- or 9-inch round cake pans.
3. In large bowl, combine cake mix, oil, eggs, sour cream, and water at low speed until moistened.
4. Beat at highest speed 2 minutes.
5. Stir in chocolate chips.
6. Pour batter into prepared pans.
7. Bake at 350F for 45 to 55 minutes or until toothpick inserted in center comes out clean.
8. Cool cake in pans 15 minutes; invert onto cooling racks to cool completely.

For Frosting
1. In small bowl, combine all frosting ingredients.
2. Beat at medium speed until smooth and creamy.
3. Fill and frost cake.
4. Garnish with mandarin oranges, if desired.

Yield: 16 servings

GHIRARDELLI CHOCOLATE CAKE

Cake
6 ounces Ghirardelli milk chocolate
1/2 cup boiling water
1 cup butter, softened
1-1/2 cups sugar
4 egg yolks
4 egg whites
1 teaspoon vanilla
1/2 teaspoon salt
1 teaspoon baking soda
2-1/2 cups sifted cake flour
1 cup buttermilk

Frosting
3 tablespoons butter
2 ounces powdered sugar
1/8 teaspoon salt
1/2 teaspoon vanilla
4 tablespoons hot milk
1/2 small carton whipping cream

For Cake
1. Melt chocolate in boiling water. Cool.
2. Cream butter and sugar until light.
3. Add egg yolks, one at a time, beating until very smooth.
4. Add chocolate and vanilla.
5. Sift flour, salt, and soda.
6. Add alternately with buttermilk to chocolate mixture, beating well after each addition.
7. Beat egg whites until stiff and fold into batter.
8. Pour batter into 3 greased 8- or 9-inch cake pans.
9. Bake at 350F for 30 to 40 minutes, or until toothpick inserted in center comes out clean.
10. Cool on wire racks.
11. Frost with chocolate frosting.

For Frosting
1. Melt chocolate over top of double boiler.
2. Cream butter and sugar together.
3. Add chocolate, vanilla, and salt.
4. Add enough of the milk to make a good spreading consistency.
5. Spread frosting between bottom 2 layers of cake.
6. Whip cream and spread between top 2 layers.
7. Frost top and sides of cake with chocolate frosting.
8. Garnish with shaved chocolate.

Yield: 16 servings

AUNT TRESA'S DEVIL'S FOOD CAKE

3 ounces (3 squares) unsweetened chocolate
1 cup cold water
2 cups sugar
1/2 cup vegetable shortening
2 eggs
2 cups all-purpose flour
1/2 cup buttermilk
1 teapsoon baking soda
1 teaspoon salt

1. Preheat the oven to 325F.
2. Grease and flour a 13x9x2-inch pan or three 8-inch round cake pans.
3. In a small saucepan, bring the chocolate and cold water to a boil over moderate heat.
4. Remove from the heat and stir to melt the chocolate. Set aside.
5. In a large bowl, cream together the sugar, shortening, and 1 of the eggs until light and fluffy.
6. Beat in the remaining egg.
7. Add the flour alternately with the chocolate, beginning and ending with the flour.
8. Add the buttermilk, baking soda, and salt; mix well.
9. Divide the batter among the prepared pans; bake for 25 to 30 minutes for the 8-inch pans or 40 to 45 minutes for the rectangular pan, until a toothpick inserted in the center comes out clean.
10. Cool on a rack for at least 10 minutes; unmold the cake; allow to cool completely.
11. Top with your favorite chocolate frosting.

Yield: 12 servings

PEANUT BUTTER PIE

Note: This same recipe can be used with a fudge sauce.

1 small jar smooth peanut butter
8 ounces cream cheese
2 cups powdered sugar
18 ounces Cool Whip
3 graham cracker crusts

1. Cream peanut butter, cream cheese, and powdered sugar.
2. Add cool whip; blend until smooth. Pour into graham cracker custs.
3. Seal in zip-lock bags and freeze.

Fudge Sauce
12 ounces semisweet chocolate chips
1 cup butter
1 box powdered sugar
2-2/3 cups evaporated milk
2 teaspoons vanilla

1. Combine all sauce ingredients in heavy saucepan.
2. Cook over low heat until smooth. Let cool.
3. Place about a quarter-inch of sauce in bottom of crust and add peanut butter mixture on top.
4. Seal in zip-lock bags and freeze.

Yield: 3 pies; 24 servings

BANANA SPLIT PIE

2 cups graham crackers, crushed
1/2 cup margarine, softened
3 cups confectioner's sugar
1 (8-ounce) package cream cheese, softened
1 egg
6 bananas, sliced lengthwise
1 (20-ounce) can crushed pineapple
1 box non-dairy whipped topping, whipped
1/2 cup pecans, finely chopped

1. Combine graham cracker crumbs and margarine; form a crust in a 9x13-inch pan.
2. Mix sugar, cream cheese, and egg; spread over crust.
3. Add bananas, pineapple, and topping in layers.
4. Sprinkle with nuts; refrigerate.

Yield: 12 servings

INCREDIBLE PUMPKIN PIE

3/4 cup milk
2 cups canned pumpkin
1-1/2 cups brown sugar
1/8 teaspoon salt
3/4 teaspoon ginger
3/4 teaspoon cinnamon
1/3 teaspooon nutmeg
5 egg yolks
2 envelopes unflavored gelatin
1/3 cup cold water
5 egg whites
1-1/2 cups heavy cream
1/3 cup sugar
1 baked 10-inch pie shell
Caramelized Almonds (see recipe below)
Butterscotch sauce (ice cream topping)
Whipped cream

1. Heat milk with pumpkin, brown sugar, salt, and spices.
2. Beat egg yolks slightly; add hot mixture gradually to yolks.
3. Mix well; cook in double boiler until thick, stirring constantly.
4. Soften gelatin in cold water; add to hot custard.
5. Stir until dissolved.
6. Cool until it begins to thicken.
7. Beat egg whites until stiff but not dry.
8. Fold in custard.
9. Cool a little while, but not until set.
10. Whip cream.
11. Fold the 1/3 cup sugar into whipped cream; then fold cream into pumpkin mixture.
12. Chill until very thick; pour into baked pie shell. (If making your own pie shell, add toasted sesame seeds to dough before baking.)
13. Chill until set.
14. Before serving, sprinkle each piece with Caramelized Almonds, dribble with butterscotch sauce, and top with whipped cream. This pie is not complete without the almonds, sauce, and whipped cream.

Yield: 8 servings

Caramelized Almonds

Note: These almonds will keep indefinitely in an airtight container. They are also delicious on coffee ice cream.

1/2 cup sugar
1 cup slivered blanched almonds

1. Stir sugar and almonds constantly in heavy skillet until a light caramel color.
2. Spread on greased cookie sheet.
3. Break apart when crisp.

ALMOND-CRUSTED KEY LIME PIE

Crust
1/2 cup margarine or butter
1 cup all-purpose or unbleached flour
1/2 cup chopped blanched almonds
1/4 cup sugar

Filling
3 eggs, separated
1 (14-ounce) can sweetened condensed milk
1 teaspoon grated lime peel
1/3 cup lime juice (2 limes)
Whipping cream, whipped and sweetened, if desired

For Crust
1. In large skillet, melt margarine.
2. Lightly spoon flour into measuring cup; level off.
3. Combine flour and remaining crust ingredients in melted margarine.
4. Cook over medium-high heat for 3 to 4 minutes, or until mixture is medium-golden brown and crumbly, stirring constantly.
5. Reserve 1/4 cup crumb mixture for topping.
6. Using back of fork, press remaining mixture firmly into bottom and up sides of 9-inch pie pan.

For Filling
1. In large bowl, beat egg whites until stiff peaks form; set aside.
2. In small bowl, beat egg yolks.
3. Gradually add condensed milk; mix well.
4. Stir in lime peel.
5. Add lime juice a little at a time, stirring after each addition.
6. Fold mixture into egg whites.
7. Pour into crust; top with reserved crumbs.
8. Freeze about 3 hours or until set. (For longer storage, wrap in foil.)
9. Allow to soften a few minutes before serving.
10. Serve with whipped cream, if desired.

Yield: 8 servings

FRESH FRUIT PIE

Crust
1/4 cup butter or margarine, softened
1/4 cup sugar
1 egg yolk
1 cup flour

Filling
1/2 cup sugar
3 tablespoons cornstarch
1-1/2 cups orange juice
1/4 cup lemon juice
1 teaspoon grated lemon rind
6 cups assorted fresh fruit, cut up

For Crust
1. Cream butter and sugar.
2. Add egg yolk.
3. With pastry blender, cut in flour until crumbs form.
4. Press into a 9-inch pie plate.
5. Bake in a 400F oven for 8 minutes or until edge is brown. Cool.

For Filling
1. In saucepan, mix sugar and cornstarch.
2. Gradually stir in orange juice until smooth.
3. Stirring constantly, bring to a boil over medium heat and boil 1 minute.
4. Remove from heat; stir in lemon juice and grated rind. Cool completely.
5. Fold in fresh fruit.
6. Turn mixture into crust; chill at least 4 hours.

Yield: 8 servings

STRAWBERRY-LIME PIE

2 envelopes unflavored gelatin
1 (6-ounce) can frozen limeade concentrate
1/3 cup sugar
1 teaspoon grated lime rind
1 cup diced, fresh, California strawberries
1 cup whipping cream, whipped
Green food coloring (optional)
1 baked 9-inch pie shell

1.   Soften the gelatin in 1/2 cup of cold water.
2.   Combine the limeade concentrate, sugar, and 3/4 cup of water in a small saucepan; cook over low heat, stirring constantly, until the concentrate melts and the sugar dissolves.
3.   Add the gelatin; stir until dissolved.
4.   Chill until syrupy; stir in the lime rind and strawberries.
5.   Fold in the whipped cream until blended; tint a pale green with food coloring, if desired.
6.   Chill until mixture mounds when dropped from a spoon; place in the pie shell.
7.   Chill for 2 to 3 hours or until firm.
8.   Garnish with additional sliced strawberries.

Yield: 6 to 8 servings

BEST-EVER PECAN PIE

1 cup dark brown sugar
1 cup light corn syrup
1/3 cup melted butter
1/3 teaspoon salt
1 teaspoon vanilla
3 eggs, slightly beaten
1 9-inch deep-dish pie shell, unbaked
1 heaping cup pecan halves

1.   Preheat oven to 350F.
2.   In a large mixing bowl, combine the brown sugar, corn syrup, melted butter, salt, and vanilla; stir well.
3.   Add the eggs; beat with an electric hand mixer for 2 to 3 minutes.
4.   Pour the mixture into pie shell.
5.   Sprinkle the pecan halves evenly over the top.
6.   Bake at 350F for 45 minutes or until pie is firm.
7.   Let the pie cool before slicing and serving.

Yield: 8 servings

KEY LIME PIE

1 tablespoon unflavored gelatin
1 cup sugar, divided
1/4 teaspoon salt
4 eggs, separated
1/2 cup lime juice
1/4 cup water
1 teaspoon grated lime peel
Green food coloring (optional)
1 cup whipping cream, whipped
1 baked 9-inch pie shell

1. Mix the gelatin, 1/2 cup sugar, and salt in a saucepan.
2. Beat egg yolks, lime juice, and water together and stir into gelatin mixture.
3. Cook over medium heat, stirring constantly, until mixture comes to a boil.
4. Remove from heat; stir in grated peel.
5. Add enough food coloring for a pale green color, if desired.
6. Chill, stirring occasionally, until thickened.
7. Beat egg whites until soft peaks form.
8. Add remaining sugar gradually; beat until stiff peaks form.
9. Fold gelatin mixture into egg whites; fold in whipped cream.
10. Spoon into pastry shell; chill until firm.
11. Spread with additional whipped cream; sprinkle additional grated lime peel around edge of pie.

Yield: 8 servings

PARFAIT APPLE PIE

1 9-inch baked pie shell
2 (12-ounce) packages frozen escalloped apples
2 tablespoons rum
1 quart vanilla ice cream

1. Bake escalloped apples following package directions.
2. Cool for 1/2 hour.
3. Combine apples and rum.
4. Spoon ice cream into pie shell; top with apples.
5. Serve at once.

Yield: 8 servings

AMARETTO PIE

1 cup sweetened condensed milk
1 tablespoon Grand Marnier
1 tablespoon Amaretto
2 tablespoons Creme de Cacao
1 cup whipping cream, whipped
1 9-inch Oreo cookie crust

1. Mix condensed milk, Grand Marnier, Amaretto, and Creme de Cacao.
2. Fold into whipped cream. Pour into crust.
3. Freeze at least 4 hours.

Yield: Enough for 10 people or 1 SAS Institute employee

BITS 'O BRICKLE ICE CREAM PIE AND SAUCE

Pie
1 prepared 9-inch graham cracker pie shell
1/2 gallon vanilla ice cream, softened to spoon easily but not melted
6 ounces Bits 'O Brickle

Sauce
1-1/2 cups sugar
1 cup evaporated milk
6 ounces Bits 'O Brickle
1/4 cup butter
1/4 cup light corn syrup
Dash of salt

For Pie
1. Spoon 1/2 of softened ice cream into prepared pie shell.
2. Sprinkle Bits 'O Brickle on top.
3. Heap with remaining ice cream and freeze.

For Sauce
1. Combine sugar, milk, butter, syrup, and salt.
2. Bring to a boil over low heat.
3. Boil 1 minute.
4. Remove from heat; cool slightly before adding remaining Bits 'O Brickle.
5. Cool, stirring occasionally; chill.

To Serve
1. Cut pie into 8 wedges.
2. Stir sauce well; spoon over individual pie wedges. Remaining sauce may be refrigerated in a tightly-covered container for use as a topping.

Yield: 8 servings

COFFEE TOFFEE PIE

Note: Freezes well.

Crust
1 cup flour
1 cup chopped walnuts
1 ounce semisweet chocolate, ground
Dash salt
1/4 pound cold butter
1 egg

Filling
1 ounce unsweetened chocolate, melted
1/2 cup butter
3/4 cup brown sugar
2 teaspoons instant coffee
2 eggs
1 cup whipping cream
2 tablespoons Kahlua
1 tablespoon powdered sugar

For Crust
1. Combine dry ingredients.
2. Cut in butter.
3. Add egg and work in with hands.
4. Press into a 9-inch pie plate.
5. Prick several times with fork; bake at 375F for 12 minutes or until brown.
6. Cool on wire rack.

For Filling
1. Melt chocolate in top of double boiler or in microwave; set aside to cool.
2. Cream butter and sugar together; beat for 2 minutes.
3. Add cooled chocolate and instant coffee.
4. Add eggs individually; beat until smooth.
5. Pour into cooled crust; refrigerate at least 2 hours to set.
6. Garnish with cream whipped with Kahlua and powdered sugar.

Yield: 8 servings

APPLE PRALINE PIE

Crust
1 (15-ounce) package Pillsbury All-Ready Pie Crusts
1 teaspoon flour

Filling
6 cups thinly sliced, peeled apples
3/4 cup sugar
1/4 cup flour
1 teaspoon cinnamon
1/4 teaspoon salt
2 tablespoons margarine or butter

Topping
1/4 cup margarine or butter
1/2 cup firmly packed brown sugar
2 tablespoons half-and-half
1/2 cup chopped pecans

For Crust
1. Prepare pie crust according to package directions for two-crust pie.
2. Roll out two crusts and put one in a 9-inch pie pan.

For Filling
1. Heat oven to 350F.
2. In large bowl, combine apples, sugar, flour, cinnamon, and salt; toss lightly.
3. Spoon apple mixture into pastry-lined pan.
4. Dot with butter.
5. Top with second crust and flute; cut slits in several places.
6. Bake at 350F for 50 to 55 minutes or until apples are tender and crust is lightly browned. Remove from oven.

For Topping
1. Melt margarine in small saucepan; stir in brown sugar and half-and-half.
2. Heat slowly to boiling.
3. Remove from heat; stir in pecans.
4. Spread over top of pie.
5. Place on cookie sheet.
6. Return to oven; bake 5 minutes longer or until topping bubbles.
7. Cool at least 1 hour before serving.

Yield: 8 servings

BLUEBERRY WALNUT PIE

Crust
2-1/2 cups graham cracker crumbs
1/2 cup finely chopped walnuts
1/4 cup plus 2 tablespoons (3/4 stick) butter, melted
3 tablespoons honey
1/2 teaspoon cinnamon

Filling
6 egg yolks
1 cup blueberry juice (drained from canned blueberries)
1 cup whipping cream
1/2 cup sugar
1/2 teapsoon cinnamon
2 tablespoons fresh lemon juice
1 teaspoon vanilla

Mousse
1/4 cup blueberry juice (drained from canned blueberries)
1 envelope unflavored gelatin

Topping
1 cup whipping cream
2 cups canned blueberries
1 cup walnuts, chopped and toasted
Whipped cream (garnish)
1. Preheat oven to 350F.
2. Combine graham cracker crumbs, 1/2 cup finely chopped walnuts, butter, honey, and cinnamon in large bowl; mix well.
3. Press into 10-inch deep-dish pie pan.
4. Bake 10 minutes. Let cool while preparing filling.
5. Combine egg yolks, 1 cup blueberry juice, 1 cup whipping cream, sugar, and cinnamon in 2-quart saucepan.
6. Cook over medium heat, whisking constantly, until mixture coats back of spoon or registers 180F - about 8-10 minutes; do not boil.
7. Immediately pour into large bowl of electric mixer.
8. Add lemon juice and vanilla; beat on low speed until egg yolk mixture begins to cool - approximately 3 to 5 minutes.
9. Meanwhile, combine 1/4 cup blueberry juice and gelatin in small saucepan; stir over low heat until gelatin is dissolved - about 2 minutes.
10. Add small amount of cooling yolk mixture and blend well.
11. Refrigerate, stirring frequently, until mousse just begins to thicken and set.
12. Whip 1 cup cream in large bowl of electric mixer until stiff peaks form.
13. Fold cream and blueberries into mousse.
14. Spoon into prepared crust.
15. Cover entire top of pie with chopped, toasted walnuts.
16. Refrigerate until completely set - about 2 to 3 hours.
17. Top each serving with whipped cream.

Yield: 8 to 10 servings

BLUEBERRY CREAM CHEESE PIE

Crust
1-1/2 cups fine graham cracker crumbs
1/2 cup finely ground walnuts
1/4 cup confectioner's sugar, sifted
1 stick unsalted butter, melted
1/2 teaspoon cinnamon

Filling
8 ounces cream cheese, softened
1 tablespoon dairy sour cream
2 tablespoons fresh lemon juice
1-1/2 tablespoons grated lemon rind
3/4 cup confectioner's sugar, sifted
3 large eggs, beaten lightly

Topping
1/4 cup granulated sugar
1 tablespoon cornstarch
2 tablespoons fresh lemon juice
2 cups blueberries, picked over

For Crust
1. In a bowl, combine graham cracker crumbs, walnuts, confectioner's sugar, butter, and cinnamon.
2. Press the mixture into a 9-inch pie plate.

For Filling
1. In a bowl with an electric mixer, beat cream cheese with sour cream, lemon juice, and lemon rind until the mixture is smooth and light - about 3 minutes.
2. Pour the filling into the shell; smooth the top.
3. Bake the pie in a preheated moderate oven (350F) for 35 to 40 minutes or until it is just set.
4. Let cool for 1 hour.

For Topping
1. In a stainless steel or enameled saucepan, combine sugar, cornstarch, a pinch of salt, 1/2 cup water, lemon juice, and blueberries.
2. Bring the mixture to a simmer, stirring constantly; simmer for 3 minutes or until the syrup is thick and clear.
3. Let the topping cool for 10 minutes; spread evenly over pie.

Yield: 8 servings

BROWNIE PIE

Chocolate Crust
1 cup all-purpose flour
1/4 cup sugar
1/4 teaspoon salt
6 tablespoons cold unsalted butter, cut into 12 pieces
3 tablespoons unsweetened cocoa, preferably Dutch-process
1/2 teaspoon vanilla extract
2 to 3 tablespoons ice water

Filling
4 ounces unsweetened chocolate
1 stick (4 ounces) unsalted butter
3 eggs
1 cup sugar
1/4 teaspoon salt
1 teaspoon vanilla extract
2/3 cup all-purpose flour
1/2 teaspoon baking powder
1 cup walnuts, coarsely chopped (optional)

Topping
1/2 cup heavy cream

For Crust
1. Preheat the oven to 325F.
2. Lightly butter a 9-inch pie pan.
3. In a medium bowl, blend together the flour, sugar, and salt.
4. Cut in the butter until the mixture is crumbly.
5. Lightly stir in the cocoa and vanilla extract.
6. Using a fork to toss and mix, add just enough of the ice water to make a dough that holds together when pressed between your fingers--it should still be slightly crumbly.
7. Gather the dough together; press it evenly into the prepared pie pan.
8. Trim the edges evenly; chill the crust while you make the filling.

For Filling
1. In a small heavy saucepan, melt the chocolate and butter over low heat.
2. Stir the mixture until blended; set it off the heat to cool slightly.
3. In a mixing bowl, beat the eggs until fluffy - about 2 minutes.
4. Gradually beat in the sugar.
5. Beat in the salt, vanilla, and melted chocolate.
6. Sift the flour with the baking powder, then gently mix the dry ingredients into the chocolate/egg mixture--do not overmix.
7. If you're including the chopped nuts, add them now; stir for a moment.
8. Pour the filling into the chocolate crust.
9. Bake the pie in the center of the oven for 20 minutes, or until the edges of the filling are set while the center is still slightly moist.
10. Cool on a rack.

For Topping
1. Just before serving, whip the cream until stiff; spread it on top of the pie.

Yield: 8 servings

FUDGE MACAROON PIE

Crust
2 cups coconut
2 tablespoons margarine or butter, melted

Filling
1 can Pillsbury Frosting Supreme Ready-to-Spread Chocolate Fudge
  Frosting
1/2 cup flour
1/2 cup dairy sour cream
2 eggs

Topping
1 cup whipping cream
1/4 cup powdered sugar
3 tablespoons cocoa

1. Heat oven to 325F.
2. Grease and flour a 9-inch pie pan.
3. In small bowl, combine coconut and margarine; press in bottom and up sides of prepared pie pan.
4. In medium bowl, combine all filling ingredients; beat 1 minute at highest speed.
5. Pour filling into crust.
6. Bake at 325F for 40 to 50 minutes or until filling is set and center is firm to the touch.
7. Cool completely.
8. In small bowl, beat all topping ingredients until stiff peaks form.
9. Spread evenly over top of pie.
10. Store covered in refrigerator.

Yield: 8 servings

CHOCOLATE SEDUCTION

1 10-inch deep-dish pie shell, unbaked
1 cup (2 sticks) butter
5 ounces unsweetened chocolate
2-1/2 cups sugar
1/2 cup half-and-half
4 eggs, room temperature
1 egg yolk, room temperature
1-1/2 teaspoons vanilla
Whipped cream and chocolate leaves (optional)

1. Preheat oven to 425F.
2. Bake deep-dish pie shell 5 minutes.
3. Set crust aside.
4. Reduce oven temperature to 350F.
5. Melt butter and chocolate in top of double boiler over gently simmering water, stirring frequently.
6. Add sugar and half-and-half; stir until sugar dissolves and mixture is smooth.
7. Remove from over water.
8. Beat eggs and yolk to blend in small bowl.
9. Gradually add to chocolate mixture, stirring until thick and smooth.
10. Blend in vanilla.
11. Pour into crust.
12. Bake until completely set - about 35 minutes.
13. Serve warm, or cool completely and decorate with whipped cream and
chocolate leaves, if desired.

Yield: 8 to 10 servings

QUICKIE BROWNIE PIE

Note: The best way to make this, if you can, is to use the
recipe on the Gharadelli Chocolate box for brownies and top it with
Dickenson's preserves.

1 package good-quality brownie mix
Raspberry preserves

1. Make up brownie mix according to directions on box.
2. Place in decorative pie plate and bake according to box.
3. As soon as the brownie comes out of the oven, spread with raspberry
preserves.

Yield: 8 servings

CHOCOLATE WALNUT PIE

1 recipe of pie crust
3 eggs
1/2 cup sugar
1 teaspoon vanilla
1/8 teaspoon salt
1-1/4 cups light corn syrup
1 (6-ounce) package (1 cup) semisweet chocolate chips
2/3 cup coarsely chopped walnuts

1. Prepare pie crust for filled crust using 9-inch pie pan.
2. Heat oven to 350F.
3. In large bowl, beat eggs.
4. Add sugar, vanilla, and salt; blend well.
5. Add corn syrup; beat just until blended.
6. Stir in chocolate chips and walnuts.
7. Pour into pastry-lined pan.
8. Bake at 350F for 40 to 45 minutes or until filling is deep golden brown.
9. Cool at least 1 hour before serving.
10. Serve with whipped topping, if desired.

Yield: 8 servings

FRENCH SILK CHOCOLATE PIE

1 baked 9-inch pie crust
3/4 cup butter, softened
3/4 cup plus 1/3 cup sugar
2 squares unsweetened chocolate, melted
1 teaspoon vanilla
3 eggs
Sweetened whipped cream to garnish
Shaved chocolate to garnish

1. Cream butter and sugar.
2. Blend in melted and cooled chocolate and vanilla.
3. Add eggs, one at a time, beating 5 minutes after each addition at medium speed.
4. Pour into cooled crust; refrigerate overnight.
5. Top with whipped cream and shaved chocolate before serving.

Yield: 8 to 10 servings

CAPITAL ROOM CHOCOLATE FUDGE PIE

6 whole eggs
2-1/2 cups sugar
1/2 cup melted margarine
5-1/2 ounces melted chocolate
1/2 teaspoon vanilla extract
6 ounces black or English walnut pieces
2 9-inch pie shells, baked at 350 for 5 minutes

1. Whip eggs on medium speed for 10 minutes.
2. Add sugar to eggs.
3. Slowly mix melted margarine, chocolate, vanilla extract, and nuts
to beaten eggs.
4. Pour mixture into two 9-inch pie crusts.
5. Bake in a 375F oven for 40 minutes or until done. Remember that the
filling underneath the crust will be soft, like a half-baked brownie.

Yield: 16 servings

ROCKY MOUNTAIN PIE

2 eggs
1/2 cup unsifted flour
1/2 cup sugar
1/2 cup firmly packed brown sugar
1 cup butter, melted and cooled to room temperature
1 (6-ounce) package (1 cup) semisweet chocolate morsels
1 cup chopped walnuts
1 9-inch unbaked pie shell
Whipped cream or ice cream (optional)

1. Preheat oven to 325F.
2. In large bowl, beat eggs until foamy; beat in flour, sugar, and
brown sugar until well blended.
3. Blend in melted butter.
4. Stir in semisweet chocolate morsels and walnuts.
5. Pour into pie shell.
6. Bake at 325F one hour. Remove from oven.
7. Serve warm with whipped cream or ice cream.

Yield: 6 to 8 servings

DOUBLE CHOCOLATE TART

Note: Can be prepared 1 day ahead.

Crust
Bordeaux cookies
Hazelnuts
2 tablespoons sugar
2 tablespoons butter, melted

Filling
1/2 cup (1 stick) unsalted butter, cut into 8 pieces
2 ounces unsweetened chocolate, coarsely chopped
1 cup sugar
2 eggs
1/2 teaspoon vanilla
Pinch of salt
1/2 cup all-purpose flour

1/4 cup strained raspberry jam or orange marmalade

Topping
3 ounces semisweet chocolate, coarsely chopped
1/2 ounce unsweetened chocolate, coarsely chopped
3 to 4 tablespoons water or coffee
Powdered sugar (optional)

For Crust
1. Combine ingredients for crust; press into 9-inch pie pan.
2. Bake at 350F for 10 minutes.
3. Set aside.

For Filling
1. Melt 1/4 cup butter with chocolate in top of double boiler over hot (but not boiling) water.
2. Remove from over water; stir until smooth.
3. Cream remaining 1/4 cup butter and sugar in processor until light and fluffy.
4. Mix in eggs, vanilla, and salt.
5. Blend in chocolate mixture, stopping occasionally to scrape down sides of work bowl.
6. Add flour in batches, blending well.
7. Spread jam over bottom of cooled crust. Top with filling.
8. Bake until knife inserted in center comes out clean - about 25 minutes.
9. Cool on rack until warm - about 15 minutes.

For Topping
1. Melt semisweet chocolate, unsweetened chocolate, and water in top of double boiler over hot (but not boiling) water.
2. Remove from over water; stir until smooth.
3. Spread on top of tart.
4. Sift powdered sugar over tart, if desired.
5. Store at room temperature.

Yield: 8 servings

LIGHT CHESS PIE WITH CHOCOLATE AND RASPBERRIES

3 extra-large eggs, separated, room temperature
3/4 cup sugar
1/3 cup dairy sour cream
1/4 cup cake flour
1-1/2 tablespoons fresh lemon juice
1/2 teaspoon vanilla
Pinch of cream of tartar
1 9-inch deep-dish pie shell, baked
2 tablespoons (1/4 stick) butter
2 teapoons dark rum
1/4 cup semisweet chocolate chips
1 ounce semisweet chocolate
1/2 pint fresh raspberries or halved strawberries
1 cup whipping cream, whipped

1. Preheat oven to 375F.
2. Blend yolks in large bowl of electric mixer.
3. Gradually add sugar; beat until pale yellow and ribbon forms when beaters are lifted.
4. Blend in sour cream, flour, lemon juice, and vanilla.
5. Beat whites with cream of tartar in another bowl until stiff but not dry.
6. Gently fold 1/4 of whites into yolk mixture to lighten; fold in remaining whites.
7. Pour mixture into crust.
8. Bake until center puffs and browns - 17 to 19 minutes.
9. Let cool completely on wire rack (center of pie will fall as it cools).
10. Heat butter and rum in heavy small saucepan until butter melts.
11. Remove from heat; stir in chocolate chips until smooth.
12. Spread evenly over pie.
13. Cool until chocolate sets.
14. Shave 1 ounce semisweet chocolate onto waxed paper, using vegetable peeler.
15. Refrigerate until chilled.
16. Just before serving, top pie with berries.
17. Pipe whipped cream decoratively over berries and crust.
18. Sprinkle top of pie with shaved chocolate.

Yield: 6 servings

GIRDLE-BUSTER PIE

20 Oreo cookies, crushed
1/4 cup butter or margarine, melted
1 quart vanilla ice cream
2 tablespoons butter or margarine
2 squares unsweetened chocolate
1/2 cup sugar
1 (5-1/3-ounce) can evaporated milk
1 teaspoon vanilla extract
Whipped cream for topping
Toasted slivered almonds

1. Mix cookies with melted butter, press into a 9-inch pie plate; freeze.
2. Spoon in slightly softened ice cream; refreeze.
3. Combine butter, chocolate, sugar, and milk in saucepan; simmer on low heat until slightly thickened. Cool. Add vanilla.
4. Spread over pie; refreeze.
5. At serving time, top generously with sweetened whipped cream and sprinkle with slivered almonds.

Yield: 8 servings

CHOCOLATE CHIP PECAN PIE

1/2 cup butter, room temperature
1 cup sugar
2 eggs
1 teaspoon vanilla
1 cup all-purpose flour
1 (12-ounce) package semisweet chocolate chips
1 cup coarsely chopped pecans
1 unbaked 10-inch pie shell
Unsweetened whipped cream (optional)

1. Preheat oven to 325F.
2. Cream butter and sugar in large bowl until fluffy.
3. Beat in eggs and vanilla.
4. Add flour; blend until smooth.
5. Stir in chocolate chips and pecans.
6. Turn mixture into pie shell.
7. Bake until center is set and top golden - about 50 minutes.
8. Serve warm or at room temperature.
9. Garnish with whipped cream, if desired.

Yield: 8 to 10 servings

CHOCOLATE CHESS PIE

2-1/2 cups sugar
7 tablespoons cocoa
4 eggs
1-1/4 cups evaporated milk
1 tablespoon vanilla
1 stick margarine, melted
2 9-inch unbaked pie crusts
Sweetened whipped cream (for garnish)

1. Preheat oven to 375F.
2. Put first 6 ingredients in blender; mix well.
3. Pour into pie shells.
4. Bake 35 to 40 minutes or until the top of the pie has puffed up like a souffle. The center will still be shaky.
5. Do not overbake.
6. Serve garnished with sweetened whipped cream.

Yield: 2 pies; 16 servings

CHOCOLATE FUDGE PIE

6 whole eggs
2-1/2 cups sugar
1/2 cup melted margarine
5-1/2 ounces chocolate, melted
1/4 teaspoon vanilla extract
6 ounces black or English walnut pieces
2 of your favorite 9-inch unbaked pie crusts

1. Whip egg on medium speed for 10 minutes.
2. Add sugar to eggs.
3. Mix melted margarine, chocolate, vanilla extract, and nuts to beaten eggs slowly.
4. Pour mixture into two pie crusts.
5. Bake in a 375F oven for 40 minutes or until done. Remember that the filling underneath the thin crust will be soft, like a half-baked brownie.

Yield: 2 pies, 16 servings

CHOCOLATE AMARETTO MOUSSE PIE

1 (12-ounce) package semisweet chocolate pieces
1/4 cup butter
1 (14-ounce) can sweetened condensed milk
1/4 teaspoon salt
1/4 cup water
1/4 cup Amaretto
2 cups heavy cream
Sliced almonds for garnish (optional)

1. Line a 9-inch plate with aluminum foil; press the foil firmly against the surface of the plate, making the foil as smooth as possible.
2. Melt 1 cup of the chocolate pieces with 2 tablespoons of the butter in small saucepan over very low heat.
3. Pour into foil-lined plate and quickly smooth over the bottom and up the side.
4. Place in the freezer until it is firm - about 30 minutes.
5. Meanwhile, prepare filling by combining remaining chocolate and butter with sweetened condensed milk and salt in medium-sized saucepan.
6. Cook, stirring constantly, over low heat until chocolate is melted.
7. Stir in water gradually.
8. Cook, stirring constantly, over medium heat for 5 minutes.
9. Add Amaretto; cook and stir again for 5 minutes or until thickened.
10. Cool to room temperature.
11. To hasten cooling, place pan over ice and water, stirring occasionally, for 10 minutes or until cooled.
12. Beat cream in a medium-sized bowl until stiff.
13. Remove beaters; refrigerate 1/2 cup for garnish.
14. Stir a part of the whipped cream into chocolate mixture to loosen slightly; fold in remainder.
15. When chocolate shell is firm, lift gently from pan with foil.
16. Carefully peel off foil and place shell on serving plate.
17. Spoon the filling into the shell; garnish with the sliced almonds and reserved whipped cream.
18. Chill until set - about 3-1/2 hours.

Yield: 8 servings

GRASSHOPPER PIE

Chocolate Cookie Crust
1-1/2 cups chocolate wafer crumbs
1/4 cup margarine or butter, melted

Filling
3 cups miniature marshmallows or 32 large marshmallows
1/2 cup milk
1-1/2 cups chilled whipping cream
1/4 cup green Creme de Menthe
3 tablespoons white Creme de Cacio
Few drops green food color (optional)

For Chocolate Cookie Crust
1. Heat oven to 350F.
2. Mix chocolate wafer crumbs and margarine in ungreased 9-inch pie pan.
3. Press evenly against bottom and sides of pan.
4. Bake 10 minutes. Cool.

For Filling
1. Heat marshmallows and milk in saucepan over low heat, stirring occasionally, until mixture mounds slightly when dropped from a spoon.
2. In chilled bowl, beat whipping cream until stiff.
3. Stir marshmallow mixture until blended; stir in Creme de Menthe and Creme de Cacao.
4. Fold into whipped cream.
5. Fold in food color.
6. Pour into pie crust.
7. If desired, sprinkle grated semisweet chocolate over top.
8. Refrigerate at least 4 hours.

Variation:
Brandy Alexander Pie
Substitute 1/4 cup dark Creme de Cacao for the Creme de Menthe and 3 tablespoons Brandy for the white Creme de Cacao. Omit green food color.

Yield: 6 to 8 servings

Microwave Recipe
1/4 cup margarine
16 to 18 Oreo cookies, crushed
35 large marshmallows
1/2 cup milk
1/4 cup Creme de Menthe
1/4 cup white Creme de Cacao
2 cups whipped topping
Chocolate curls to garnish
Whipped topping to garnish

1. Melt margarine in 9-inch pie plate for 30 seconds on high.
2. Add crushed Oreos and press to cover bottom and sides of plate.
3. Cook 1-1/2 to 2 minutes over high heat.
4. In 2-quart bowl, heat marshmallows and milk on high for 2 to 2-1/2

minutes or until marshmallows begin to melt.
5. Stir until completely melted.
6. Cool 5 minutes.
7. Add liqueurs.
8. Refrigerate until partially thickened.
9. Fold in whipped topping.
10. Spoon into pie plate and freeze.
11. Garnish with additional topping and chocolate curls.

Yield: 6 to 8 servings

RIBBON ALASKA PIE

Note: This is such a pretty dessert. If the thought of preparing a Baked Alaska scares you, try this as a substitute on your menu.

2 pints peppermint stick ice cream
2 9-inch baked pie shells
2 tablespoons butter
1 cup sugar
2 ounces unsweetened chocolate
1 (6-ounce) can evaporated milk
1 teaspoon vanilla extract
3 egg whites
1-1/2 teaspoons vanilla extract
1/4 teaspoon cream of tartar
6 tablespoons sugar

1. Combine butter, 1 cup sugar, chocolate, and milk in saucepan.
2. Cook over low heat until chocolate melts and sauce is well blended.
3. Add the 1 teaspoon vanilla and chill.
4. Soften ice cream and spread half into each of the pie shells.
5. Freeze until firm.
6. Divide fudge in half and pour over the pies.
7. Freeze while making meringue.
8. Beat egg whites until stiff but not dry.
9. Gradually add sugar, vanilla, and cream of tartar, beating until stiff peaks form.
10. Spread meringue over pies.
11. Sprinkle top of pies with peppermint stick candy.
12. Bake at 450F just until meringue browns.
13. Serve immediately or freeze until ready to serve.

Yield: 2 pies; 16 servings

SAS INSTITUTE'S FAVORITE CHEESECAKE

Note: Cheesecake really does have to ripen. Plan ahead so that this one will be at its best. Whenever we serve this one it is our biggest seller and we cannot keep cutting it fast enough. I think that the best part about it is that it is so easy. Please take the time to add the eggs one at a time; it really does make a difference.

Crust
1 package Pepperidge Farm Bordeaux Cookies
2 tablespoons melted butter

Filling
4 (8-ounce) packages cream cheese, room temperature
2 cups sugar
6 eggs, beaten one at a time
2 teaspoons vanilla
1 (16-ounce) carton dairy sour cream

1. Generously grease bottom only of 9-inch springform pan with butter.
2. Lightly crush cookies; combine with melted butter. The more you crush the cookies, the softer the crust will be. I like to break them up with my hands so that the crust will still be crunchy.
3. Lightly press cookie mixture in bottom of springform pan.
4. Cream cream cheese and gradually add sugar.
5. Add eggs, one at a time.
6. Add vanilla.
7. Fold in sour cream.
8. Pour into pan and bake for 45 minutes at 375F.
9. Turn oven off and let the cake cool in the oven for 1 hour.
Cake needs to ripen for at least 8 hours. It really is much better if you can make it a day ahead.

Yield: 16 servings

Variation:
Chocolate Cheesecake
For the crust, use chocolate wafers and increase butter to 1/4 cup. For the filling, use 1 pound chocolate Neufchatel cheese and 1 pound cream cheese. You may want to decrease the amount of sugar just a little bit since the Neufchatel is a little sweeter than the cream cheese.

FANTASTIC CHOKAHLUA CHEESECAKE

Chocolate Crumb Crust
1-1/3 cups chocolate wafer crumbs
1 tablespoon sugar
4 tablespoons unsalted butter, room temperature

Mocha Sauce
1 (8-ounce) jar chocolate ice cream topping
1 tablespoon instant coffee

Topping
Sour cream or Cream Fraiche (optional)

Cheesecake
1-1/2 cups (9 ounces) semisweet chocolate pieces
2 tablespoons butter
1/4 cup Kahlua
1 pound cream cheese, softened and cut into small pieces
2 large eggs
1/3 cup sugar
1/4 teaspoon salt
1 cup dairy sour cream

For Crust
1. Combine wafer crumbs, sugar, and butter, mixing well.
2. Put mixture in an even layer over bottom of a 9-inch springform pan.

For Mocha Sauce
Slowly heat topping; stir in coffee to dissolve.

For Cheesecake
3. Preheat oven to 325F.
4. Slowly heat chocolate, butter, and Kahlua in a small saucepan, stirring until chocolate melts and mixture is smooth. Set aside and cool slightly.
5. Add softened cream cheese, continuing to beat until smooth.
6. Beat in eggs; then beat in sugar, salt, and sour cream.
7. Gradually beat in chocolate mixture.
8. Pour into chocolate crumb crust.
9. Bake for 40 minutes, or just until filling is barely set in center.
10. Remove from oven; let stand at room temperature at least 1 hour.
11. If desired, before serving, spread on a thin layer of sour cream or Cream Fraiche and drizzle Mocha Sauce over top of cake.
12. Cut in small slices with a thin sharp knife dipped in cold water.
13. Refrigerate leftovers.

Yield: 12 servings

AMARETTO CHEESECAKE

Crust
1-1/2 cups crushed plain chocolate wafer cookies
1/3 cup ground almonds
1/4 cup Amaretto
2-3 tablespoons melted butter

Filling
1 pound ricotta cheese
8 ounces softened cream cheese
4 eggs
1/3 cup Amaretto liqueur
1 cup sugar
1/4 teaspoon salt
1/2 teaspoon freshly grated orange rind

For Crust
1. Combine all ingredients.
2. Mix well.
3. Press firmly into the bottom of a 9- or 10-inch springform pan.

For Filling
1. Combine all ingredients in a large bowl.
2. Beat for at least 5 minutes with an electric mixer at high speed.
3. Scrape the sides and bottom of the bowl often.
4. Pour the batter into the crust-lined pan.
5. Bake in the center of a 325F oven for 1 hour.
6. Turn off oven, open the door; leave the cake in for another 15 minutes.
7. Remove; let cool; cover the pan tightly with food-wrap; chill at least 8 hours before serving.

Yield: 16 servings

CHOCOLATE CHEESECAKE

Note: If all the batter won't fit in your springform pan, put 2/3
in the springform and 1/3 in an 8-inch square pan.

Crust
18 to 20 Nabisco Famous Wafers (or any chocolate wafer), crushed
1/2 cup margarine, melted
1/2 teaspoon cinnamon

Filling
3 (8-ounce) packages cream cheese, room temperature
1 cup sugar
4 eggs
16 ounces semisweet chocolate chips
1 teaspoon vanilla
2 tablespoons cocoa
3 cups dairy sour cream
1/4 cup butter, melted
1. Combine all crust ingredients; press on the bottom and sides of
a springform pan.
2. Mix together sugar and eggs until light.
3. Add cream cheese gradually, beating well after each addition.
4. Melt chocolate chips.
5. Add to egg mixture with vanilla, cocoa, and sour cream, beating
constantly.
6. Add melted butter, mixing well.
7. Bake at 350F for 1 hour.
8. Chill overnight.

Yield: 16 servings

MOCHA CHOCOLATE CHIP CHEESECAKE

Crust
1-1/2 cups chocolate wafer crumbs (about 24 wafers)
6 tablespoons (3/4 stick) butter, room temperature
1/3 cup sugar

Cake
1-1/2 pounds cream cheese, room temperature
1 cup sugar
4 eggs, room temperature
1/3 cup whipping cream
1 tablespoon instant coffee powder
1 teaspoon vanilla
1 cup miniature chocolate chips
(Or use our cheesecake recipe and add the coffee powder and chips)

1. Position rack in center of oven and preheat at 200F.
2. Butter bottom and sides of 9-1/2-inch springform pan.
3. Combine crumbs, butter, and 1/3 cup sugar in medium bowl and mix well.
4. Pat evenly onto bottom and sides of prepared pan. Set aside.
5. Beat cream cheese in large bowl of electric mixer until fluffy.
6. Blend in 1 cup sugar.
7. Add eggs one at a time, beating well after each addition.
8. Add cream, coffee, and vanilla; beat 2 minutes.
9. Turn mixture into prepared crust.
10. Top with chocolate chips and swirl through with spatula.
11. Set pan on baking sheet. Bake until tester inserted in center comes out clean - about 2 hours (cake will appear soft).
12. Cool completely on rack.
13. Chill thoroughly before serving.

Yield: 10 to 12 servings

THE LAZY GOURMET'S PECAN GLAZED TORTE

Cake
6 ounces semisweet chocolate, grated
8 tablespoons (1 stick) unsalted butter, softened
1/2 cup sugar
4 eggs, separated, at room temperature
1 cup finely chopped pecans
1/4 cup all-purpose flour
18 pecan halves, for decoration

Chocolate Glaze
4 tablespoons unsalted butter
4 ounces semisweet chocolate
2 tablespoons heavy cream
1 tablespoon coffee liqueur, such as Kahlua

For Cake
1. Preheat the oven to 350F.
2. Generously butter a 9-inch cake pan.
3. Melt the chocolate in the top of a double boiler over hot, not simmering, water. Set aside.
4. In a large bowl, beat the butter until very smooth.
5. Gradually add the sugar; beat until fluffy.
6. Add the egg yolks one at a time, incorporating completely after each yolk is added.
7. Add the melted chocolate; combine thoroughly.
8. In a small paper bag or bowl, combine the pecans with the flour; shake to coat the nuts.
9. Add the mixture to the batter; blend.
10. Beat the egg whites until stiff peaks form; gently fold them into the batter.
11. Pour into the prepared cake pan and bake for 25 minutes; remove cake from the pan. Cool completely.

For Chocolate Glaze
1. In a small saucepan, melt together the butter and chocolate over very low heat.
2. Combine the cream with the liqueur; stir them into the chocolate mixture.
3. Place the cake on a rack set over a plate, which will catch the glaze drippings.
4. Pour the glaze over the cooled cake, tilting the rack to ensure that the top of the cake and some of the sides are coated with glaze.
5. Carefully transfer the cake to a clean serving plate; decorate with the pecan halves.
6. Refrigerate, covered; serve chilled.

Yield: 6 to 8 servings

RASPBERRY RIBBON TORTE

Pastry
2 cups flour
1/4 teaspoon salt
1 cup butter
4-6 tablespoons water
3 tablespoons sugar

Filling
3 (3/4-ounce) packages instant vanilla pudding mix
1-1/2 cups milk
2 tablespoons cornstarch
1/4 cup water
1 (10-ounce) package frozen raspberries, thawed

Topping
1/4 cup finely ground almonds
1 cup whipping cream, whipped
2 tablespoons sugar
1/4 teaspoon almond extract

1. Heat oven to 450F.
2. Lightly spoon flour into measuring cup; level off in medium bowl; combine measured flour and salt.
3. Using a pastry blender or fork, cut in butter until particles are size of small peas.
4. Add ice water 1 tablespoon at a time to mixture, stirring with fork until dough is moist enough to hold together.
5. Form into ball; cover.
6. Chill 30 minutes or until dough is easy to handle.
7. Divide dough into 6 equal parts; shape each part into ball.
8. Flatten balls; smooth edges; roll each lightly on well floured surface from center to edge into 9-inch circle.
9. Transfer to ungreased cookie sheet; prick generously with fork.
10. Sprinkle each circle with 1-1/2 tablespoons sugar.
11. Bake at 450F for 5-7 minutes.

For Filling
1. In small bowl, beat pudding mix and milk at medium speed until thickened - about 5 minutes.
2. Chill.
3. In medium saucepan, blend cornstarch and water; add thawed raspberries.
4. Cook over medium heat until thick, stirring constantly - about 5 minutes.
5. Refrigerate 1 to 2 hours.
6. Alternately spread raspberry and vanilla fillings between the cooled pastry circles, ending with a thin layer of vanilla on top.
7. Sprinkle with almonds.

For Topping
1. In small bowl, combine whipped cream, sugar, and almond extract; mix well.

2. Spread on sides and 1 inch around outer edge of torte.
3. Refrigerate; serve within 4 hours.

Yield: 16 servings

OUR ICE CREAM SUNDAE PIE

Crust
13 Pepperidge Farm Bordeaux Cookies, broken
1-1/2 cups Oreo cookie pieces
2 tablespoons meleted butter

Filling
3 cups vanilla ice cream
3/4 cup Bits 'O Brickle
3 cups chocolate ice cream

Topping
10 large York Peppermint Patties
3-4 tablespoons butter or cream
1 cup heavy cream
3 tablespoons sugar

For Crust
1. Combine equal parts Bordeaux cookies and Oreos with melted butter.
2. Spread evenly over bottom and sides of 10-inch pie plate.

For Filling
1. Layer vanilla ice cream, softened, followed by Bits 'O Brickle and topped with chocolate ice cream.
2. Freeze.

For Topping
1. Melt the York Peppermint Patties with 3-4 tablespoons of butter or cream.
2. Whip and sweeten heavy cream.

To Assemble
1. Remove pie from pan to cut.
2. Cut into 10 pieces.
3. Top each with any crumbs from the pan, whipped cream, and chocolate sauce.
4. Top with a cherry.

Yield: 10 servings

CHOCOLATE INTEMPERANCE

Note: If you use a springform pan, line it with foil first so it won't leak. You may find that you need to use two brownie mixes to get all the pieces for the cake.

Cake
1 (23-ounce) package brownie mix
2 tablespoons water
3 eggs

Filling
1-1/2 pounds semisweet chocolate
1/2 cup strong coffee
3 eggs, separated
1/2 cup Tia Maria
2 tablespoons sugar
1/2 cup heavy cream

Chocolate Glaze
1/2 pound semisweet chocolate
1/3 cup water

For Cake
1. Preheat oven to 350F.
2. Grease an 11x15-inch jelly roll pan. Line it with waxed paper. Grease and lightly flour paper, shaking off any excess flour.
3. Beat ingredients together at medium speed of electric mixer until batter is smooth.
4. Spread batter evenly in jelly roll pan.
5. Bake for 10 to 12 minutes or until cake tests done.
6. Turn cake onto a rack and peel off paper. Let cool.
7. Lightly oil a 2-quart Charlotte mold and line with cooled cake.
8. Cut rounds of cake to fit both top and bottom of mold and cut a strip for the sides.
9. Place smaller round in bottom of mold.
10. Wrap strip around inside of the mold. (You will probably have to piece one section of the side to cover completely; but don't worry, any patchwork will be hidden by chocolate glaze.)
11. Spoon chilled filling mixture into mold.
12. Chill for 3 to 4 hours or until firm.
13. Unmold and cover with glaze.

For Filling
1. Melt chocolate with coffee in top of a double boiler. When chocolate is completely melted, remove pan from heat.
2. Beat egg yolks until pale yellow; stir into chocolate.
3. Gradually stir in Tia Maria. Cool mixture.
4. In a separate bowl, beat egg whites, gradually adding sugar until whites are stiff.
5. Whip cream.
6. Gently fold whipped cream into cooled chocolate mixture; fold in egg whites.

For Chocolate Glaze

1. Melt chocolate in water; stir until smooth.
2. Spread over top of mousse-cake; drizzle down sides.
3. Chill again.
4. Serve in slender slices--it's indecently opulent.

Yield: 8 to 10 servings

STRAWBERRY SHORTCAKE

Note: If you want to be a real piggy-wig about the whole thing,
you can split the biscuits when they come out of the oven and butter
both the top and bottom.

Use your imagination when you assemble the shortcakes. Definitely
layer biscuit bottom, strawberries, whipped cream, top biscuit, whipped
cream and then strawberries. If there is any syrup in the strawberry
bowl, dribble that on top.

2 cups sifted all-purpose flour
3 teaspoon double-acting baking powder
3/4 teaspoon salt
5 tablespoon granulated sugar
1 teaspoon grated lemon or orange rind
1/2 cup shortening
1 egg beaten
Butter or margarine
Sliced strawberries
1 cup heavy cream, whipped

1. Preheat oven to 450 degrees.
2. Sift together flour, baking powder, salt, sugar, and rind.
3. With pastry blender or 2 knives, cut shortening scissor-fashion
into flour mixture until like corn meal.
4. Add beatened egg, then enough milk to make easily-handled dough.
5. Drop by large spoonfuls onto cookie sheet. Recipe should make about
6 biscuits.
6. As soon as the biscuits come out of the oven, sprinkle sugar on top.

Yield: 6 servings

CHOCOLATE STRAWBERRY PATCH

Genoise
8 eggs, room temperature
1-1/3 cups sugar
1 teaspoon vanilla extract
1 cup sifted cake flour (not self-rising)
1/2 cup sifted unsweetened cocoa powder, preferably Dutch process
1/4 teaspoon salt
1/4 pound (1 stick) unsalted butter, melted and cooled

Chocolate Buttercream and Cake Fiili..g
4 egg yolks
1 cup sifted confectioner's sugar
1/4 teaspoon salt
6 ounces bittersweet or semisweet chocolate, melted and cooled slightly
1 tablespoon instant espresso coffee powder dissolved in 1 tablespoon
    hot water
3/4 pound (3 sticks) unsalted butter, room temperature
1/3 cup dark rum
1 cup red raspberry jam

Bittersweet Chocolate Glaze
1/4 pound (1 stick) unsalted butter
1 cup unsweetened cocoa powder
1 teaspoon instant espresso coffee powder
1 cup sugar
2/3 cup heavy cream
3 pints fresh strawberries, rinsed and hulled
1/2 cup red currant jelly

For Genoise
1. Preheat the oven to 350F.
2. Butter a 12-inch springform pan. Dust with flour and shake out the excess.
3. In a large mixing bowl set over (not touching) a pan of simmering water, beat the eggs with a whisk or electric mixer for 1 minute.
4. Beat in the sugar and vanilla. Continue beating until the sugar has dissolved and the mixture is just barely warm to the touch.
5. Remove from the heat and beat at high speed until tripled in volume, cooled, and the mixture forms a ribbon when the beaters are lifted - about 10 minutes.
6. Sift together the flour, cocoa, and salt. Sift again.
7. One-third at a time, quickly fold the flour mixture into the egg mixture.
8. Fold in the butter and then quickly spread the batter into the prepared pan.
9. Bake for 30 to 35 minutes, until the top springs back when lightly touched, the edges begin to pull away from the pan, and a cake tester inserted in the center comes out clean.
10. Cool for 10 minutes and then remove the sides of the pan.
11. Cool on a rack.

For Chocolate Buttercream

1. In a medium mixing bowl, beat together the egg yolks, confectioner's sugar, and salt until very light and the mixture forms a ribbon when the beaters are lifted - about 5 minutes.
2. Beat in the melted chocolate and dissolved coffee.
3. Beat in the butter, two tablespoons at a time, until smooth and fluffy.

For Glaze
1. In a small saucepan, combine the butter, cocoa, coffee, sugar, and cream.
2. Cook over low heat, stirring constantly, until smooth - about 5 minutes.
3. Remove from the heat and let cool for 3 to 5 minutes.

To Assemble
1. Using a long, serrated knife, horizontally split the cake in half.
2. Place the layers, cut side up, on your work surface.
3. Splash the cut surfaces of both layers evenly with the rum.
4. Spread the raspberry jam over the bottom layer.
5. Spread the buttercream over the jam so it is about 1/2-inch thick.
6. Put the top layer in place, cut side down.
7. Cover with plastic wrap; chill several hours or overnight, until the buttercream has set. (The recipe can be prepared a day ahead to this point.)
8. Pour the warm glaze over the top and sides of the cake. Spread the glaze with a small spatula.
9. Using the largest strawberries around the top outside edge, arrange the strawberries all over the top of the cake.
10. In a small saucepan, melt the jelly over low heat. Brush the berries with the warm jelly.
11. Refrigerate until set and serve chilled.

Yield: 16 servings

MEXICAN CHOCOLATE FREEZE

Crust
1/2 cup margarine or butter
1 cup all-purpose or unbleached flour
1/2 cup chopped blanched almonds
1/4 cup sugar
2 tablespoons cocoa

Filling
1 quart (4 cups) coffee ice cream, softened
1 pint (2 cups) chocolate ice cream, softened
1/4 teaspoon cinnamon
1/8 teaspoon cloves

1. Melt margarine in a large skillet.
2. Lightly spoon flour into measuring cup; level off.
3. Combine flour and remaining crust ingredients with melted margarine.
4. Cook over medium-high heat 3 to 4 minutes or until mixture is crumbly, stirring constantly.
5. Reserve 3/4 cup of mixture for topping.
6. Sprinkle remaining mixture into bottom of 9-inch square or 11x7-inch pan. Cool completely.
7. Spoon half of coffee ice cream onto crumbs.
8. In small bowl, combine chocolate ice cream and spices; spoon over coffee ice cream.
9. Spread remaining coffee ice cream over chocolate ice cream.
10. Sprinkle with reserved crumbs.
11. Cover; freeze until firm.

Yield: 9 to 12 servings

WHITE CHOCOLATE ALMOND TORTE

Note: This is a terrific quick recipe. Don't let the length of
the list of ingredients scare you. It is very impressive to serve and
delicious. One short cut: use whipped dairy topping and flavor it
with the almond extract. You can also use sherry or amaretto to
flavor the cake and topping.

Cake
1-3/4 cups all-purpose flour
1-3/4 cups sugar
1-1/4 teaspoon baking soda
1 teaspoon salt
1/4 teaspoon baking powder
2/3 cup butter, softened
4 ounces (4 squares) unsweetened chocolate, melted and cooled, or
   4 envelopes premelted unsweetened baking chocolate
1-1/4 cups water
1 teaspoon almond extract
3 eggs

Filling
8 ounces white chocolate or vanilla flavor candy coating, melted and
   cooled
3/4 cup butter
1/4 teaspoon almond extract
1/2 cup chopped almonds

Filling and Topping
1 pint (2 cups) whipping cream, whipped
1 tablespoon sugar
1/4 teaspoon almond extract

1.   Heat oven to 350 degrees.
2.   Grease and flour four 8- or 9-inch round pans.
3.   In a large bowl, blend all cake ingredients at low speed until
moistened.
4.   Beat at highest speed for 3 minutes.
5.   Pour batter into prepared pans (layers will be very thin).
6.   Bake for 15 to 18 minutes or until toothpick inserted in center
comes out clean.
7.   Cool cake in pans 10 minutes. Invert onto cooling racks to cool
completely.
8.   In medium bowl, combine all filling ingredients except almonds; beat
until smooth and creamy.
9.   Stir in almonds.
10. In medium bowl, blend sugar and almond extract into whipped cream
for filling and topping.
11. Place one cake layer on serving plate; spread with half of white
chocolate filling.
12. Top with second cake layer and spread with one third of the whippd
cream filling.
13. Repeat cake layers, using remaining white chocolate filling and
ending with topping of whipped cream. Frost sides with whipped cream.
14. If desired, garnish with chocolate curls or shavings.
15. Cover and chill.
Yield: 12 servings

HOTEL HERSHEY DERBY PIE

1 cup granulated sugar
4 tablespoons cornstarch
2 eggs, lightly beaten
1/2 cup (1 stick) butter or margarine, melted and cooled
3 tablespoons bourbon or 1 teaspoon vanilla
1 (6-ounce) package semisweet chocolate pieces
1 cup finely chopped pecans
1 9-inch unbaked pie shell

Derby Whipped Cream
1/2 cup heavy cream
2 tablespoons confectioner's sugar
1 teaspoon bourbon or 1/2 teaspoon vanilla

For Pie
1. Combine sugar and cornstarch in a medium-size bowl; beat in eggs; mix in butter, bourbon, chocolate bits, and pecans.
2. Pour into pastry shell.
3. Bake in a moderate oven (350F) for 40 minutes or until puffy and lightly browned.
4. Cool pie completely on wire rack.
5. Cut pie into slim wedges (it's very rich); top each portion with a dollop of Derby Whipped Cream.

For Derby Whipped Cream
1. Beat heavy cream with sugar in a small bowl to soft peaks.
2. Add bourbon or vanilla; beat to stiff peaks.

Yield: 8 servings

APPLE DUMPLINGS WITH HARD SAUCE

Apple Dumplings
1-1/2 packages (9-1/2- to 11-ounce size) pie crust mix
3 tablespoons butter or margarine, softened
3 tablespoons granulated sugar
1 tablespoon dark raisins
2 tablespoons chopped walnuts
3/4 teaspoon ground cinnamon
6 large baking apples (4 pounds), such as Rome Beauty or Granny Smith
2 tablespoons lemon juice
Whole cloves
1 egg yolk

Hard Sauce
1/2 cup butter or regular margarine, softened
1 teaspoon vanilla extract
1-1/4 cups unsifted confectioner's sugar

1. Make pastry as package label directs.
2. Form pastry into a flat, 8-inch round; wrap in waxed paper; refrigerate.
3. In small bowl, combine 3 tablespoons butter, granulated sugar, raisins, walnuts, and cinnamon; blend with fork.
4. Core apples with corer.
5. Pare apples; brush with lemon juice.
6. Using spoon, fill hollows with raisin/walnut mixture.
7. Preheat oven to 425F.
8. Grease well a shallow, 15-1/2x10-1/2x1-inch baking pan.
9. On lightly floured pastry cloth or floured surface, divide pastry evenly into sixths.
10. Form each piece into a round ball.
11. Flatten each piece; then roll out from center into an 8-1/2 inch square.
12. Trim edges, using pastry wheel for decorative edge. Save trimmings.
13. Place an apple in center of each square; brush edges lightly with water.
14. Bring each corner of square to top of apple; pinch edges of pastry together firmly to cover apple completely.
15. Re-roll trimming 1/4-inch thick.
16. With knife, cut out 24 leaves, 1-3/4-inches long and 3/4-inch wide.
17. Brush one end of each leaf lightly with water.
18. Press leaves on top of dumplings; put clove in center.
19. Arrange in pan.
20. Brush with yolk mixed with 1 tablespoon water.
21. Bake, brushing once with juices in pan, 40 minutes, or until pastry is browned and apples are tender when tested with a wooden pick.
22. With broad spatula, remove dumplings to serving dishes.
23. Serve warm, topped with Hard Sauce.

For Hard Sauce
1. In medium bowl, using portable electric beater, cream butter until light.
2. At low speed, add vanilla and confectioner's sugar; beat until smooth.

Yield: 6 servings

HAZELNUT TORTE

Note: Chocolate, hazelnuts, and raspberries--what could be better?

Torte Layers
7 eggs
1/4 teaspoon salt
1 cup granulated sugar
1 teaspoon vanilla extract
1-1/4 cups ground hazelnuts
1-1/4 cups ground pecans
1/4 cup packaged dry bread crumbs
1 teaspoon baking powder
1/2 teaspoon salt

Filling
1 cup heavy cream, chilled
1/2 cup confectioner's sugar
1 teaspoon vanilla extract

Chocolate Frosting
4 squares (4 ounces) unsweetened chocolate
1/4 cup butter or regular margarine
3 cups sifted confectioner's sugar
1/2 cup hot water
1 teaspoon vanilla extract

1 cup raspberry preserves
1/2 cup whole hazelnuts

Coffee Frosting
2 teaspoons instant coffee
2 tablespoons hot water
1/4 cup butter or margarine, softened
1-3/4 cups sifted (sift before measuring) confectioner's sugar

For Cake
1. Separate eggs, putting whites into large bowl of electric mixer, yolks in smaller one.
2. Let whites warm to room temperature - about 1 hour.
3. Preheat oven to 375F.
4. Line bottom of three 8-inch round cake pans with circles of waxed paper.
5. With mixer at high speed, beat whites with 1/4 teaspoon salt until soft peaks form when beater is slowly raised.
6. Gradually beat in 1/2 cup granulated sugar, 2 tablespoons at a time, beating until stiff peaks form.
7. With same beater, beat yolks until thick and light.
8. Gradually beat in rest of granulated sugar, beating until thick - about 3 minutes; beat in vanilla.
9. Combine ground nuts, crumbs, baking powder and 1/2 teaspoon salt; turn into yolk mixture; mix well.
10. With an under-and-over motion, fold into the egg whites just to

combine.

11. Pour into prepared pans, dividing evenly; smooth surfaces.

12. Bake 25 minutes, or until surface springs back when gently pressed with fingertip.

13. To cool, hang each pan upside down between two other pans - 1 hour.

For Filling
1. In medium bowl, combine cream, confectioner's sugar, and vanilla.
2. Beat until stiff; refrigerate.

For Chocolate Frosting
1. In top of double boiler, over hot water, melt chocolate and butter.
2. Remove from water; add confectioner's sugar, the hot water, and vanilla; mix until smooth.
3. Set in larger bowl of ice cubes to chill. Stir until thickened.

For Coffee Frosting
1. In medium bowl, dissolve coffee in hot water. Add butter and confectioner's sugar.
2. Mix until smooth.

To Assemble
1. Loosen sides of layers from pans with spatula.
2. Turn out of pans; peel off paper.
3. On plate, asssemble layers, spreading each layer with half raspberry preserves, then with half of filling.
4. Frost torte with chocolate frosting.
5. Chop hazelnuts, reserving 6 whole ones for top.
6. Decorate sides of cake with chopped hazelnuts; refrigerate 1 hour.
7. Place coffee frosting in pastry bag with number 4 star tip.
8. Decorate, making border around bottom of cake and three even triangles on top.
9. Place whole hazelnuts in center.
10. For easier cutting, refrigerate 2 hours before serving.

Yield: 12 servings

BUCH DE NOEL

Note: This is the most beautiful holiday dessert. When decorating the top, let your imagination run wild. If you can find some candied Angelica, it makes perfect holly leaves with some pieces of candied cherry for the berries.

Cake
8 ounces semisweet chocolate
1/3 cup water
8 egg yolks
1 cup sugar
Pinch of salt
8 egg whites

Icing
7 ounces semisweet chocolate
1 ounce unsweetened chocolate
11 tablespoons butter, softened
2 cups sifted, powdered sugar
1 egg yolk
3/4 cup dairy sour cream

Flavored Whipped Cream
1 cup whipping cream
2 tablespoons sugar
1 tablespoon Grand Marnier

Meringue Mushrooms
3 egg whites
1/4 teaspoon cream of tartar
Pinch of salt
1-1/3 cups sugar
1/3 cup water

For Cake
1. Grease a 10x14-inch jelly roll pan and line with wax paper. Grease the wax paper.
2. Heat the chocolate with the water until chocolate is melted. Cool.
3. Beat together egg yolks with sugar and salt until pale yellow and fluffy, but not stiff.
4. Fold in cooled chocolate.
5. Beat egg whites until stiff peaks form.
6. Stir a little of the egg whites into the chocolate mixture to lighten.
7. Fold remaining egg whites into the chocolate mixture.
8. Spread batter in prepared pan.
9. Bake at 375F for 15 to 20 minutes.
10. While cake is baking, sprinkle a clean tea towel with powdered sugar.
11. Take cake out of the oven; flip onto the tea towel.
12. Remove pan and wax paper.
13. Trim edges off of cake.

14. While still hot, roll cake and towel up like a jelly roll.
15. Let cool.

For Icing
1. Melt chocolates.
2. Fold in sour cream.
3. Cream together butter and powdered sugar.
4. Beat egg into sugar mixture.
5. Mix chocolate into sugar mixture.
6. Refrigerate a little if needed.

For Flavored Whipped Cream
1. Combine all ingredients.
2. Beat until peaks form when beater is lifted.

For Meringue Mushrooms
1. Beat egg whites until foamy stiff.
2. Boil together sugar and water until 138F on candy thermometer. (Put lid on pan and let steam wash down the sides.)
3. Turn on mixer with egg in it and slowly pour in sugar.
4. Continue beating until meringue reaches a marshmallow-like consistency.
5. Using a pastry bag, squirt meringue onto a buttered and dusted cookie sheet, making round blobs and 1-1/2-inch stips.
6. Bake at 200F for 1 hour.
7. Make a hole in the bottom of each round (this is the mushroom top) and insert the tip of a long strip (this is the stem). Glue together with water.

To Assemble
1. Unroll cake.
2. Spread cake with flavored whipped cream.
3. Roll cake back up.
4. Place cake on platter.
5. Frost with icing, reserving some for decorating.
6. Put reserved icing in a pastry bag.
7. Using a jagged tip, pipe bark onto your cake.
8. Decorate with mushrooms.
9. Sprinkle log with powdered sugar; dust mushrooms with cocoa.
10. Slice on a angle to look like a log.

Yield: 12 servings

MARQUISE AU CHOCOLAT

Note: This dessert is best made a day ahead of time. It will keep up to one week in the refrigerator.

1 to 2 packages lady fingers
1/2 pound (2 sticks) unsalted butter
4 ounces bittersweet chocolate, such as Callebaut
3 cups heavy cream
1 cup plus 2 tablespoons confectioner's sugar, sifted
1/2 cup plus 3 tablespoons unsweetened cocoa, sifted
8 egg yolks
2 tablespoons flavored liqueur, such as Grand Marnier
Chocolate Buttercream (optional for decorating)

1. Line the bottom and sides of a medium loaf pan with the ladyfingers. Set aside.
2. In a heavy saucepan, melt together the butter and chocolate over very low heat.
3. When the chocolate is almost melted, remove the pan from the heat and stir the mixture to melt the remaining chocolate. Set aside.
4. In a bowl, whip the cream until it just begins to stiffen.
5. Quickly add the confectioner's sugar and the cocoa and beat until the mixture is combined thoroughly; do not overbeat. Set aside but do not refrigerate.
6. In a bowl that is set over, but not touching, hot water, beat together the yolks and liqueur, whisking constantly until thickened.
7. Add the butter/chocolate mixture and pour into the bowl of a food processor.
8. Process until combined.
9. Add the whipped cream and mix just until combined.
10. Pour the mixture into the prepared mold and refrigerate for at least 6 hours or overnight.
11. To serve, set the mold in a pan of hot water for a minute or two; invert on a serving platter to unmold.
12. Decorate, if desired, by piping Chocolate Buttercream between the ladyfingers.

Yield: 6 to 8 servings

APPLE PANDOWDY

Apples
6 tart apples, peeled, cored, and sliced thin
1/2 cup packed, dark brown sugar
1/4 cup granulated sugar
1/4 teaspoon ground nutmeg
1/2 teaspoon ground cinnamon
1/8 teaspoon ground cloves
1/4 teaspoon salt

Biscuit Dough
1-1/2 cups flour
1-1/2 tablespoons sugar
2-1/4 teaspoons baking powder
3/4 teaspoon salt
1/2 cup chilled, unsalted butter, cut into 10 pieces
6 to 9 tablespoons milk

1 cup chilled heavy cream, whipped and lightly sweetened with sugar

1. Preheat oven to 350F.
2. In a large mixing bowl, toss apples, both sugars, nutmeg, cinnamon, cloves, and salt to combine.
3. Put apple mixture into a buttered, 9-inch baking dish.
4. For the dough, sift flour, sugar, baking powder, and salt into a large mixing bowl.
5. Rub butter in with your fingers or cut in with a pastry blender until mixture resembles coarse meal.
6. Sprinkle with 6 tablespoons of the milk and toss with fork.
7. Add more milk if necessary to make a soft dough.
8. On a lightly floured surface, roll dough 1-inch larger than baking dish.
9. Dough sould be about 1/4-inch thick.
10. Lay dough over baking dish with apples.
11. Flute or otherwise secure dough to edge of dish.
12. Bake until crust is golden brown and apples are soft and bubbly - 40 to 45 minutes.
13. Serve warm or at room temperature, garnished with whipped cream.
Yield: 8 servings

EDNA BIRDSON'S BLUEBERRY BUCKLE

3/4 cup sugar
1/4 cup shortening
1 egg, beaten
1/2 cup milk
2 cups sifted flour
3/4 teaspoon salt
2 teaspoons baking powder
2 cups blueberries

Topping
1/2 cup sugar
1/3 cup flour
1 teaspoon cinnamon
1 cup butter

1. Cream sugar and shortening; beat in egg and milk, then sifted dry ingredients.
2. Gently stir in berries.
3. Turn into greased 9x13-inch pan.
4. Combine topping ingredients.
5. Sprinkle crumbled topping over batter.
6. Bake 35 minutes at 350F.

Yield: 16 servings

FRUIT COBBLER

1 pint blueberries
2 pounds peaches, peeled and sliced
3/4 cup plus 2 tablespoons plus 1 tablespoon sugar
1 cup flour
1 teaspoon baking powder
1/2 teaspoon salt
1 egg
5-1/3 tablespoons melted butter
1 teaspoon cinnamon

1. Preheat oven to 375F.
2. Butter 9x13-inch pan.
3. Lay blueberries in pan; top with peaches; sprinkle 2 tablespoons sugar on top.
4. Combine dry ingredients; add egg.
6. Sprinkle or crumble on top of fruit.
7. Combine cinnamon and 1 tablespoon sugar.
8. Sprinkle on top of cobbler.
9. Bake at 375F for 15 minutes.
10. Increase oven temperature to 400F and bake for 12 more minutes.

Yield: 10 to 12 servings

GERMAN PEACH PUDDING

Note: This recipe is very special to me because of the woman who gave it to me. I used to work with her, and she had a kind of sad story but was always interested in you and loved jokes and happiness. She would be so pleased that her recipe was making so many people happy.

In the summertime, when peaches are fresh, this is my standard company dessert; it is fast and easy. Usually I make it up in the afternoon, cover it with film and let it sit until we sit down for dinner. During dinner it bakes and I am able to serve it hot! If dinner is on the heavy side, serve it alone, if you can afford the space, serve it over a scoop of good vanilla ice cream. Enjoy!

4 cups sliced peaches
1 cup sugar

Topping
1/2 cup butter
2/3 cup sugar
1 egg
1 cup flour
1 teaspoon baking powder

1. Place peaches and sugar in bottom of pie plate. I never measure; I just fill the plate with sliced peaches and sprinkle some sugar and cinnamon over them. I don't use anywhere near 1 cup of sugar. The more sugar you use, the juicier the cobbler will be.
2. Cream butter and sugar.
3. Add the egg, the flour, and the baking powder.
4. Dip and spread over the top of the peaches. It is not necessary to make the topping even, because it sort of evens out while it bakes. The thicker parts tend to get puddingy and the thin parts get crunchy. It's all wonderful.
5. Bake at 350F for 30 to 35 minutes.

Yield: 6 servings

MILE HIGH STRAWBERRY CLOUD

Cookie Crust
1 stick butter or margarine
2 tablespoons sugar
1 cup unsifted flour

Filling
1/2 pint heavy cream
2 egg whites, room temperature
1 cup sugar
1 tablespoon lemon juice
1 (10-ounce) package frozen, sliced strawberries, partially thawed
Whole fresh strawberries for garnish

For Cookie Crust
1. Mix together all ingredients with electric mixer until crumbly.
2. Press dough together with hands until it can be formed into a ball.
3. Press dough evenly onto bottom of an 8x8-inch square pan.
4. Bake in oven preheated to 375F about 15 minutes or until golden brown. Cool.

For Filling
1. Whip cream until stiff.
2. Beat egg whites until foamy.
3. Gradually add sugar to egg whites, beating until stiff.
4. Add lemon juice, strawberries, and strawberry juice.
5. Beat at high speed with electric mixer 15 minutes. Scrape down sides of bowl frequently with rubber spatula.
6. Fold in whipped cream.
7. Spoon mixture onto cookie crumb crust.
8. Freeze until firm.
9. Just before serving, garnish with whole strawberries.

Yield: 8 servings

APRICOT AND STRAWBERRY STRIP

2 cups sifted all-purpose flour
1/4 cup sugar
1/2 teaspoon salt
3/4 cup butter
4 tablespoons cold water
1 egg, beaten
2 pints small strawberries, hulled and washed
1/3 cup sugar
1/2 teaspoon arrowroot
1 teaspoon vanilla extract
1/2 cup apricot preserves

1. Sift flour, 1/4 cup sugar, and salt in mixing bowl.
2. Cut in butter with pastry blender until the mixture resembles corn-meal.
3. Sprinkle water over the surface.
4. Stir with fork until flour is moistened and pastry clings together.
5. Roll on lightly floured board to a 7x14-inch rectangle. Pastry should be free moving. If it sticks, loosen with spatula and lightly flour underneath.
6. Trim edges evenly.
7. Fold in half lengthwise.
8. Lift with spatula and place on a cookie sheet.
9. Unfold.
10. Cut 1/2-inch wide strip from each long side.
11. Moisten edges of rectangle.
12. Place strips on long moistened edges.
13. Score edges with back of knife blade.
14. Brush with egg.
15. Bake in 375F oven for 25 minutes. Cool.
16. Toss strawberries with the 1/3 cup sugar.
17. Let stand 30 minutes.
18. Drain juice adding water if necessary to make 1/3 cup.
19. Mix juice with arrowroot and vanilla.
20. Bring to a boil, stirring constantly.
21. Simmer 1 minute. Remove from heat; cool.
22. Spread apricot preserves on bottom of pastry strip.
23. Arrange strawberries over top.
24. Pour juice mixture over all.

Yield: 6 to 8 servings

LEMON MERINGUE TART

Sweet Crust Pastry
1-1/2 cups unbleached pastry flour or all-purpose flour
1/3 cup sugar
3 egg yolks
1/2 teaspoon vanilla
1/4 teaspoon salt
7 tablespoons unsalted butter

Lemon Filling
1 cup sugar
2/3 cup strained, fresh lemon juice
3 eggs
3 egg yolks
1 teaspoon finely grated lemon peel
1/2 cup (1 stick) unsalted butter, cut into tablespoon-sized pieces,
   room temperature

Meringue
2/3 cup sugar
2 egg whites, room temperature

For Sweet Crust Pastry
1. Sift flour onto work surface; make well in center.
2. Mix sugar, yolks, vanilla, and salt in well, using fingertips until sugar and salt dissolve.
3. Pound butter with rolling pin to soften.
4. Break into pieces; work into sugar mixture using fingertips.
5. Using pastry cutter or dough scraper, cut flour into sugar mixture until well blended.
6. Gather into a ball.
7. With heel of hand, push small pieces of dough down onto surface away from you to blend butter and flour thoroughly.
8. Gather into ball.
9. Wrap in plastic.
10. Refrigerate at least 2 hours or up to 3 days.
11. Roll dough out on lightly-floured surface to thickness of 1/8-inch.
12. Fit into 9-1/2-inch tart pan with removable bottom. Trim edges.
13. Cover with plastic wrap; refrigerate 1 hour.
14. Preheat oven to 400F.
15. Lightly butter foil; set buttered side down in shell.
16. Fill with dried beans or pie weights.
17. Bake until pastry is set - about 15 minutes.
18. Remove foil and weights.
19. Bake 6 to 8 minutes until brown.

For Lemon Filling
1. Whisk sugar, lemon juice, eggs, yolks, and peel in top of nonaluminum double boiler set over boiling water until mixture thickens enough to coat the back of the spoon - about 10 minutes; do not let mixture boil.
2. Remove from heat.
3. Whisk in butter 1 tablespoon at a time, completely incorporating each before adding next. (Can be prepared up to 2 weeks ahead and

refrigerated.)
3. Pour filling into crust.
4. Cool to room temperature.

For Meringue
1. Preheat broiler.
2. Whisk sugar and whites in stainless steel bowl set over saucepan of boiling water until slowly dissolving ribbon forms when whisk is lifted - about 10 minutes.
3. Remove from heat and beat with electric mixer until whites are cool and stiff.
4. Spoon into pastry bag fitted with star tip.
5. Pipe design atop tart, covering completely.
6. Broil until meringue is lightly browned - about 1 minute.
7. Serve immediately.

Yield: 8 servings

TORTILLA TORTE

Note: This recipe must be made ahead.

1 (12-ounce) package (2 cups) semisweet chocolate pieces
3 cups dairy sour cream
10 (7- or 8-inch) flour tortillas
1/4 cup sifted powdered sugar
Chocolate curls
Fresh strawberries (optional)

1. In a medium saucepan, melt the chocolate pieces over low heat, stirring occasionally.
2. Stir in 2 cups of the sour cream.
3. Remove from heat. Cool.
4. Place one tortilla onto a serving plate.
5. Spread about 1/3 cup of the chocolate mixture atop.
6. Repeat with eight of the remaining tortillas.
7. Top with the 10th tortilla.
8. In a small bowl, stir together the remaining 1 cup sour cream and the powdered sugar.
9. Spread on top of the torte.
10. Cover and chill overnight.
11. Before serving, garnish with chocolate curls and strawberries.

Yield: 6 to 8 servings

CHOCOLATE CREAM TORTE

1 cup unsalted butter, room temperature
16 ounces bittersweet chocolate, melted and cooled
3/4 cup confectioner's sugar
1 tablespoon vanilla
2 cups heavy cream, whipped
1/4 cup cocoa
2 tablespoons confectioner's sugar
8 candied rose petals
8 candied violets

1. Line the bottom of a 9-inch springform pan with wax paper.
2. Combine butter, chocolate, the 3/4 cup confectioner's sugar, and vanilla in a large mixing bowl; beat until smooth.
3. Set aside 1 cup of whipped cream; cover and refrigerate it for frosting.
4. Fold the remaining whipped cream into the chocolate mixture on the lowest speed; beat just to combine.
5. Spread the mixture into the prepared pan; cover; chill at least 6 hours, or freeze.
6. Run a knife dipped into warm water around the edge of the cake.
7. Release the springform; gently turn the cake upside down onto a platter.
8. Peel off wax paper.
9. Spread or pipe whipped cream over top and sides.
10 Sift the cocoa and remaining 2 tablespoons of confectioner's sugar together; sift over top.
11 Garnish with candied flowers.

Yield: 12 servings

RASPBERRY MARZIPAN TART

Cake
1-1/4 cups all-purpose or unbleached flour
1/3 cup sugar
1 teaspoon baking powder
1/2 cup unsalted butter, margarine or butter, softened
1 egg
1/4 cup Kraft raspberry preserves

Filling
1/3 cup sugar
1/2 cup unsalted butter, margarine, or butter, softened
1/2 teaspoon almond extract
2 eggs
1 cup grated or finely chopped almonds
1/4 cup Kraft raspberry preserves

Glaze
1/2 cup powdered sugar
2 to 3 teaspoons lemon juice

For Cake
1. Heat oven to 350F.
2. Grease 9-inch round cake pan or 9-inch pie pan.
3. Lightly spoon flour into measuring cup; level off.
4. In large bowl, combine flour, 1/3 cup sugar, baking powder, 1/2 cup butter, and egg with pastry blender until dough forms.
5. Press dough over bottom and up sides of prepared pan; spread 1/4 cup preserves over dough.
6. Chill while preparing filling.

For Filling
1. In small bowl, cream 1/3 cup sugar, 1/2 cup butter, and almond extract until light and fluffy.
2. Add eggs, 1 at a time, beating well after each.
3. Stir in almonds.
4. Spoon filling over preserves layer; spread gently.
5. Bake at 350F for 40 to 50 minutes or until deep golden brown.
6. Cool 2 hours.
7. Spread with 1/4 cup preserves.

For Glaze
1. In small bowl, blend glaze ingredients until smooth.
2. Drizzle over tart.

Yield: 16 servings

PEACH-RASPBERRY TART

Pate Brisee
3/4 cup cold unsalted butter
2-1/2 cups unbleached all-purpose flour
6 to 8 tablespoons ice water
1/2 teaspoon salt
2 large egg yolks
1/3 cup sugar

Tart
Pate Brisee
Water
Ice water
2-1/2 pounds peaches
2 tablespoons lemon juice
1/3 cup sugar
3 tablespoons cornstarch
1/2 cup fresh red raspberries
2 teaspoons butter, melted
1 large egg

For Pate Brisee
1. Cut butter into flour with pastry blender or two knives in medium bowl until mixture resembles coarse crumbs.
2. Mix 6 tablespoons of the water and the salt in small bowl until salt dissolves; beat in egg yolks.
3. Gradually drizzle water mixture over flour mixture while stirring and tossing with fork until dough cleans sides of bowl. Use additional water if dough is too dry and crumbly.
4. Shape into ball.
5. Refrigerate, wrapped in plastic, at least 45 minutes or overnight.
6. Trace 9-inch circle on piece of waxed paper.
7. Roll out a third of the Pate Brisee on lightly floured surface into a 9x5x1/8-inch rectangle.
8. Cut lengthwise with fluted pastry wheel into 1/2-inch wide strips.
9. Weave strips on waxed paper in lattice pattern to fit the circle.
10. Refrigerate, covered with plastic wrap, until firm - about 30 minutes.

For Tart
1. Heat 3 quarts water in large Dutch oven to simmering.
2. Fill large bowl with ice water.
3. Blanch 3 peaches at a time in simmering water until skins loosen - about 10 seconds; remove immediately to ice water with slotted spoon.
4. Working with one peach at a time, peel, pit, and cut into 1/3-inch thick slices; toss in lemon juice in large bowl.
5. Drain peaches, discarding lemon juice.
6. Mix sugar and cornstarch in small bowl; sprinkle over peaches.
7. Toss gently; reserve.
8. Place one oven rack in lower third of oven; place second rack in center of oven.
9. Heat oven to 425F.
10. Roll out remaining Pate Brisee on lightly floured surface into a

13-inch circle, 3/16-inch thick.

11. Fold circle in half; ease and unfold into 9x1-inch tart pan with removable bottom.

12. Press dough gently against bottom and sides of pan, starting at center and easing out any air pockets as you work.

13. Spoon half the reserved peaches into tart shell; sprinkle with half the raspberries.

14. Mound remaining reserved peaches in center; sprinkle with remaining raspberries.

15. Drizzle butter over fruit.

16. Brush edges of tart shell lightly with water.

17. Carefully slide firm lattice off waxed paper onto pie; let stand a few minutes to soften slightly.

18. Press and crimp ends of strips against edges of tart shell where they meet to seal.

19. Trim pastry flush with rim of pan.

20. Beat egg and 1 tablespoon water in small bowl; brush on lattice.

21. Bake on lower oven rack 30 minutes.

22. Reduce oven temperature to 375F; transfer tart to center oven rack.

23. Continue baking until juices are bubbling in center and lattice is brown, 15 to 20 minutes longer.

24. Cool on wire rack to room temperature.

25. To unmold tart, place palm of hand on bottom of tart pan, letting rim of pan fall away; slide tart onto serving plate.

Yield: 6 servings

STRAWBERRIES WITH ALMOND CREAM

1 (4-serving) package vanilla instant pudding mix
2 cups whipping cream
1 cup milk
1/2 teaspoon almond extract
2 pints strawberries, hulled

1. In large bowl with mixer at low speed, beat instant pudding, cream, milk, and almond extract until blended.

2. Increase speed to high and beat until soft peaks form.

3. Spoon mixture in center of a chilled bowl; arrange strawberries around mixture.

Yield: 6 to 8 servings

CHOCOLATE ALMOND STRUDEL

8 ounces bittersweet chocolate, coarsely chopped
1-1/4 cups slivered almonds
1-1/2 teaspoons cinnamon
1/4 pound (1 stick) unsalted butter, melted
6 sheets filo dough
1-1/2 cups fresh bread crumbs
2 teaspoons sugar
Heavy cream, for serving

1. Preheat the oven to 375F.
2. In a bowl, combine the chocolate, 1 cup almonds, and 1 teaspoon cinnamon; set aside.
3. Cover 6 sheets of filo dough with a dampened, but not too wet, tea towel.
4. In a bowl, combine the bread crumbs with the sugar and the remaining 1/2 teaspoon cinnamon. Toss to distribute evenly.
5. Using a pastry brush, brush one side of one sheet of filo dough with melted butter.
6. Sprinkle with 2 rounded tablespoons of the bread crumb mixture.
7. Continue layering in this fashion until all 6 sheets of dough have been layered, buttered, and crumbed.
8. Spread the filling along the lower third of the top sheet of pastry.
9. Roll up, folding in the ends, so that the roll is neatly packed and the filling is contained.
10. Set the roll on a baking sheet.
11. Roll the remaining 1/4 cup almonds in the remaining butter; gently spread the nuts over the top of the strudel.
12. Bake for 45 minutes until golden brown.
13. Serve warm, with each slice in its own pool of heavy cream, if desired.

Yield: 8 servings

COFFEE DACQUOISE

Meringue
1-1/2 cups hazelnuts
3/4 cup sugar
1 tablespoon cornstarch
6 egg whites, stiffly beaten
1/4 teaspoon cream of tartar

Coffee Buttercream
6 egg yolks
6 tablespoons sugar
2 teaspoons vanilla
2 cups (1 pound) unsalted butter, at room temperature
3 tablespoons instant coffee
2 tablespoons coffee liqueur

Whipped Cream
1 cup (1/2 pint) heavy cream
2 tablespoons confectioner's sugar
1 teaspoon vanilla

For Meringue
1. Toast the hazelnuts in a baking pan at 350F for 15 minutes.
2. Cool; then finely grind in a food processor.
3. Mix the nuts, sugar, and cornstarch together.
4. Beat the egg whites with cream of tartar until stiff.
5. Fold in the nut mixture.
6. Line two cookie sheets with foil.
7, Shape meringue mixture into 10-inch rounds on each sheet.
8. Bake at 350F for 20 to 25 minutes, until golden brown and crisp.
Cool.

For Coffee Buttercream
1. Blend the egg yolks, sugar, and vanilla until smooth.
2. Add the butter 1 tablespoon at a time.
3, Mix the instant coffee and liqueur together; blend into the buttercream.
4. Chill until spreadable.

For Whipped Cream
1. Whip the heavy cream, sugar, and vanilla until thick.
2. Set aside.

To Assemble
1. Put the buttercream into a pastry bag with a star tip.
2. Put one of the layers on a serving platter.
3, Using half of the buttercream, pipe a border around the edge.
4. Fill the center with the whipped cream; top with the second
layer.
5. Pipe the remaining buttercream around its edges.
6. Garnish the center with confectioner's sugar and hazelnuts.
7. Chill.

Yield: 10 servings

CHOCOLATE-ORANGE CREAM PUFF

Cream Puff Strip
4 tablespoons unsalted butter
1/8 teaspoon salt
1/2 cup sifted all-purpose flour
2 eggs

Cream Filling
1/4 cup golden raisins
1/4 cup Cointreau or other orange liqueur
1 cup heavy cream, chilled
2 tablespoons sugar
3/4 teaspoon vanilla extract
2 tablespoons grated orange zest

Assembly
2 ounces semisweet chocolate, melted
2 tablespoons confectioner's sugar

For Cream Puff Strip
1. Preheat oven to 400F.
2. Butter a 15x11-inch jelly roll pan.
3. In a medium saucepan, combine the butter, sugar, and salt with 1/2 cup of water.
4. Bring to a boil over moderately high heat.
5. Add the flour all at once; beat with a wooden spoon over low heat until the mixture masses and pulls away from the sides of the pan - about 1 minute.
6. Remove from the heat and continue beating for 2 minutes longer to cool the mixture slightly.
7. Add the eggs, beating them in 1 at a time, until the mixture is smooth and has a satiny sheen.
8. Spoon onto the prepared jelly roll pan in an even strip about 2 inches wide and 15 inches long.
9. Bake in the preheated oven until puffed and golden brown - about 35 minutes.
10. Remove from the oven; let cool on a wire rack.

For Cream Filling
1. In a small saucepan, combine the raisins and Cointreau.
2. Cook over low heat until warmed through.
3. Remove from the heat and let stand for 1 hour to plump raisins.
4. Drain the raisins, reserving the liqueur.
5. Beat the cream until soft peaks form.
6. Add the sugar, vanilla, and the reserved liqueur; beat until stiff peaks form.
7. Fold in the orange zest and raisins.

To Assemble
1. With a serrated knife, split the pastry strip horizontally in half.
2. Spread the cream filling over the bottom.
3. Cover with the top half of the pastry.
4. Spread or drizzle the melted chocolate over the top.
5. Sift the confectioner's sugar over the chocolate.

Yield: 6 servings

COFFEE TOFFEE CLOUD

Meringue
6 egg whites
1/2 teaspoon cream of tartar
Dash salt
2 cups sugar

Filling and Topping
1 pint (2 cups) whipping cream, well chilled
1/2 cup powdered sugar
1/3 cup cocoa
9 little Heath Candy Bars, coarsely crushed (reserve 3 tablespoons)

For Meringue
1. Heat oven to 275F.
2. Line 2 cookie sheets with brown or parchment paper.
3. In large bowl, beat egg whites, cream of tartar, and salt until foamy.
4. Add sugar gradually, beating until stiff and glossy (do not over-beat).
5. Spread half of mixture into an 8-inch circle on prepared cookie sheet; repeat with remaining mixture on other cookie sheet.
6. Bake at 275F for 50 to 60 minutes or until crisp and very light, golden-brown around edges.
7. Turn oven off; leave meringue in closed oven for 2 hours.
8. Remove from oven; cool completely.

For Filling and Topping
1. In medium bowl, combine cream, sugar, and cocoa.
2. Beat at highest speed until stiff peaks form.
3. Fold in crushed candy.

To Assemble
1. Place one meringue layer on serving plate.
2. Spread with half of filling.
3. Repeat layers.
4. Sprinkle with reserved crushed candy.
5. Chill.

Yield: 12 to 16 servings

CHOCOLATE MINT SWIRL MOUSSE

6 ounces semisweet chocolate, broken into bits
3/4 cup skim milk
1/2 teaspoon unflavored gelatin
2 eggs, room temperature
1 teaspoon powdered instant coffee
1/2 cup heavy cream
1 tablespoon confectioner's sugar
1/2 teaspoon mint extract
1/2 drop green food coloring (optional)

1. In a double boiler, melt the chocolate over hot, but not boiling, water.
2. When partially melted, stir with a spoon until smooth.
3. In a small saucepan, combine the milk with the gelatin; heat to scalding.
4. Stir well to dissolve the gelatin completely.
5. In a blender, combine the eggs with the coffee; process for a few seconds until blended.
6. Add the melted chocolate and hot milk; process at high speed for 2 minutes.
7. Transfer to a bowl; cover; refrigerate until very cold and thick.
8. In a small bowl, combine the heavy cream, sugar, mint extract, and green food coloring, if desired. (To tint whipping cream, immerse a toothpick clean and repeat the process until a very light but pleasing color is achieved. Remember, a little food coloring goes a long way.)
9. Whip the mint mousse mixture until stiff.
10. Spoon 1 tablespoon of the mint mousse into the center of a glass dessert dish.
11. Spoon 2 heaping tablespoons of the chocolate mousse on either side of the mint mousse.
12. Using the handle of a teaspoon, swirl the mixtures together to create a marbleized pattern.
13. Repeat the procedure until all the servings are assembled.
14. Chill until serving time.

Yield: 10 servings

STRAWBERRY SHERBET

2 quarts fresh or frozen strawberries
2 cups sugar
1-1/3 cups milk
1/3 cup lemon or orange juice*
1/8 teaspoon cinnamon

1. Blend together all ingredients.
2. Freeze until ready to serve.

*Use less sugar if you use orange juice.

Yield: 4 servings

ALMOND GRAPE CUSTARD

Note: This recipe was given to me by a Scottish neighbor. It's different from anything else I've ever had and is a wonderful blending of flavors.

Fruit Filling
1 (3-ounce) package of lemon-flavored gelatin
1/2 cup sugar
1 cup boiling water
1 cup dairy sour cream
1 cup halved green grapes

Almond Crust
1/2 cup butter or margarine
1 cup flour
1/2 cup diced roasted almonds
1/4 cup sugar

1. Dissolve gelatin and sugar in water.
2 Add sour cream and mix well.
3. Refrigerate until firm but not set - about 1 hour.
4. Fold in fruit.
5. Melt butter and add rest of the crust ingredients to form a ball.
6. Stirring constantly, cook over medium heat 3 to 5 minutes (until golden and crumbly).
7. Put all but 1/2 cup crust mixture into 8x8-inch pan.
8. Lightly press. Refrigerate.
9. Pour filling over crust.
10. Chill 3 hours.
11. Sprinkle reserved crumbs on top.

Yield: 6-8 servings

ALMOND FLOAT

1 envelope unflavored gelatin
1/3 cup cold water
3/4 cup boiling water
1/3 cup granulated sugar
1 cup milk
1-1/2 teaspoons almond extract
Berries or other fruit in season--mandarin oranges are good
1/3 cup sugar
2 cups water
1/2 teaspoon almond extract

1. Soften gelatin in cold water.
2. Add boiling water; stir until gelatin is dissolved.
3. Add sugar, milk, and 1-1/2 teaspoons extract; mix well.
4. Chill in square pan until set.
5. Cut into squares or diamonds; put into glass bowl.
6. Add fruit.
7. Make a syrup using the 1/3 cup sugar, 2 cups water, and 1/2 teaspoon almond extract.
8. Add enough to the bowl to make the mixture float.
9. Garnish with fresh mint. Store in refrigerator until serving time.

Yield: 4 to 6 servings

MOUSSE AU CHOCOLAT

6 ounces semisweet chocolate
1/4 cup light or heavy cream or milk
1 teaspoon vanilla or 1 tablespoon brandy
Dash of salt
4 egg yolks, slightly beaten
4 egg whites
1/4 cup sugar

1. Melt chocolate in saucepan over very low heat, stirring constantly.
2. Remove from heat; blend in cream, vanilla, and salt.
3. Gradually add to egg yolks, beating with wire whip until thick and creamy.
4. Beat egg whites until foamy throughout.
5. Gradually beat in sugar; continue beating until mixture will form stiff peaks.
6. Gently but thoroughly fold into chocolate mixture.
7. Spoon into individual dessert dishes or serving bowls.
8. Chill at least 2 hours.

Yield: 8 to 10 servings

CHOCOLATE CITRUS SAUCERY

Note: These little cups are so pretty and delicious. It is a perfect dessert for a buffet.

Chocolate Sauce
3 ounces unsweetened baking chocolate
1/2 cup milk, scalded
3/4 cup sugar
1 teaspoon vanilla extract

Citrus Cream
6 ounces orange gelatin
1 cup boiling water
2 cups vanilla ice cream
3 cups Cool Whip

For Chocolate Sauce
1. Place ingredients in blender container in the order given.
2. Blend at medium speed for 30 seconds; scrape and blend on high speed until smooth.

For Citrus Cream
1. Completely dissolve gelatin in water.
2. Whip gelatin on medium speed, gradually adding softened ice cream.
3. Beat until smooth on high speed.
4. On low, quickly blend whipped topping into gelatin mixture.

To Assemble
1. Layer citrus cream into lined muffin tins.
2. Layer chocolate sauce over citrus cream.
3. Freeze until ready to serve.

Yield: 6 servings

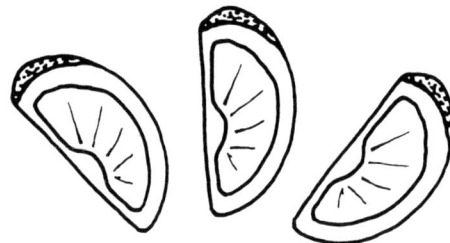

CHOCOLATE SATIN MOUSSE

Mousse
1 cup heavy cream, chilled
1 pound semisweet chocolate, broken into small pieces
4 tablespoons unsalted butter, cut into 4 pieces
1/3 cup brewed, strong coffee, room temperature
2 egg yolks
1/3 cup Creme de Cacao, Kahlua, or Tia Maria
4 egg whites, room temperature
4 tablespoons sugar

Custard Sauce
7 egg yolks
1 cup milk
1 cup half-and-half cream
1/2 cup sugar
1 to 1-1/4 teaspoons vanilla extract
Brandy or cognac, if desired

For Mousse
1. In a chilled small mixing bowl, beat the cream until stiff peaks form; refrigerate.
2. Pour water into the bottom of a double boiler; set the empty top in place.
3. Place over moderate heat; bring the water to a simmer.
4. When the top is heated by the hot water, remove it and let cool for exactly 1 minute.
5. Add the chocolate, butter, and coffee.
6. Place over simmering water and stir with a rubber spatula until about three-fourths melted.
7. Remove the top of the double boiler from the heat; stir until melted.
8. Pour the mixture into a large bowl.
9. In a small bowl, combine the egg yolks and the Creme de Cacao.
10. Gradually whisk the yolks into the chocolate mixture. Set aside.
11. In a medium bowl, beat the egg whites until soft peaks form.
12. One tablespoon at a time, add the sugar, beating constantly until stiff, but not dry, peaks form.
13. Gently but thoroughly fold the whites into the chocolate mixture.
14. Fold the whipped cream into the chocolate mixture until no streaks show.
15. Pour the mousse into a flat 9- or 10-inch dish that is at least 3 inches deep.
16. Cover with plastic wrap; refrigerate until firm - at least 6 hours or overnight.

For Custard Sauce

1. Off the heat, in a large, nonaluminum saucepan, combine the egg yolks and 1/2 cup of the milk.
2. Whisk thoroughly and set aside.
3. In another large saucepan, combine the remaining 1/2 cup milk with the half-and-half and the sugar.
4. Cook over low heat, stirring occasionally, until the mixture comes to a simmer.
5. Beating constantly with a whisk, slowly add the half-and-half mixture to the reserved egg yolk mixture.
6. Cook, stirring constantly over low heat, until the mixture thickens to the consistency of unbeaten heavy cream and coats a spoon - 5 to 10 minutes.
7. Remove from heat.
8. Strain the custard sauce into a bowl; allow to cool to lukewarm.
9. Add the vanilla and a bit of brandy, if you are using it.
10. Cover with plastic wrap placed directly on the surface; refrigerate until chilled - about 4 hours. (If you choose, you can chill the sauce quickly by setting the bowl over ice.)

Yield: 8 to 12 servings

MOUSSE AU CHOCOLAT A L'ORANGE

18 ounces semisweet chocolate, coarsely chopped
Grated zest of 1 orange
10 egg yolks, beaten until slightly foamy
10 egg whites
1/2 cup coarsely chopped hazelnuts or almonds (optional)
1 ounce semisweet chocolate, grated (optional)
Unsweetened whipped cream, for garnish

1. In a double boiler, melt the chopped chocolate with 3/4 cup of water.
2. Remove from heat; whisk the chocolate until smooth.
3. Add the orange zest; let cool to room temperature.
4. Beat the egg yolks again lightly with a whisk; add them, a little at a time, to the cooled chocolate, mixing thoroughly after each addition.
5. Beat the whites until firm peaks form.
6. Vigorously beat a large dollop of the whites into the chocolate mixture, then beat in the nuts and/or grated chocolate, if desired.
7. Gently fold the remaining whites into the mixture.
8. Carefully spoon the mousse into tall dessert glasses (or use a handsome glass bowl); refrigerate for at least an hour.
9. If desired, serve with unsweetened whipped cream.

Yield: 12 servings

TRIPLE-CHOCOLATE SILK

Note: This is the most impressive dessert. It takes a little
bit of time to make it, but is fail-proof. If the gelatin gets too
thick, simply reheat it a little. It takes a lot of bowls, but it is
wonderful.

Vegetable oil
1 tablespoon unflavored gelatin
1/4 cup cold water
5 large egg yolks, room temperature
1/2 cup sugar
1 cup half-and-half cream, scalded
3 ounces white chocolate, finely ground
3 ounces milk chocolate, broken into small pieces
3 ounces semisweet chocolate, broken into small pieces
1-3/4 cups whipping cream, well chilled
Bittersweet Chocolate Sauce (recipe follows)

1. Brush inside of 6-cup souffle dish lightly with oil; reserve.
2. Soften gelatin in cold water; reserve.
3. Beat egg yolks and sugar with whisk in medium mixer bowl until mixture becomes pale yellow and forms a ribbon. (Mixture dropped from
raised whisk falls in even stream that stacks up on itself like a ribbon
before sinking into rest of mixture).
4. Gradually whisk the scalded half-and-half into yolk mixture.
5. Transfer yolk mixture to heavy, 2-quart nonaluminum saucepan; cook,
stirring constantly with wooden spoon, over low heat, until mixture
thickens and coats spoon - 10 to 12 minutes (do not boil).
6. Remove from heat.
7. Add reserved gelatin mixture to yolk mixture; stir until gelatin
completely dissolves.
8. Strain yolk mixture into 1-quart measuring container.
9. Transfer 1/3 of mixture to each of 3 small mixing bowls.
10. Working quickly, immediately whisk white chocolate into first bowl,
milk chocolate into second bowl, and semisweet chocolate into third
bowl.
11. Return to white chocolate mixture; whisk again to be sure white
chocolate is completely melted and thoroughly blended.
12. Cover bowl with lightly-buttered plastic wrap (with plastic touching custard); refrigerate.
13. Whisk; cover; refrigerate milk chocolate mixture and semisweet
chocolate mixture, following the same procedures for white chocolate
mixture.
14. Whip 1 cup of the cream in chilled, small mixer bowl until stiff
peaks form.
15. Remove white chocolate mixture from refrigerator. (As each of the
3 chocolate mixtures is removed from refrigerator, it should be thick,
but still viscous--similar to the consistency of unbeaten egg whites.
If too thick, set bowl over small amount of simmering water and stir
only until of proper consistency.)
16. Fold 1/2 of the beaten cream into white chocolate mixture; refrigerate remaining beaten cream.
17. Pour white chocolate mixture into reserved souffle dish; smooth top

and tap dish lightly on counter to settle mixture and eliminate air bubbles.

18. Cover dish with plastic wrap; freeze until set - no longer than 10 to 15 minutes.

19. Fold remaining beaten cream into milk chocolate mixture; pour into souffle dish over set white chocolate layer.

20. Smooth top with back of spoon and press gently to eliminate air bubbles.

21. Cover with plastic wrap and freeze until milk chocolate layer is set - no longer than 10 to 15 minutes.

22. Meanwhile, whip remaining 3/4 cup cream in chilled mixer bowl until stiff peaks form.

23. Fold beaten cream into semisweet chocolate mixture; pour into souffle dish over set milk chocolate layer.

24. Smooth top with back of spoon; press gently to eliminate air bubbles.

25. Cover with plastic wrap and refrigerate until Silk is completely firm, at least 4 hours or overnight. (Do not freeze.)

26, Prepare Bittersweet Chocolate Sauce.

27. Just before serving, rub bottom and sides of souffle dish with a hot damp towel until Silk loosens.

28. Invert souffle dish onto lightly oiled plate and remove souffle dish.

29. Refrigerate until Silk is firm again - about 5 minutes.

30. To serve, cut Silk into 8 wedges.

31. Pour about 1/4 cup Bittersweet Chocolate Sauce onto a large plate; tilt plate as needed to coat with sauce.

32. Place 1 wedge of Silk in center of plate on sauce.

33. Repeat for remaining servings.

34. Serve immediately.

For Bittersweet Chocolate Sauce

1 cup cold water
1/2 cup sugar
6 ounces bittersweet chocolate, broken into small pieces
2 ounces unsweetened chocolate, broken into small pieces
1/4 cup lightly salted butter, cut into 4 pieces
1 tablespoon cognac or brandy

1. Combine water and sugar in 1-quart, nonaluminum saucepan; heat over low heat to simmering.

2. Cover mixture and simmer 5 minutes.

3. Uncover; remove from heat; cool to lukewarm.

4. Melt bittersweet and unsweetened chocolates with butter.

5. Gradually stir lukewarm sugar-syrup into chocolate mixture; stir in cognac.

6. Keep sauce at room temperature until serving time - up to 4 hours. (Do not refrigerate: chocolate will harden.)

Yield: 8 servings

BAKLAVA

1 pound filo dough
1 pound pecans
1 pound butter, clarified
1/2 teaspoon to 1 tablespoon cinnamon
2-3 tablespoons sugar, to taste
Cloves

Syrup
3 cups sugar
2 cups water
Juice of 1 small lemon
1 stick cinnamon

1. Chop pecans and mix them with sugar and cinnamon. The nuts should be coarse but powdery.
2. Preheat oven to moderate (350F).
3. Place 1 pastry in a well-buttered baking pan; brush with butter.
4. Place second pastry sheet on top of the first; butter again.
5. Repeat until 6 or so layers of buttered pastry sheets have been built up.
6. Sprinkle top pastry sheet evenly with pecan mixture and place one or two buttered pastry sheets over this.
7. Repeat this process until all ingredients have been used, ending with 6 perfect pastry sheets, as on the bottom.
8. Brush top with remaining butter.
9. Cut lines on a 45 degree diagonal, the length of the pan to make diamond-shaped pieces.
10. Upon completion, place 1 clove in the center of each piece.
11. Bake in moderate oven for about 45 minutes to 1 hour or until golden brown.
12. Boil sugar, water, and lemon juice with cinnamon stick for about 10 minutes.
13. Pour hot syrup over cooled baklava or cooled syrup over hot baklava.
14. Allow to stand several hours before serving.

Yield: 24 to 30 pieces

CHOCOLATE CARAMEL LAYER SQUARES

Note: This recipe has never failed to get lots of requests for the recipe. It's so easy and so gooey good.

1 (14-ounce) bag caramels
2/3 cup evaporated milk
1 German chocolate cake mix
3/4 cup butter, softened
1 cup nuts, chopped
1 (6-ounce) bag chocolate chips

1. Combine caramels and 1/3 cup evaporated milk in double boiler and melt caramels. Remove from heat.
2. Combine cake mix, 1/3 cup evaporated milk, and butter.
3. Add nuts.
4. Put 1/2 of the mixture into a greased 9x13-inch pan.
5. Bake 6 minutes at 350F.
6. Remove from oven; sprinkle with chips.
7. Pour caramel on top of chips.
8. Top with remaining mixture.
9. Bake at 350F for 18-20 minutes or until done.
10. Let cool before cutting.

Tip: When applying the second layer of mix, just dab it on in little blobs of batter. Don't try to spread it out; it will smooth out during baking.

Yield: 24 squares

SWEET CRESCENTS

1/2 cup chopped salted cocktail peanuts
1/2 cup coconut flakes
1/2 cup brown sugar
1/2 cup granulated sugar
1 package won ton wrappers
1 egg, beaten

1. Mix peanuts, coconut, brown sugar, and granulated sugar.
2. Fold won ton squares into triangles.
3. Round off the top corner with scissors.
4. Place 1 teaspoon filling in center.
5. Moisten edges with beaten egg and seal.
6. Deep fry in hot oil until golden, turning once.
7. Drain and cool.
8. Store in air-tight container.
9. Serve crescents as dessert with ice cream or sherbet.

Yield: 8 to 10 dozen

MINT BROWNIES

Note: These will stay moist for a long time. They look very pretty on a tray served with a small white cookie; Russian Tea cookies are good. These are so rich that you can cut them into very small pieces.

Brownies
4 eggs
2 cups sugar
1 cup cocoa
1 cup flour
1/2 teaspoon peppermint extract
1 teaspoon vanilla
1 cup butter or margarine

Icing
2-3/4 cups confectioner's sugar
1 stick butter or margarine, melted
1/2 teaspoon peppermint extract
3-5 drops green food coloring to desired color
Milk, as needed

Chocolate Topping
3 ounces unsweetened chocolate
3 ounces butter

For Brownies
1. Grease 9x13-inch pan.
2. Beat eggs and sugar.
3. Add cocoa, flour, peppermint extract, vanilla, and butter.
4. Beat well.
5. Pour into pan; bake at 350F for 30 minutes.
6. Cool.

For Icing
1. Cream confectioner's sugar with butter, extract, and food coloring.
2. Add milk until mixture is spreadable.
3. Spread icing on brownies as soon as they come out of the oven.
Some of the butter may separate, but it will go back together when cool.
4. Refrigerate for at least 30 minutes.

For Chocolate Topping
1. Melt unsweetened chocolate with butter.
2. Spread on top of mint layer.
3. Cool 30 minutes before cutting.

Yield: 48 small squares

TWEED BROWNIES

6 ounces white chocolate
1/4 pound (1 stick) unsalted butter, cut into 6 pieces
2 eggs, room temperature
3/4 cup sugar
1/2 teaspoon salt
1-1/2 teaspoons vanilla extract
1/2 teaspoon almond extract
1 cup sifted all-purpose flour
1/2 cup semisweet chocolate mini-morsels
1/2 cup chopped blanched almonds (about 2 ounces)

1. Preheat the oven to 350F.
2. Generously grease an 8- or 9-inch square baking pan.
3. Line the bottom and 2 sides with parchment or foil and grease the paper and sides of the pan.
4. Finely chop half of the white chocolate so that the bits are about the size of cooked rice or barley. Set aside.
5. In a double boiler, melt the remaining white chocolate over simmering water.
6. When the chocolate is soft, add the butter, one piece at a time, stirring until melted before adding more butter.
7. When all of the butter is incorporated, set aside to cool slightly.
8. In a large mixing bowl, beat eggs with an electric mixer until light in color.
9. Gradually add the sugar; beat until the mixture is very thick.
10. When the beaters are lifted, the batter should leave a trail on the surface that lasts for 10 seconds before it dissolves.
11. Beat in the salt, vanilla, and almond extract.
12. Using a rubber spatula, fold in the chocolate mixture.
13. One-half cup at a time, fold in the flour, the finely chopped white chocolate, 1/4 cup of the mini-morsels, and almonds.
14. Spoon the mixture into the prepared pan; smooth the top.
15. Sprinkle with the remaining 1/4 cup mini-morsels.
16. Bake in the center of the oven for 30 to 35 minutes, until the top is dry and a toothpick inserted near the center comes out clean.
17. Cool the brownies in the pan on a rack.
18. Unmold the brownies; remove the paper.
19. Trim away any dry edges before cutting.

Yield: 30 to 36 brownies

KAHLUA CHOCOLATE WALNUT SQUARES

Chocolate Walnut Squares
1-1/4 cups sifted all-purpose flour
3/4 teaspoon baking powder
1/2 teaspoon salt
1/2 cup soft butter or margarine
3/4 cup packed brown sugar
1 large egg
1/4 cup Kahlua
1 cup semisweet chocolate pieces
1/3 cup chopped walnuts
1 tablespoon Kahlua, for tops of bars

Brown Butter Icing
2 tablespoons butter
1 tablespoon Kahlua
2 teaspoons milk or light cream
1-1/3 cups sifted powdered sugar

For Chocolate Walnut Squares
1. Re-sift flour with baking powder and salt.
2. Cream butter, sugar, and egg together well.
3. Stir in Kahlua, then flour mixture, blending well.
4. Fold in chocolate pieces and walnuts.
5. Spread evenly on greased baking pan (7x11x1-1/2 inches).
6. Bake in moderate oven (350F) 30 minutes, or until top springs back when touched lightly in center.
7. Remove from oven; cool in pan 15 minutes; brush top with remaining tablespoon of Kahlua.
8. When cold, spread with Brown Butter Icing.
9. When icing is set, cut into 1-3/4x1-1/2-inch bars.

For Brown Butter Icing
1. Place butter in saucepan over low heat.
2. Heat until lightly browned.
3. Remove; add Kahlua, milk, and powdered sugar.
4. Beat until smooth.

Yield: 2 dozen

LEMON SQUARES

NOTE: This is one of those classic recipes that shows up at many baby showers and picnics. It will melt in your mouth with a tangy sweetness.

Crust
2 sticks butter or margarine
2 cups flour
1/2 cup powdered sugar

Topping
1/2 cup lemon juice
4 eggs
2 cups sugar
1 teaspoon baking powder
1/4 cup flour
Powdered sugar

For Crust
1. Cream butter and sugar. Add flour and gently combine; don't over-work, or the crust will be tough. Crust should just hold together.
2. Press into 9x13 pan.
3. Bake at 350F for 15 minutes. Crust should be golden, not browned.

For Topping
1. Mix together lemon juice, eggs, sugar, baking powder, and flour.
2. Pour over crust; bake for an additional 20-25 minutes at 350F.
3. Remove from oven; cool.
4. Sprinkle with powdered sugar.
5. Cut into squares.

Yield: 24 squares

COCOA-WHITE CHOCOLATE CHUNK BAR COOKIES

Note: This was our combination of a white chocolate chunk cookie recipe with some depraved ideas we had. It turned out even better than we anticipated. Try them, you'll love them!

8 tablespoons (1 stick) unsalted butter, room temperature
1/2 cup packed dark brown sugar
1/2 cup granulated sugar
1 teaspoon vanilla extract
1/2 teaspoon salt
1/3 cup unsweetened cocoa powder
1 egg
1/2 teaspoon baking soda
1 cup all-purpose flour
12 ounces (2 cups) coarsely chopped white chocolate bars (four 3-ounce chocolate bars, such as Lindt or Tobler)
3/4 to 1 bag caramels or 3/4 to 1 jar caramel ice cream topping

1. In large bowl, combine the butter, brown sugar, sugar, vanilla, and salt.
2. Beat with a spoon until fluffy.
3. Beat in the cocoa, then the egg and baking soda.
4. Stir in the flour.
5. Transfer to a bowl just large enough to hold the batter; cover and refrigerate until firm - 4 hours or overnight.
6. Preheat the oven to 325F.
7. Lightly grease a 13x9-inch pan.
8. Press half of cookie dough into bottom of pan.
9. Bake for 10 minutes.
10. While cookie crust is baking, melt caramels over low heat adding a little cream (if desired) to make melting easier.
11. When cookie crust comes out of the oven, pour melted caramel over crust; sprinkle with white chocolate chunks.
12. Dot top of cookies with remaining dough.
13. Return cookies to oven; bake for 15 to 20 minutes or until top is slightly crusty and springs back to the touch.
14. Cool for at least 30 minutes before cutting.
15. Cut into small pieces - they're very rich!

Yield: 30 bars

TWO-LAYER BROWNIES

Note: When you are in a jam for a quick dessert, this idea will really come in handy. Always put the blond brownies on the bottom because its batter is thicker.

1 package blond brownie mix
1 package chocolate brownie mix

1. Preheat oven to 350F.
2. Grease two 13x9-inch pans.
3. Make blond brownies according to package directions.
4. Divide batter in half; spread evenly over the bottom of the pans.
5. Make chocolate brownies according to package directions.
6. Divide batter in half; spread over blond batter. You may have to dot the chocolate batter on top of the blond if it is too hard to spread.
7. Bake according to package directions.

Yield: 48 brownies

CHATTANOOGA CHOCOLATE PEANUT BARS

1-1/2 cups unsifted flour
3/4 teaspoon baking powder
1/4 teaspoon salt
1/2 cup chunky peanut butter
1/4 cup butter, softened
3/4 cup firmly packed brown sugar
3 tablespoons milk
1 teaspoon vanilla
1 egg
6 squares semisweet chocolate, melted

1. Mix flour, baking powder, and salt.
2. Cream peanut butter and butter.
3. Add milk and vanilla.
4. Add egg; blend well.
5. Add flour mixture, blending well.
6. Spread about 2/3 of the dough in the bottom of greased and floured 13x9-inch pan.
7. Drizzle most of the chocolate over the dough.
8. Gently pat remaining dough into the pan.
9. Drizzle with remaining chocolate.
10. Bake at 375F for 18-20 minutes, or until golden brown.
11. Cool 10 minutes; cut into bars or squares.

Yield: 2 dozen

TRUFFLES

3 ounces semisweet chocolate
5 tablespoons unsalted butter
1 egg yolk
2/3 cup sifted confectioner's sugar
1 teaspoon vanilla
Coating*

1. Melt chocolate in saucepan over very low heat, stirring constantly; cool.
2. Cream butter with egg yolk.
3. Gradually add sugar, blending well.
4. Stir in chocolate and vanilla.
5. Chill until firm enough to handle.
6. Shape into balls that are about 1 inch in diameter.
7. Roll in coating; chill.
8. Store in refrigerator.

*Use finely chopped nuts, toasted coconut, cocoa, or a mixture of equal parts of ground semisweet chocolate and chocolate wafer crumbs.

Yield: 30 pieces

KAHLUA TRUFFLES

12 ounces semisweet chocolate
4 egg yolks
1/3 cup Kahlua
2/3 cup butter, unsalted
Cocoa, not sweetened
Ground almonds

1. Melt chocolate in top of double boiler over simmering water.
2. Remove from heat; cool to room temperature.
3. Add yolks, one at a time, stirring constantly until thoroughly blended.
4. Mix in Kahlua; return to simmering water for 2-3 minutes, stirring constantly.
5. Pour mixture into bowl of electric mixture.
6. Beat in butter, a tablespoon at a time.
7. Continue beating mixture until it is fluffy in texture.
8. Cover with plastic wrap; refrigerate for 4 to 5 hours or overnight.
9. Roll into 3/4-inch balls, then in bitter cocoa or nuts.
10. Refrigerate until ready to use. To freeze, place in a container with wax paper.

Yield: 3 dozen

DORCHESTER FUDGE

1 (8-ounce) package semisweet chocolate
1-1/2 cups sugar
2/3 cup evaporated milk
1/2 cup marshmallow topping
1/2 cup chopped nuts*
1/4 cup butter, softened
1/2 teaspoon vanilla
1. Cut each chocolate square into 4 pieces.
2. Combine sugar and evaporated milk in saucepan.
3. Stir over medium heat until mixture comes to a full rolling boil; boil 5 minutes, stirring constantly.
4. Add chocolate to remaining ingredients.
5. Carefully add boiling sugar syrup; stir until chocolate melts and mixture is smooth.
6. Pour into buttered, 8-inch square pan.
7. Chill; cut into squares.

Yield: 36 pieces

*For variations, substitute:
Peanut Butter Fudge--1/2 cup peanut butter for butter and nuts
Coconut Fudge--1 cup coconut for the nuts
Mocha-Almond Fudge--1/2 cup chopped, toasted almonds for the nuts
 and add 2 teaspoons instant coffee

Index

Additional copies of *Recipes from Pennies*
may be obtained by calling Publications Sales
at 919/467-8000, Extension 7001.